Celebrate

Also by Lucia van der Post

Things I Wish My Mother Had Told Me

Celebrate

The Art of the Special Occasion

LUCIA VAN DER POST

JOHN MURRAY

First published in Great Britain in 2009 by John Murray (Publishers)
An Hachette UK Company

I

A CIP catalogue record for this title is available from the British Library

ISBN 978-0-7195-2297-0

Book design by Janette Revill

Typeset in Adobe Caslon by Palimpsest Book Production Limited,
Grangemouth, Stirlingshire

Printed and bound by Clays Ltd, St Ives plc

John Murray policy is to use papers that are natural, renewable and recyclable
products and made from wood grown in sustainable forests. The logging and
manufacturing processes are expected to conform to the environmental
regulations of the country of origin.

John Murray (Publishers)
338 Euston Road
London NW1 3BH

www.johnmurray.co.uk

For my husband Neil Crichton-Miller, my children Emma and David, their spouses Mark and Becky, and all five of our grandsons – ten very good reasons for having had so much cause to celebrate.

Contents

6 The Wedding   153

Introduction

scarcely remember a time when it has been more important to celebrate the things that really matter in life. If there's an upside to the economic upheavals that sometimes come to try us – and there is – it has to be that it makes us reappraise the things that truly make a difference to our sense of well-being and happiness. Nobody with half a wit needs telling that money doesn't buy happiness – we all know that – but money can sometimes assume too large a role in people's lives. We've all discovered from personal experience that what makes us happy more than anything else – way above posh yachts, private planes and meals in swanky restaurants – is having people we care about in our lives. This belief lies at the core of *Celebrate* – the idea that those of us who are lucky enough to have people we love, who have friends and families, have lots to celebrate, and we should never forget it.

This book isn't about swanky, high-falutin', show-off entertaining – leave that to those who think it matters. It's about ideas and suggestions for celebrating the great adventure that is life. All through our lives, if we are lucky, there are events that are worth making special, some momentous, others less so – there are birthdays and Christmases, Valentine's day and Halloween, and there are the great rites of passage, the big stepping stones, such as weddings and christenings and funerals. They all speak of the human need for ritual, of the necessity of acknowledging their importance in proper ways. If we ignored these fundamental human needs, if we took no trouble and never bothered to put together these life-enhancing gatherings, our lives would be the poorer – fewer friendships would be honoured, fewer love affairs would take off, fewer important thank-yous would be said, and there would be fewer opportunities for fun, which matters greatly, too.

So, it is important in these early days of the twenty-first century that we acknowledge how privileged we are to have a rich history that gives shape and meaning to many of our celebrations, for none of them has sprung up unbidden or without reason. These rituals connect us in a deep way with all those who have gone before us, and yet we can do the celebrating in very contemporary ways.

Everywhere I read that kitchen suppers, staying in, seeing friends, having picnics, playing games, making things together, having adventures are all much more in evidence than the showy, full-blown catered affairs that used to require butlers, elaborate decorations, endless imported entertainment. Hurrah! This book is an attempt to make organising these occasions easier, with advice on everything from planning and plotting to what to do about flowers, decorations and presents. Since I'm rather fond of food and drink, almost every chapter is crammed with suggestions about how and what to serve, and if there is a strong bias towards the sort of comforting, deeply satisfying food that you seldom get from most posh caterers, well, I make no apologies for that – it always seems to me so much more enjoyable than dainty bits of coulis and tricky little towers of this and that.

There's lots of practical information and a mass of truly useful websites and niche services, which I hope will help you to bring off the party, picnic or intimate dinner that you long for. It's the sort of book I wish I'd had to hand on many an occasion during a life that's been happily filled with lots of things to celebrate. If it inspires any of you to see more of your friends and families, to make the most of life's big moments, to create some truly memorable celebrations for those you care about, then I shall be more than happy.

The New Year's Eve Party

New Year's eve is like every other night; there is no pause in the march of the universe, no breathless moment of silence among created things that the passage of another twelve months may be noted; and yet no man has quite the same thoughts this evening that come with the coming of darkness on other nights. Hamilton Wright Mabie

Some people love New Year's Eve and reserve their greatest celebration of the year for the night the old year passes and the next one arrives. Others dread it, overcome by the melancholy thought that yet another year will shortly be irretrievably gone forever. Yet others try to behave as if nothing at all is happening. As one of our friends put it, 'We don't "do" New Year's Eve.' Others, though, can't escape the feeling of somehow being a failure if they're not doing anything, or haven't been invited anywhere. The thought that everybody else is having so much more fun than you are is dispiriting. This, no doubt, accounts for the fact that so many people solve what they perceive to be a problem by heading for snow or sun, where professionals put on a show and you don't have to worry your head about a thing.

I have, through the years, been to many different sorts of New Year's Eve parties and they've varied from wonderful to downright hideous. The worst were nightmarish, where the house was so packed with people that one could scarcely move, nobody bothered to introduce you to anybody and one was left to mill around, searching for a drink and hoping for a bit of food. Eventually, around midnight, something would happen but by then one had usually lost the will to live.

Those I've enjoyed most were in the Scottish Highlands or down in Dorset when we've been away – say with a group of friends and family, where all ages mingled. The food was lovely but unfussy – what could be better than smoked salmon or oysters, roast grouse, pheasant or guinea fowl, followed by Atholl Brose? The wines were well chosen, and afterwards everyone joined in games of various sorts until the clock struck midnight.

Others I've loved include millennium eve, which we spent with some old, close friends who had invited a wide circle of people, most of whom had known each other for years and been on lots of holidays together, whose children knew each other too. The gathering was large but also warm, fun and truly celebratory, with competitions, games, dressing up and a few other jollities. A better time couldn't have been had.

For me, though, the nicest, best way of all to bring in the New Year is to spend it with a smallish group of close friends where somebody has taken rather more trouble than is usual with the drink and the food, and warmth and familiarity are a major part of its charm.

The only way to spend New Year's Eve is either quietly with friends or in a brothel. Otherwise when the evening ends and people pair off, someone is bound to be left in tears. W.H. Auden

Glamorous Parties

There are, though, other, more extravagant, parties which are obviously fun – in a completely different sort of way. At the Amanpuri Hotel on the Thai island of Phuket, New Year regularly attracts a group of international jet-setters. The Duchess of York, David Tang and their ilk used to gather there every New Year – a date that, for them, seemed to be a solemn commitment. It is said that there is no harder hotel in the world to get into than the Amanpuri at that time of year.

Among celebrities it's become rather fashionable to host spectacular New Year's Eve parties, although celebs being celebs, they tend to be a bit competitive. In 2007, in the bad old, free-spending days, Jay-Z declared that he wanted to throw the most extravagant New Year's Eve party ever, and to that end spent a million pounds on fireworks for a midnight display at the Palms Hotel in Las Vegas. He had in mind that Paris and Nicky Hilton were hosting a bash in Vegas's LAX nightclub, where Pamela Anderson had been paid to turn up. Ah, well . . .

No sign of austere times either when Roman Abramovich celebrated the end of 2008 – he pulled out all the stops at his Snowmass estate in Colorado with an indoor ice rink for guests, who included F1 champion Lewis Hamilton and his girlfriend Nicole Scherzinger, who performed with her group, the Pussycat Dolls.

Or how about the themed New Year's Eve party, organised by one of Her Majesty's ambassadors to Moscow during the Cold War. He and his family threw a shipwreck party in the late 1970s, and everyone had to wear what they would be wearing if a ship were going down – some women wore nightdresses and the naval attaché wore his full uniform except for his trousers. Somehow, knowing that the 'enemy' was just outside made it seem even more precious to be having their own kind of fun. As they celebrated, they could hear the popping of champagne corks from the militia outside and saw the fireworks, which were in one colour only – a flaming red.

In Russia, New Year is bigger than the Orthodox Christmas, which is more of a low-key, family affair, falling on 7 January. In past years, the oligarchs became famous for glittering Great Gatsby-style parties, with no expense spared. Metals tycoon Vladimir Potanin, for instance, paid George Michael £1.7 million to perform for less than an hour at a private bash on New Year's Eve, while in 2008, Pravda reported that a group of 150 New Russians paid €700,000 a ticket to engage Whitney Houston, Mariah Carey and Justin Timberlake to entertain them on a flight to Iceland, en route to a 'Lord of the Rings' party!

New Year's is a harmless annual institution, of no particular use to anybody save as a scapegoat for promiscuous drunks, and friendly calls and humbug resolutions. Mark Twain

Beauty

If you're going to what you hope will be a terrific New Year's Eve party, you will want to look your best. Since New Year comes right after Christmas, with its food-based treats and time spent indoors, the skin often looks peaky, but such are the wonders of the beauty world, some excellent quick fixes are available.

Home Facials

Masks really do revive the vitality of the skin, unclogging the pores, removing dead cells, which are the chief culprit in making the skin look dull, and generally introducing a glow. Here are some of the best.

* The Organic Pharmacy's Collagen Boost Masque (£35) is one of my favourites.

* Steep Clean Mask (£32) from BlissLondon is a 15-minute do-it-yourself facial in a tube.

* Clarins Pure and Radiant Mask (£18) consists of a lovely green paste that you smear over your face. It really perks up the skin.

* Beauty therapist Lucy Sarpe, many a Notting Hill mummy's secret treat, swears by the Avene Soothing Moisture Mask (£18). She says using this is the best thing you can ever do for your skin, because it is totally rehydrating and revives dull and listless areas. She says it is important to massage the preparation into your face slowly – works instantly.

* Decleor Source d'Eclat Radiance Revealing Peel-Off Mask (£25) is great for dull skin types, leaving the skin looking more radiant.

* Neal's Yard's White Tea Enriching Facial Mask (£21.50) and Rose Formula Antioxidant Facial Mask (£21.60) have ardent fans.

* The Guinot range, in particular the Guinot Moisture Supplying Radiance Mask, the Guinot Fresh Radiance Peel-off Mask and the Guinot Refreshing and Renewing Mask (all £25), is also popular.

✳ The best and cheapest beauty treatment of all is a good long walk – gives the skin no end of a glow. And if you still look peaky, remember that Guerlain does the most fantastic bronzers – swirl a brush over its Terracotta Bronzing Powder and you'll instantly look glowy and golden.

SPA BREAKS

If you fancy getting away for a day or two of indulgent cosseting, here are some suggestions:

* AGHADOE HEIGHTS, Killarney, Co Kerry
  (www.aghadoeheights.com)
* HARTWELL HOUSE, Aylesbury, Buckinghamshire
  (www.hartwell-house.com)
* CALCOT MANOR, Tetbury, Gloucestershire
  (www.calcotmanor.co.uk)
* THE SCOTSMAN, Edinburgh (www.thescotsmanhotel.co.uk)

Day Spas

Many big hotels around the country have terrific day spas, into which you can pop for a single treatment or, if you can afford the time and money, a full day of treats. Some of them offer special 'festive packages'. Here, to give some idea, is what the spa at Brown's Hotel (www.brownshotel.com) in London offers in the way of a post-Christmas beauty revival package:

* The Mistle 'Toes' pedicure (90 minutes £85), which could get your pins ready for dancing the night away, includes massage, exfoliation, a paraffin foot wrap and nail trimming and painting. They use delicious-smelling ingredients, such as fig and cinnamon.

* The Red Carpet package (220 minutes £295) is very indulgent, including a luxurious facial, revitalising eye and lip treatment and an aromatic manicure and pedicure.

Boho types love Cowshed (www.cowshedonline.com) at Clarendon Cross, but there are other branches in Shoreditch and Soho. It's where the fashionable young set meet for beauty treatments, but it's also a nice place for coffee or lunch. You can drink fresh juices and gossip while having a manicure or pedicure. Look online for a list of UK stockists of their lovely products. Here is a selection of what they have to offer:

* The Cowgroom is the best party preparation. Two therapists work together and all treatments begin with the feet and an invigorating exfoliation with peppermint salt scrub. This is followed by a forehead pressure-point massage and a de-stressing shoulder massage to prepare you for your chosen treatment. The 30-minute treatment (£75) includes a speedy facial (which still cleanses, exfoliates and steams and you get a mask), a collagen eye treatment (which reduces puffiness and combats fine lines), eyebrow tidy, manicure, pedicure and a foot and leg massage. That should get you in great shape for a party. The 60-minute treatment (£105) includes the full Hot Stone Cowshed Facial.

* Serious facials are a speciality and you may prefer to go for one of these. I love the Anti-aging Vitamin C Facial (75 minutes £90), which leaves the skin looking luminous, and the Micro Polish Facial (60 minutes £75), which is the one to go for if your skin feels dry and dull.

More Fabulous Facials

* I'm an ardent fan of the Rose Crystal Lymphatic Facial to be had at the Organic Pharmacy (www.theorganic pharmacy.com). It includes deep cleansing, exfoliation,

steaming, extraction and four luxurious masks (Rose Hip, Seaweed, Honey and Jasmine and Collagen) as well as massage of the hands, arms, feet, face, décolleté and scalp, which incorporates a nourishing hair serum. The result is really glowing skin (and very messy hair – book a hair appointment for afterwards). It takes an hour and a half and costs £100.

* Many a fashionable Londoner swears by the Triple Oxygen Facial Mask at Bliss (www.blisslondon.co.uk). Bliss has lots of beauty pick-me-ups – including a hangover herbie, in case you feel in need of something for the morning after the night before – but the oxygen facial is usually agreed to be the gold standard.

* For a good old-fashioned facial and massage, Lucy Sarpe is much revered by all who've tried her. Top-to-toe treatment (pedicure, manicure, facial and massage) costs £125, and she can get you ready for a party in a couple of hours. An hour's facial costs £50. She works from home in the Bayswater area (telephone 07799 534288 for an appointment).

* Sophie Hunter (www.sophiehunterhealthandbeauty.co.uk) is another name hotly exchanged. Go for her Fundamental Facial (70 minutes £75), which includes cleanse, tone, peel, extract, massage and mask using Sophie Hunter Health & Beauty natural product range based on royal jelly and honey. She also offers a facial using the products of uber-modish aesthetician Dr Sebagh (90 minutes £125).

* The fabulous Anastasia Achilleos has taken over the Method Spa inside 21, the Home House extension at 21 Portman

Square, London – it is open to non-members as well as members. Her bespoke facials and treatments are divine (telephone 020 7670 2037).

* If you haven't had your eyelashes tinted or your eyebrows shaped, and want to try it, queen of the eye area is Linda Meredith (www.lindameredith.com). She also does an amazing, crystal-clear oxygen facial, which seems to bring the whole skin alive.

Hair and Beauty

Some hairdressers these days have spas attached so that you can do the whole beauty thing all at once, swanning serenely from washbasin to spa table.

* Joseph has a beauty salon upstairs at Hari's (www.haris salon.com). Besides being a dab hand with the scissors, Hari offers two special facials – one using the products of the legendary Ole Henriksen ('facialist to the stars' as Hari calls him), which have all sorts of lovely natural ingredients, and the Haute Couture Dauphin facial. Both are terrific.

* Paul Edmonds (www.pauledmonds.com) is a magician with hair but he also has a beautiful spa, offering some fantastic facials. Environ is a beauty brand that the world of fashion, stage and screen has recently discovered, and he offers a facial using its products. He also offers a Hydradermie facial, using products by Guinot, which lifts and firms the jawline and neck, drains toxins and helps smooth wrinkles.

* Richard Ward (www.richardward.co.uk), another hair stylist to the fashionable crew – he has long done the terrific cuts and highlights for Trinny and Susannah – has all sorts of holistic and other treatments. You can have everything from a massage to a manicure, pedicure and a facial.

* Aveda (www.aveda.co.uk) has a whole host of salons across the UK, offering both hair and spa treatments.

What to Do?

One can't write anything about New Year's Eve without giving honourable mention to Scotland, the home of Hogmanay, which has a special place in the heart of every Scot. The traditional New Year's Eve in grander houses involves playing Scottish music, dancing reels, dining off smoked salmon, pheasant, haggis and other specialities, and frequently continuing to party right into the next day.

The drawback of dancing reels is that you need plenty of room and at least twelve people. In bigger houses (in Edinburgh's New Town the houses have famously large rooms) it's easy – families often combine forces and celebrate together in the house of the family with the largest room. Otherwise, halls can be hired, and ticketed events are not hard to find. It makes it all much more fun if the men wear kilts, and the women long dresses with tartan sashes. Non-Scots wear their party outfits, with some tartan touches. The singing of Robbie Burns's poem 'Auld Lang Syne' while linking crossed arms in a circle has been taken up by many

English-speaking nations, but it always has a special resonance when sung on its home ground.

Once midnight has struck, the age-old custom of 'first-footing' comes into play, and not just in Scotland. This involves trying to be the first person to cross the threshold of a friend or neighbour (a tall, dark-haired male brings the most luck), and should be accompanied by the giving of symbolic gifts – it used to be coal, but these days it might be shortbread, whisky or a rich fruit cake. The first-foot is supposed to set the luck for the rest of the year.

Haste ye back, we loue you dearly, call again you're welcome here. May your days be free from sorrow, and your friends be ever near. May the paths o'er which you wander, be to you a joy each day. Haste ye back we loue you dearly, haste ye back on friendship's way.

Sung by Andy Stewart and the cast at the end of each edition of 'The White Heather Club', a television show that ran every New Year's Eve from 1957–68

If Not Scotland, Where?

These days, many cities around the world stage special, all-inclusive celebrations, so that everybody can take part. Sydney, the first large city to see in the New Year because of its geographical position, always has spectacular fireworks that light up the harbour, the opera house and the bridge, and is a family-friendly occasion. New York has a great party atmosphere in Times Square. Fireworks by the Thames in London, and the Tyne in Newcastle, are also fabulous, and people still traditionally gather in Trafalgar Square. All over the country, towns and cities invite the general public to join in, and the atmosphere is usually happy and upbeat.

Renting somewhere with friends and toasting the occasion in foreign climes is not a bad way to start the new year, and can become a habit. Some friends of ours always go to the Swiss Alps, where they ski all day and celebrate the Swiss way in restaurants and cafés all night – very carefree. Others party in rented houses in Cape Town, where it's high summer and beach picnics become part of the newly established rituals.

The Russian National Group (www.russia-travel.com) runs tours at this time of year, during which you can sample such wonderful specialities as troika rides and a visit to the ballet. Included is a New Year's Eve party in Tsarskoe Selo, near St Petersburg, and if you're looking for a big, extravagant celebration, that's certainly what you get. As well as spending the evening in a fabulous palace, you are entertained with music, ballet, opera and choral singing. After cocktails, you are given an Imperial dinner, prepared by French chefs, and watch fireworks at midnight – not cheap, but a serious extravaganza.

What to Eat?

While the New Year's Eve formula I like best is a smallish dinner party with good friends, I recognise that human nature comes in very varied packages and others may well prefer other forms of celebration. The difficulty is that while hanging around waiting for the clock to strike, food is needed. So here are some ideas.

Small Eats

* Canapé kits have recently become a Christmas speciality and there's every reason to suppose they'll go on being popular. Forman & Field (www.formanandfield.com) have a kit for serving buckwheat blinis and smoked salmon. It comes with proper blinis, generous portions of smoked salmon and small tubs of the essential extras – crème fraiche, chopped shallots and capers. Its Tartare Shots (developed by an ex Roux brothers chef) are also delicious – heavy shot glasses filled with salmon and orange, beetroot and gravadlax, or smoked tuna with capers. Neither of those is cheap (£17.95 for 18 blinis and £19.95 for six shot glasses and their contents) but they are dead easy to serve.

* Both Marks & Spencer (www.marksandspencer.com) and Waitrose (www.waitrose.com) have good catering divisions and offer a variety of canapés and I have to say that they are not quite as delicious as the finest home-made *but* – and it's a very big *but* – they are efficient, trouble-free and not all that expensive. In other words, a very acceptable

halfway house. If you have masses of people coming and know you won't have time to fiddle, they're a godsend. Marks & Spencer's mini bacon, mint and pea frittatas are really good if heated in a hot oven for between five and eight minutes, and it would be wonderfully retro to serve their mini cheeseburgers – they need a bit of cooking and assembly but not too much. Waitrose has miniature portions of roast beef with horseradish sauce and yorkshire puddings, which are ready to heat. They also have sushi, mini-fishcakes and tapas.

* www.effortless-eating.com has a changing seasonal menu of fabulous starters (beef carpaccio with shaved parmesan, rocket and lemon dressing, or crab, shelled pea and broad bean salad with parmesan wafers), which are elegant though not particularly cheap.

* Crostini aren't hard to make. Slice a ciabatta into rounds, brush with oil on both sides and toast in a hot oven until golden (about ten minutes). Then top with Stilton, guacamole, smoked salmon, gravadlax or anything else you fancy.

* Spread bruschetta with wonderfully good salmon pâté. Marks & Spencer sell one at this time of year, made with nothing but salmon, dill and some cream, and Forman & Field's smoked wild salmon pâté is good, too.

Cold Spread

Another tack is to lay out lots of gorgeous breads – Poilane's country loaf, rye bread, walnut or olive loaves (I buy ours from Richard Polo's Exeter Street Bakery in London, but

there are now lots of places that sell interesting breads). Put
out salamis, ham, prosciutto, cheeses and, if you can find it,
the lovely Italian mostardo di frutta, which is traditionally
used to perk up boiled meats, rather like chutney. Galicia in
London's Portobello Road does gorgeous Spanish hams.
Italian antipasti is perfect party food and it's worth knowing
about Savoria (www.savoria.co.uk), which imports wonderful
Sicilian bottarga di tonno rosso (divine shaved over pasta),
hams, cheeses and olive oils as well as truffles in season. Lay
out big bowls of tomatoes, olives, celery, gherkins, and let
people help themselves.

Hot Food

Later in the evening, you could come up with one gorgeous
hot dish – a delicious fish soup with all the trimmings would
be fabulous, or a divine fish pie, or lamb cooked long and
tenderly with haricot beans. For a big party, where proper
food is needed, I'm prejudiced in favour of comforting
dishes, such as lasagnes and cottage pies (see page 349).
They're relatively easy to make in quantity, heat up well and
are well behaved, not requiring last-minute attention, and
they're generally liked by all ages from small children up to
octogenarians. If you don't have time to make them, try
those available from www.effortless-eating.com – they come
in great big white china containers and taste thrillingly
home-made.

Puddings

It is again the simple things that appeal to all ages – meringues, profiteroles (both dead easy to make at home by simply following recipes), trifles, jellies, chocolate cake (see page 88).

MOROCCAN THEME

It can be fun to theme an evening. Food from North Africa is spicy and enticing – try delicious spicy fishcakes with a chermoula sauce, followed by a tagine (either lamb or chicken) accompanied by a salad of some sort (sliced fennel, orange and red onion makes a good refreshing one in winter). For pudding, I love izmiri, a Middle Eastern fruit salad of dried fruits soaked in rose or orange water overnight and then gently cooked (in the same liquid with perhaps some lemon rind, cinnamon and nutmeg) until softened and finally topped with toasted almonds and served with yoghurt.

Dinner Party Menu

If you're doing an intimate dinner for, say, six, eight or ten of your closest friends, then I think the food needs to be slightly grander than for a big party. I'd start with the best smoked salmon you can find (see Fergus Granville's notes on page 25), served either plain with gorgeous bread (I love it with Irish soda bread) or on blinis with sour cream and some caviar (I think Danish lumpfish roe is perfectly fine, but if you can afford the vertiginous prices of oscietra, beluga or sevruga that would, of course, be a divine treat). Other alternatives are a good borscht with some sour cream, hot smoked eel fillets, crab and avocado salad (mix the crab and avocado together in quite lumpy pieces, mark out in circles with a cookie cutter and serve on a bed of rocket) or – if you love it – foie gras (see sources on pages 22–23) and brioche with a glass of a delicious Sauternes.

Potted shrimps are always wonderful. I love Baxter's (www.baxterspottedshrimps.co.uk) and those from the Fish Society (www.thefishsociety.co.uk), which is a wonderful source of fresh fish, from Dover soles to more exotic species. I have just discovered that www.effortless-eating.com also sells them, beautifully potted in great big glass kilner jars for either four to six or eight to ten people, and they look particularly inviting.

For a main course, I'd go for simply cooked game of some kind – pheasant, duck or guinea fowl – accompanied by red cabbage, roasted parsnips and either finely cut game chips or roasted potatoes. (The BBC website has a delicious recipe for roasted guinea fowl – go to www.bbcgoodfood.com/recipes and in the search box, enter: guinea fowl with mustard and lemon roots.) It's a good time to do something heavenly with Jerusalem artichokes as well – sauté the peeled and sliced artichokes in some olive oil until golden brown and cooked through, then toss some garlic, parsley and walnuts into the pan and cook for a few more minutes. Those in Scotland might choose haggis or braised venison.

Follow this with some fabulous cheeses and a delicious pud, such as a walnut and prune tart, or, for those who are feeling overfed from Christmas, some poached fruit – plums, figs, quinces if you can find them – with amaretti ice cream. You can always buy in delicious ice creams – most farmers' markets sell them and there's always Green & Black's fabulous chocolate ones.

And finally, don't forget, too, that a wonderful and yet simple way to end a fine meal is by offering around Cantuccini biscuits to dip into a glass of Vin Santo, that delicious sweet amber Tuscan wine.

J. Sheekey's Shellfish Cocktail

This wonderful starter has many fans.
Here is the recipe in quantities for four people.
(The Head Chef at J. Sheekey Oyster Bar is Richard Kirkwood.
Check out the restaurant at www.j-sheekey.co.uk.)

6oz/175g cooked Atlantic prawns
5oz/150g cooked lobster
5oz/150g cooked white crabmeat
4 cooked Dublin Bay prawns
1 head Iceberg lettuce
1 head red endive
4 spring onions
½ cucumber
18fl oz/½ litre mayonnaise
12oz/350g tomato ketchup
1 tsp Tabasco sauce

splash of Worcestershire sauce
½ juiced lemon
splash of cognac

1. Prepare seafood: peel Atlantic prawns, removing heads; dice lobster meat; check crabmeat for any bits of shell; remove shells from tails of Dublin Bay prawns, keeping heads intact.
2. Shred lettuce and endive together.
3. Peel cucumber and cut into thin slices (the size of a matchstick); thinly slice spring onions at an angle.
4. Place lettuce and endive into the base of a glass and add a small amount of each shellfish.
5. Add more lettuce, endive, cucumber and spring onion.
6. Place remainder of shellfish on top of lettuce, except for the prawn tail.
7. Make Marie Rose sauce: mix mayonnaise, tomato ketchup, Tabasco, Worcestershire sauce, lemon and cognac together; pour a large spoonful over seafood mix.
8. Place one Dublin Bay prawn on top.

Foie Gras

Too rich for every day, as a once-a-year treat I love it, but some people hate the very idea, worried about the conditions in which the geese that provide the swollen livers are kept. They may be interested to know that Waitrose has developed a faux gras, which is made from goose or duck livers, blended with goose or duck fat, obtained from birds that live normal lives, wandering round the farm paddocks. It doesn't taste quite the same as foie gras, but at least allows one to eat it with a clear conscience.

One of *The Times* cookery writers, Sheila Keating, brought to her readers' attention a Spanish goose liver, produced by Eduardo de Sousa, a farmer from just north of Seville. His geese, apparently, fatten themselves up in autumn by eating as much as they can, ready for the rigours involved in migrating to warmer climates. De Sousa helps the process along by putting out figs, acorns, lupins and olives on which they gorge (unforced) until their bellies touch the ground and their livers have naturally grown fat. Then they are humanely dispatched. He won an award for compassion from the Paris International Food Salon. Selfridges sells what Sheila Keating calls this 'welfare-friendly' version of cooked foie gras exclusively. Traditional foie gras (whole livers in Pinot Gris wine jelly) as well as duck liver can be bought from www.thegoodfood network.co.uk. Other foie gras en gelee and foie gras en croute can be bought from www.efoodies.co.uk.

Caviar

There is more simplicity in the man who eats caviar on impulse than in the man who eats Grape-Nuts on principle. G.K. Chesterton

Charlie Chaplin apparently once sold a thousand-word excerpt from his autobiography for 9lb/4kg of golden caviar, the most sought-after and rarefied of the sturgeon's eggs. These days, if you could find it, it would cost you about £15,000 for 2¹/₄lb/1kg, packed in a 24-carat gold tin.

If you're worried about the future of wild sturgeon, which is severely threatened, it's worth knowing that sturgeon farms are being set up all over the caviar-loving world, in France, Italy, China, the USA and, most recently, Israel. It's not a quick-fix solution, though. It takes between fifteen and twenty years before a sturgeon is mature enough to produce sufficient eggs for harvesting. A trickle of caviar from farmed sources is beginning to reach the expectant market, and it is a good deal cheaper than the wild variety – Caviar d'Aquitaine from France retails at £48 for 1oz/30g as against about £155 for the same amount of Iranian beluga – but the jury is still out on the quality.

Beluga (banned except from Iran, where it is legally caught) is the most sought-after, with the biggest eggs, which range in colour from light grey to almost black. Next comes oscietra, with its golden-brown eggs – a little smaller but with a slightly fruity note. Sevruga is the smallest sturgeon and produces the smallest eggs, which are dark grey to black in colour.

According to food writer Matthew Fort, there is no need to bother with chopped egg or onion when you serve caviar. This is how you eat it: 'Get yourself a mother-of-pearl spoon, scoop out a tidy amount from a tin that you've just opened, and place on the back of the hand between forefinger and thumb. Let it rest there for a moment or two to allow blood temperature to just warm it through slightly, and then scoop it into your mouth with lips and tongue. That's what the experts do, anyway.'

He adds, 'The correct drink is not Krug, or indeed champagne of any kind, nor vodka, no matter how well chilled, but a really crisp Muscadet, which would interfere least with the delicate and elusive qualities of great caviar.'

Where to buy it? Caviar House has joined forces with Maison Prunier (www.caviarhouse-prunier.com) to sell caviar produced on fish farms in the Bordeaux area. The sturgeon are bred in tanks in which the Caspian climate is replicated.

Smoked Salmon

Pink, slimy, floppy smoked salmon is an abomination. Pale, beautifully smoked, firm-fleshed smoked salmon is still an all-time treat. Now that there is so much disgusting stuff around, purveyed by the cheapest of high-street chains, it is worth knowing where to buy the best – and, more importantly, why it is the best. I buy my own from the Hebridean Smokehouse (www.hebrideansmokehouse.com) because it farms its own salmon in a tidal bay at North Uist, which means the food miles from harvest to production are very few. If you find yourself in North Uist you should go to Clachan, Locheport, and buy it in person. Owner Earl Granville, otherwise known as Fergus, gives us the low-down on smoked salmon today.

Fergus Granville's Philosophy

* Good fish are essential to start with – as with many other products, the end result is dependent on the raw material.

* Smoking may disguise or improve a bad fish, but only to some extent.

* Good farmed salmon must have been grown, harvested and handled properly.

* Good-quality farmed salmon come from sites that have a good tidal exchange, and are stocked at a reasonable density. The fish should be fed a relatively low-oil diet.

* Ideally, the salmon should be harvested by hand and in unstressed condition. Stressing the fish – aside from animal welfare considerations – causes a build-up of lactic acid, which results in the smoked salmon splitting and gaping.

* Once killed, careful handling is essential. For instance, a dead whole fish should not be lifted by the head or tail, because this causes dislocation of the spinal column and consequent blood-spotting in the smoked fish.

Salting, Smoking and Slicing:

* Good smoked salmon should be neither over- nor under-salted. The former may achieve a longer shelf-life at the expense of palatability, as can other additives.

* Smoking is part art and part science. The aim is to gauge environmental factors and achieve the correct percentage weight loss and flavouring. The smoke should not overwhelm completely the taste of the salmon.

* Smoking in small batches, ensuring that proper monitoring and attention to detail is possible, is important.

* Slicing by hand is preferable to slicing by machine. The hand-slicer notices and removes bones, scales and bruised areas, and uses a D-shaped cut, which incorporates sections from the whole fish in each slice – from surface (pellicle) down to skin – ensuring a balanced taste. (The surface area is likely to be smokier and saltier.) Hand slicing does not produce the oiliness caused by the vibrations of slicing machines, which use a long cut along the length of the side, coming from a necessarily uniform depth.

Bad Practice:

* Bad smoked salmon comes from salmon that have been grown at high density as fast as possible and subsequently mechanically harvested and processed.

* The fish are liable to be oily, flabby and bruised, as will be the resultant smoked salmon.

* Machine slicing worsens oiliness.

* Injecting brine, rather than dry-salting, is done for convenience and to add weight. (The fish should lose weight during this process.)

* To save time and money, and to lessen weight-loss, a shorter and more intensive smoking may be done, which results in salmon that is too smokey.

* Mass production, by its nature, doesn't lend itself to a high-quality end product.

What Should the Consumer Look Out for?

* Origin – Scottish is best, but read the small print, because fish imported from elsewhere can be processed in Scotland and called 'Scottish'.

* Hand slicing – generally better than machine-slicing.

* Wide white lines of fat with relatively big distances between them – these indicate fast-grown fish and so should be avoided.

* Oil visible in the vacuum-packed bag – a bad sign.

* Fish displaying blotchy marks, blood spots or general poor presentation – avoid.

* Gimmicky or elaborate marinades – these may be used to mask basic poor quality.

* Price – with smoked salmon, you tend to get what you pay for. Producing very good smoked salmon is labour intensive and expensive. Cheap smoked salmon made by big operators is fine as an ingredient in another dish, but to eat on its own when quality matters, go for small, relatively expensive producers.

* Qualifications – most quality marques on packaging generally relate to a minimum standard of fish production and husbandry, not the quality of smoking/slicing, and so are no practical help in choosing smoked salmon. Some smokehouses choose to publicise awards gained, noting them on the packaging, but it's not hard to amass these if you enter enough competitions. Anything less than a

Gold/Silver Great Taste Award probably doesn't give much indication of quality.

Finally, in the farmed v. wild debate, bear in mind that most wild salmon is now Alaskan/Canadian, so has food miles issues. The best farmed smoked salmon should be on a par with wild.

Cocktails

There's no doubt that young people (their livers still relatively perky) love cocktails. Here are recipes for some classics and a few less usual ones:

Pomegranate Martinis

Pomegranate is the ingredient *du jour*, purporting to be good for everything from arthritis to rejuvenation, but whatever else it may or may not do, it tastes good.

* Three parts tequila to five parts each of triple sec, lime juice and pomegranate juice

Classic Martini

This recipe won the 1951 Martini competition in Chicago.

* ½fl oz/15ml dry vermouth, 3fl oz/90ml gin, ⅓fl oz/10ml Cointreau, 2 anchovy-stuffed olives

Mojito

* Mix 5 mint leaves with half a cup of freshly chopped lime. Shake together with 60ml white rum, 20ml sugar syrup and 3 tsp of caster sugar. Add to a highball glass (tall, straight-sided) and top up with soda water and a sprig of mint.

Bloody Mary

* To 90ml of spiced tomato juice add 15ml of vodka as well as some celery salt and black pepper. Shake all together.
   Big Tom, sold by many supermarkets and other drinks outlets, is a delicious bottled spicy tomato juice. To make your own, add a dash of Worcestershire sauce, a dash of Tabasco and a squeeze of lemon juice to your usual tomato juice.

Sea Breeze

* Mix 5ml of vodka with 130ml of cranberry juice and 35ml of grapefruit juice. Add ice and garnish with a wedge of lime.

Cosmopolitan

* Mix 60ml vodka with 30ml triple sec, 30ml cranberry juice. Add ice and garnish with a wedge of lime.

Manhattan

* 5ml sweet vermouth, 3ml bourbon whiskey, dash of angostura bitters, twist of orange peel and one maraschino

cherry. Combine the vermouth, bourbon whiskey and bitters with 2–3 ice cubes in a mixing glass. Stir gently, so as not to bruise the spirits and cloud the drink. Place the cherry in a chilled cocktail glass and strain the whiskey mixture over the cherry. Rub the cut edge of the orange peel over the rim of the glass and twist it over the drink to release the oils but don't drop it in.

Champagne Cocktails

Some people hate them (Matthew Jukes, for instance, see below and speaking personally I like my champagne straight) but sometimes they add a bit of fun to the proceedings. Grand mimosas are no trouble. For every 750ml bottle of chilled champagne or sparkling wine, mix in two cups of chilled fresh orange and ¼ cup of orange liqueur, and serve straightaway. There are plenty of other champagne cocktails, of course – a Bellini is champagne and peach juice, a Kir Royal is champagne with crème de cassis while Champagne Royale is champagne mixed with a dash of black raspberry liqueur and garnished with fresh raspberries.

FUNKIN PUREES

Finally, don't forget funkin purées – used by bartenders all over the country, these are pure puréed fruits with just a dash of sugar to help preserve them – no artificial flavours, additives, colourings or preservatives at all. Choose from 22 different flavours, including pear, peach, raspberry, apple and strawberry. As well as cocktails, they can be used as a basis for sorbets or ice creams. Check the website (www.funkin.eu) for recipes. Special mixes are also available for a whole range of cocktails from Pina Colada to raspberry mojitos and passionfruit margaritas.

✤·✤

Champagne
by Matthew Jukes, of Quintessentially Wine

Champagne is the quintessential celebratory drink. More than just a synonym for celebration, it has the bounce and resilience necessary to cope with myriad gastronomic demands, but one must choose carefully. Above all, avoid champagne cocktails – an abomination – and as for Black Velvet (equal measures of champagne and Guinness), it's an insult to them both.

Bottles come in ten different sizes, from the humble quarter bottle, or snipe, up to the mighty Nebuchadnezzar with a capacity of twenty bottles. Anything above the magnum size, though, is seldom seen and, indeed, it can be dangerous to try to pour from these bottles (never mind the problems involved in chilling). The serious point is that, aside from the impression they make, magnums are regarded as being better for the champagne, because they contain the same amount of air as a regular bottle but twice the volume of liquid. Therefore, the thinking goes, the wine ages more slowly (less oxidation) and, as a result, develops greater complexity.

Insisting on the right glass for your favourite champagne should not be seen as an affectation. From a narrow point at the bottom of the bowl, the glass should flare gradually outwards, wider than the normal flute, before turning in more sharply towards the rim. A continuous stream of bubbles is stimulated by the point at the bottom while the turn-in at the top helps capture the bouquet.

WHAT TO DO ABOUT A HANGOVER

First off, you can try to mitigate the effects by matching each glass of alcohol with one of water (cue to hosts to provide enough water). Mixing drinks – whisky, say, or liqueurs, with wines – makes things much worse, and don't drink on an empty stomach. Eat as you go along, even if it's only a few nibbles with each drink.

Next morning, some people find a hearty breakfast – lots of carbs – helps. Otherwise, a very spicy Virgin Mary (i.e. a Bloody Mary without the vodka) may do the trick, or a traditional prairie oyster. For this, carefully crack one whole raw egg into a glass without breaking the yolk. Season it with Worcestershire sauce, salt and pepper, and swallow it fast so that you don't break the yolk.

Games

Games and other entertainments are a quintessential part
of many a New Year's Eve party. In our family, since my
husband has a Scottish background, we used, when his parents
were alive, to dance Scottish reels over the New Year period.
They were a lot of fun, and something to be enjoyed by all
ages. And you don't have to be Scottish. You can buy discs of
the music of all the famous reels – Dashing White Sergeant,
the Gay Gordons, the Eightsome Reel – and while it helps if
somebody knows what to do, if you're stuck you can find
instructions for more than you'll ever get around to dancing
online (www.scottishdance.net/ceilidh/dances). The provisos
are that you need space and quite a lot of people.

A good ploy to get people warmed up and in party mood
is to start with the game where one person sticks a post-it
note with the name of a famous character to the forehead of
another guest, who has to guess the name, by dint of
questioning his opposite number.

A topical quiz is always great fun. Select questions from a
book (there are always loads of quiz books around at
Christmas time), keep the end-of-year quizzes from
newspapers, or ask guests to bring along a set of ten
questions each. You can break them up into current affairs,
sport, art, literature, geography or anything else.

Charades is a great party game. This is one of several ways
to play it. Divide everyone into small teams, making sure
they're as evenly balanced in terms of age and enterprise as
possible. Each team in turn acts out a word, or the title of a

book, play, film, song or painting, in mime. Speaking is not allowed. Titles can be divided into separate words, and words into syllables, or acted as the whole thing. The teams either choose what they are going to do or pull their challenge out of a hat. The other teams have to guess what the answer is – use a stop-watch or an egg-timer to time how long it takes to guess. The quickest team wins.

Other old favourites are 'Twenty Questions', 'Murder in the Dark' (a great game if you're in a house party), backgammon and Scrabble. Packs of cards for games of whist, rummy or even bridge are a great standby. There are lots of helpful websites filled with instructions for games for every age. In particular www.partygameideas.com and www.game-daddy.com.

New Year's Day is every man's birthday.
Charles Lamb

7

Valentine's Day

When I was young, I don't remember St Valentine's Day ever figuring very much. These days, judging by the amount of tosh that appears in the newspapers in the run-up to the day, it's big. I have to confess I find the whole notion slightly naff, a rather embarrassing cliché beset with hearts, balloons, shades of pink and cheap cards, but all over the country tokens of affection and rather expensive eating rituals seem to be required, mostly, it has to be said, by the female of the species. So what to do? Nothing for it, I think, but to enter into the spirit of the thing. It would be too curmudgeonly to do anything else, and besides, it's indubitably true that St Valentine's Day does come at a pretty drear time of year. T.S. Eliot thought April the cruellest month. Me, I think it's February. St Valentine's Day does provide a splendid excuse for some jollity just when most of us could do with a bit of an uplift.

Origins

How and why 14 February came to be called St Valentine's Day and the focus of romance, when tokens of love are traditionally exchanged, is something of a mystery. It appears to have grown out of a pagan ceremony marking a young man's rite of passage in which the god Lupercus played a key role. The Catholic Church, being keener on saints than pagan gods, niftily redirected lovers' allegiance to a certain St Valentine, chosen because he was a bishop who had been martyred for persistently joining young Roman soldiers to their dearly beloveds in wedlock – the Emperor Claudius thought they made better soldiers when not distracted by the transports of marriage.

The day became associated with romance during the time of Chaucer, when the tradition of courtly love flourished. Young men started offering handwritten greetings, stating their affection, to the girls they wished to court, and so the matter of notes became a ritual. In the nineteenth century, sharp-eyed entrepreneurs spotted an opportunity, and mass-produced cards for the occasion largely took over. These days, about one billion Valentine's cards are sent each year worldwide, and when it comes to presents, it's interesting to note that in the US men spend on average twice as much as women.

Cards

I think the two classiest things to do are either to make your own, or at least to personalise the card to make it particular and special, or to buy an antique one.

* A brilliant website for personalising cards, with quite jokey, fun ideas, is www.moonpig.com.

* Photobox cards (www.photobox.co.uk) are also great – you get to choose the photograph you put on the front.

* As with Christmas and birthdays, I don't really think an email card does it, but if you're really stuck and you've missed the post, then www.pennypostcards.com allows you to choose from a whole range of rather charming antique-style ones.

You add a personal message and send it to an email address free where, of course, it arrives instantaneously.

* Antique Valentine's cards have to be seized upon when you come across them as there's a bit of serendipity involved. Some auction houses have sales of them a few weeks before the day so keep your eyes peeled. Otherwise, vintage bookshops often sell them and so do some antique shops. They are usually utterly enchanting and turn the card into something more like a real present. Lucky recipients can collect and frame them.

* If you're stuck for words, let me recommend *Love Letters* collected by Michelle Lovric (published by Weidenfeld & Nicolson). Here are some of the most eloquent love letters ever written, and the book is beautifully embellished with drawings, photographs and little envelopes bearing facsimiles of the originals of many of the letters. Dip into it for some inspiration. You could copy out something appropriate, in as beautiful a script as you can manage, inside an antique card, or one of your own making.

You can't come into the room without my feeling all over me a ripple of flame, & if, wherever you touch me, a heart beats under your touch, & if, when you hold me, & I don't speak, it's because all the words in me seem to have become throbbing pulses. Edith Wharton, novelist, to W. Morton Fullerton, journalist, early March 1908

How to Celebrate

The wonderful thing about St Valentine's Day is that you have to think of just two people. It doesn't take the planning skills of Montgomery at Alamein to organise. The real problem lies around the weight of expectation and the pressure to come up with something wild and wonderful. The other thing is that restaurants, florists, chocolate suppliers and all the rest seem to think it is a good opportunity to make financial hay. I have known couples choose to treat each other on either side of the big day to avoid the prime heists, or whisking the best-beloved away before or after but not necessarily on the day itself. There are plenty of simple ways to celebrate, though, that are just as much fun as whizzing off to Paris or Rome.

Picnics

In our Northern Hemisphere, where it's usually extremely cold in February, anything outdoors requires some planning if it's not to be an ordeal, but winter picnics, even in cities, have a certain romance about them. Cosily wrapped up with muffs, and even hot-water bottles, and with Thermoses of hot food and drinks – mulled wine, maybe, or hot chocolate – the two of you can find a special place to spend an hour or two. City parks, the gardens of stately homes, hills and woods in Dorset, the flatlands of East Anglia and lonely beaches everywhere all have a strange, melancholy, wintry beauty about them, and the wonderful thing is that not many other people will be about. There's a certain sort of best beloved who would be charmed by a hike up to some amazing peak, where, almost certainly, you could have a picnic all to yourselves. Look at pages 89–95 for suggestions for winter picnics. Check into www.the-picnic-site.com for all sorts of romantic picnic ieas.

Dinner and a Movie

I think there's nothing nicer – particularly if you're still in the early phases of a romance and if the suggestion comes from the male of the species – than a specially cooked dinner for two, followed by a fabulous romantic movie, preferably a grand old weepie – 'Casablanca', 'An Affair to Remember', 'Doctor Zhivago', 'Gone With The Wind', 'Roman Holiday'. Get them from www.lovefilm.co.uk or your local DVD shop may well have them.

   If you prefer to go out, great treats are to be had other than mainstream films. Check what's on at the National Film Society, the Electric Cinema and art cinemas dotted around the country. Followed by dinner, it makes for a wonderful evening.

Weekend Away

If you want to get away, publand has been transformed with lots of really gorgeous pubs and inns offering lovely rooms, good accommodation and great food. Think about the Yorkshire Dales, the Lake District or Dorset – to my mind, one of the most beautiful counties of all. Check www.thegoodpub guide.co.uk and Alistair Sawday's website (www.sawdays.co.uk) for a wonderful range of suggestions from inexpensive to plush.

ALTERNATIVE ROMANTIC MOVIES

Most suggestions for romantic films are the usual rather schmaltzy ones we all know and love so well. Nothing wrong with that. But if you want something more off-beat here is a list taken from www.huffingtonpost.com. As the site puts it: 'they pack a potent romantic wallop, but are a bit less obvious'.

1. 'Eyewitness' (1981): a Manhattan janitor makes himself a target for a killer by claiming to have information about a murder – in order to get closer to the TV reporter who's covering the story. This stars William Hurt and Sigourney Weaver, before they made it. A smart script and lots of personal chemistry.

2. 'The Terminator' (1984): A classic. 'I came through time for you,' Kyle Reese (Michael Biehn) tells Sarah Connor (Linda Hamilton), in a romantic moment, sandwiched between chase sequences as they flee the unstoppable Arnold Schwarzenegger. Strictly speaking, not a romantic movie, but it's hard to ignore the sweeping sentiment when the two of them finally have a few minutes together.

3. 'Brokeback Mountain' (2005): the gay cowboy movie – and one of the most heartbreaking romances ever. Heath Ledger is amazing as the tight-lipped cowboy who falls for his sheep-herding partner, Jake Gyllenhaal. They don't come more moving than this.

4. 'Crouching Tiger, Hidden Dragon' (2000): Ang Lee's martial-arts epic offers incredible visual effects and hand-to-hand acrobatics, but it's the unspoken love story between the two central characters that remains with you at the end. Very affecting.

5. 'Manhattan' (1979): lovely romantic film. A bittersweet comedy with intense feelings, outstanding performances and great comic writing, plus gorgeous Gordon Willis black-and-white photography and a Gershwin score – you can't go wrong.

6. 'City Lights' (1931): unrequited love between Charlie Chaplin, as the Little Tramp, and Virginia Cherrill, as the blind flower girl he falls for, in what may be his funniest and most touching silent feature. She thinks he's a millionaire – and so he goes to great lengths to find the money for the operation that will restore her sight. A perfect date film.

Alistair Sawday is particularly good for the little-known but terrific pub. He also features out-of-the-way country rectories – anywhere, really, that's off the beaten track.

* Malmaison hotels (www.malmaison.com) offer luxury at not-too-expensive prices – and they're always a visual pleasure, design being one of their priorities, but if you really want to be alone, a little cottage down a ramshackle lane might be just the thing. Check out the Landmark Trust (www.landmarktrust.org.uk). Their properties for rent range from the said cottage to a lighthouse, a castle or a vast stately pile.

If you want to move up a notch and stay in a truly romantic hotel, look to Mr and Mrs Smith (www.mrandmrssmith.com) for advice. In reality, Mr and Mrs Smith are James Lohan and Tamara Heber-Percy. When they fell in love, they wanted, like many a young couple before them, to get away for romantic weekends in the country, but could they find a guide that told them all the things they really wanted to know before they set off down the motorway on a long journey? They could not. It was at a particularly grim hotel in the Lake District where they were having a thoroughly miserable time – again – (Corby trouser press, magnolia kettle big enough for just two cups of tea, miniature UHT cartons and ginger biscuits, bed with a dip in the middle) that they decided to give up on all known hotel guides and do it themselves. They had one question in mind – would the hotel, pub or guest house give young couples with romance on their mind a great time?

They stayed in over a thousand hotels up and down the UK and ended up tracking down fifty-two enchanting spots for a romantic weekend, covering all sorts of moods, one for every weekend of the year. They have a knack of telling readers exactly what they want to know – which room to ask for, which table in the dining-room you'd most like to sit at, which other restaurants are worth visiting, what clothes to take, things to do in the area, as well as all the usual practical details. Bear in mind, though, that these are not cut-price hotels – they're mostly gorgeous. You can check the hotels by geographical location on the website, and also make a reservation. And incidentally, they sell a brilliant CD ('Something for the Weekend') – a compilation of some of Mr & Mrs Smith's favourite hip bands.

I can neither eat nor sleep for thinking of you my dearest love. I never touch even puddings.

Horatio Nelson to Lady Emma Hamilton, 29 January 1800

Going Farther Afield

* Eurostar (www.eurostar.com) takes you to Brussels, Lille or Paris, and you can change for Bruges, an almost perfect medieval city. Cheaper day tickets are often available if you book in advance. Amsterdam also has trendy shops and amazing museums. To make Valentine's Day a really special, probably never-to-be-repeated, occasion, take the Orient Express to Paris or Venice.

* The pyramids make a splendidly romantic setting for St Valentine's Day. If you stay at the Fairmont Towers Heliopolis (www.fairmont.com), the hotel can sometimes arrange for Dr Zahi Hawass, the head of Egypt's Supreme Council of Antiquities, to breathe some life back into the ancient stones by sharing some of his most exciting recent archaeological findings during an intimate lecture over dinner.

* One of the most romantic treats of all – particularly if a proposal is in the offing – is to whisk your beloved to Vienna and on to the dance floor at one of the many famous balls held between November and February. The Johann Strauss ball is closest to Valentine's Day, but it gets very booked up so get your skates on early. Check out www.vienna.info for everything you need to know. Tickets for the ball cost about £110 per person and there's a strict dress code – black tie for men and floor-length ball gowns for women. (www.soundofvienna.at can book a package for you.)

* For well-heeled art lovers, a special viewing of one of the world's greatest paintings – Leonardo da Vinci's 'The Last

Supper' in Milan's Santa Maria delle Grazie – is hard to beat. Usually, the mural is surrounded by eager tourists, but book into the hotel Principe di Savoia (via www.bellini travel.com) and the concierge can arrange for you to see this Renaissance masterpiece after the crowds have gone. The church can be kept open and art expert Maria Teresa Cairo is available as a guide to the complicated symbolism of the picture. Afterwards, you sit down to an intimate dinner, just the two of you, in front of the picture, lit by flickering candlelight. While on the subject of Italy, Emily Fitzroy at Bellini Travel can sort out any number of truly special experiences all over that beautiful country.

Grand Gestures

* If you want to go for the grand romantic gesture there's a website specially for you, www.theromantic.com. Lots of wonderfully daffy ideas. For instance, gather together chocolate, favourite tea, cookies, a small teddy bear, whatever else you know he/she loves, label it xxxx's Late Night Survival Pack and sticker it with a red cross and tell her to open it when things get tough at work. Pick up a smooth stone when you're out walking and have it engraved with a special message ('Ned loves Samantha' – if you don't think that's too corny – or just 'I love you').

* Inside a beautiful box leave instructions to ring a telephone number to book a massage whenever he/she feels like it (most spas offer this service). I happen to love the spa at the Mandarin Oriental Hotel and the wonderful Anastasia Achilleos at Home House in Portman Square (see pages 8–12

for more suggestions). If you want to be seriously romantic, you could organise the now fashionable massage for two. You lie side by side with a masseur(euse) apiece, and you both emerge suitably oiled and pampered (www.candyand bloom.com offer a couples massage as does www.unlisted london.com). Usually, you don't have to be a member of a health club to enjoy spa treatments, but you could tap into the web for one of the many masseurs who will come to your home.

* A trip on the London Eye (www.londoneye.com) or the Wheel of Manchester (www.worldtouristattractions.co.uk) after dark is a wonderfully romantic experience. Track down a restaurant that he/she hasn't been to before for afterwards – some of the nicest aren't always the grandest. Do some research to find a backstreet treasure.

* Taking a moviegoer to a film may not seem particularly grand, but register with www.secretcinema.org and each month you will be sent a text or an email giving you place and time, but only when you arrive at the venue will you know what you're going to see. The films are chosen by ardent film buffs and are 'challenging, stimulating and groundbreaking' – no risk of finding yourself watching 'Mamma Mia' for the third time. The snag is a showing may not coincide with Valentine's Day but does that matter? The gesture remains just as grand.

* Likewise, Intelligence Squared debates (www.intelligence squared.com) are always interesting and usually mind-expanding. These are held in London, usually at the Royal Geographical Society's Ondaatje Theatre.

Parties

* Viktor Wynd and the Last Tuesday Society (www.thelast
tuesdaysociety.org) not only throw lavish parties but hold a
series of fascinating salons and debates throughout the year.
In 2009, their Valentine's party was called 'Loss, a Night of
Misery'. They showed the saddest films in a separate room,
and had ceremonial chopping of onions at midnight. One
year, a man played a trumpet made of ice but couldn't give
an encore because it had melted by the end.

* For young girls a dateless St Valentine's often spells deep
gloom. Instead of bemoaning the lack of affection, soothe
the ego with some fun of your own. A girly do, either at
home or in a restaurant or pub, may be unconventional
but can be splendid. A pampering party with masseurs,
manicurists, facialists, pedicurists can all now easily be
hired to come to the house, and if a number of you club
together, it needn't cost a fortune (www.unlisted
london.com offers a pampering spa party service as does
www.thepamperparty.co.uk). One young girl I know,
though, does recount the time she had planned a kitschy
evening with a girlfriend who was also temporarily
manless, and they had agreed to carry a plastic rose and
meet in a restaurant, all for a laugh. Unfortunately, the
girlfriend had a work crisis and never turned up – *not* a
good evening to find yourself alone in a cheap restaurant
with a jokey rose stuck in your lapel.

* The other thing to do is to hold a party yourself. A lot of
your friends would – I'd lay a bet – be delighted to be let

off the whole 'what-the-hell-shall-we-do-tonight' kerfuffle and go to a party. You don't have to make it elaborate. Send out jokey invitations covered in pink hearts and glitter. Make – or order – a heart-shaped cake, preferably with pink icing. Cook pasta (a real spaghetti Bolognese, carefully made, is a great treat – that they're usually so lousy is because they're badly made), or order in pizza, or just lay on a variety of breads, cheeses, patés and salamis. Have big bowls of kitschy sweets lying about the place (TK Maxx sells them, as does Marks & Spencer). Serve Häagen-Dazs on sticks with the pink heart-shaped cake. Decorate the room with as many flowers as you can afford and, for drink, go for Cava, or white or red wine, as decent as you can afford. If you're up for it, you could make glitzy cocktails. Then you're done.

Romance has been elegantly defined as the offspring of fiction and love. Benjamin Disraeli

Presents

In principle, I love flowers, but for me there's something just a bit too predictable about roses, not to mention chocolates and champagne, on Valentine's Day. Bring along the champagne (if you both love it, although personally I'd prefer a sensational red Burgundy, or a crisp white Burgundy come to that), the chocolates and the roses by all means (see below), but if you're giving a present, think a little more laterally, and bring something else as well. It doesn't seem to me the sort of day on which anybody expects to be given great big consumer items – the real treat is the surprise, and doing something together, whether it be a picnic, a dinner, a visit to the opera or cosying up with a brilliant DVD.

* BOOKS: I think there's nothing more seductive than being given a meaningful book. Being introduced to a new author who gives hours of pleasure is like being invited into a different world. Roland Barthes's *Fragments d'un discours amoureux* has been described by one fan as 'a dazzling primer for every moment you are in love'. Antonia Fraser's *Anthology of Love Letters* (published by Weidenfeld & Nicholson) makes a good present, including letters to and from the great lovers of history – Heloise and Abelard, Napoleon and Josephine, Henry VIII and Anne Boleyn, Alfred de Musset and George Sand – and oh, the language! It fills one with nostalgia for more elegant times.

It's also rather wonderful to discover a book together. I remember shortly after I met my husband he had to leave to take up a scholarship for three months in America, and one of the ways we kept in touch (no mobile phones or email then) was by deciding in advance on a list of books that we'd read while apart that would somehow unite us mentally and that we could talk about afterwards. In this way, we both discovered Steinbeck with *The Grapes of Wrath*, Stephen Crane's *The Red Badge of Courage* and Dostoevsky's *The Brothers Karamazov* at the same time. There were others but those three have stayed with me all my life, and while at the time we were young, straight out of university and rather earnest, the idea can be applied to all tastes.

Old books, vintage or merely secondhand, chosen with care, are always lovely. First editions of a favourite book are a special treat.

* MUSIC: what's true for books is also true for music – to be introduced to a new singer, soloist or composer is a gift for life. I still cherish the songs of Boris Vian that a French friend gave me, the disc of jazz music another friend gave me and the wonderfully mournful Portuguese Fado yet another one introduced me to. Love songs vary but some are wonderful – in 2007 the *New York Daily News* compiled a list of the 100 greatest love songs ever written. They range from Frank Sinatra and The Beatles to The Supremes, The Bee Gees and John Travolta (you get the drift – no love songs by the troubadours here). A compilation disc including some of these could perk up the evening, and even become a permanent part of his/her life.

* KEEPSAKES: a divine little brooch, a gorgeous scarf or two beautiful antique glasses seem to me to hit the right note. Guinevere (www.guinevere.co.uk) always has lovely antiques, many of a smallish and so suitable nature. Search for somewhere similar, and probably cheaper, in your area. A poem, handwritten and framed by you, is far more touching than any jokey present from a department store. A beautiful notebook – Smythson's small ones are perfect – give great pleasure to use.

* CHOCOLATES AND CAKES: unless your dearly beloved has a taste (and why not?) for Black Magic, go for one of the delectable niche brands (see pages 82–86). Little boxes of both white and dark chocolate hearts are available from www.loving-chocolate.co.uk, and they will also do single, double (or triple!) initials, or spell out a message in chocolate. For very jolly personalised bars (spell out names, initials, messages) go to www.mychocolateindulgence.com. Konditor & Cook (www.konditorandcook.com) have all sorts of speciality cakes – for St Valentine's Day you could have a name or a message spelt on little cakes in a narrow, 3-foot/metre-long box, each one differently and separately iced with a different initial or word.

Flowers

Why is it no one ever sent me yet
One perfect limousine, do you suppose?
Ah no, it's always just my luck to get
One perfect rose. Dorothy Parker

I'm with Dorothy Parker – I don't think a single rose, no matter how perfect, cuts it. I also think that if you're going to send flowers, make sure they're gorgeous, and best make them chic – nothing that reeks of a garage forecourt. Buy masses and masses of a single flower – roses (although they won't be in season), peonies, tulips, hydrangeas, lilies – or a huge multi-stemmed orchid in a big chunky pot (www.crocus.co.uk) and deliver them in person. Go to a flower market – for Londoners, Nine Elms in Battersea is fantastic – and you can buy in such abundance that you will appear wonderfully generous.

If you're having them sent – and there is something wildly wonderful about a huge bunch of flowers arriving at the office desk, so good for the self-esteem – choose your florist with care. Floristry, fortunately, has come along in leaps and bounds, and even the chain stores have got in designers to make sure their bunches are up to scratch. Marks & Spencer and John Lewis have upped the taste levels, hiring (at great expense I imagine) floral experts such as Jane Packer and Paula Pryke to be the taste police. So, these days, for a very reasonable outlay, you can get a more than decent collection of flowers, and you can order them twenty-fours a day from the John Lewis website (www.johnlewis.com).

If you want to mix different sorts of flowers, stick to one colour, unless you have a very practised eye. The chic florists mix colours with great panache but mostly, if you observe closely, just two – they might mix white or cream with pinks or purples but nothing else. Otherwise, they take one shade – say pink – and then have several gradations of the colour, ranging from pale to very deep. A few go for contrasts – mixing red with purple and adding in some orange, which can look wonderful, but it takes a masterly eye. Colours that look good together are whites, lime greens and creams; pinks and reds; lilacs and all shades of blue.

You could take a leaf out of the chic florist Ercole Moroni at Alexander McQueens. He belongs to the simple school of floristry. In spring, he loves lots of bulbs. He takes, for instance, a massed group consisting of pots of baby hyacinths, daffodils or other spring flowers grown from bulbs. Apart from anything else they smell divine.

FAVOURITE FLORISTS

* **Inwater (www.inwater.uk.com)** does cutting-edge floristry – immersing flowers in water, twisting them round bowls, that sort of thing.
* **Rob van Helden (www.rvhfloraldesign.com)** comes with pretty grand provenance (he does Elton John's galas and was the florist for Pierce Brosnan's and Claudia Schiffer's weddings). He sends out divine bouquets.
* **Robbie Honey (www.robbiehoney.com)** does lovely flowers and will do you proud for St Valentine's Day. (One year, he and Jamie Oliver did a pod-cast featuring food and flowers.)
* **Wild at Heart (www.wildatheart.com)**, founded by Nikki Tibbles, does beautiful bouquets, with brilliantly mixed colours, from £45. She also plants bulbs in vintage containers, and since February is peak bulb time, it could be the perfect solution – less obvious and much more long-lasting than roses.

If you've left everything too late and are reduced to buying flowers at the petrol station forecourt, you can try to rescue the situation by removing the naff bits (the baby's breath or the flower in the ghastly colour), cutting the stems so that the bunch turns into something like a proper bouquet, and tieing with rough string or ribbon – perks them up no end.

The Meaning of Flowers

Traditionally, different flowers convey a distinctive message. Roses are the symbol of love and so are thought to be the most appropriate flower for St Valentine's Day. However, to those who are aware of the code (few among us, I'd guess), it's not just the rose that matters – colour is important, too. Red is the lover's rose, standing for enduring passion; white signifies humility and innocence while yellow expresses friendship and joy. Pink is the rose for gratitude, appreciation and admiration; orange is for enthusiasm and desire; lilac and purple roses represent enchantment and love at first sight.

Since roses aren't in season in February, it's a tricky time of year to deal with this complicated code and, in my view, long-stemmed hot-house roses aren't greatly to be desired. However, www.realflowers.co.uk grows proper country roses in the UK during the summer, and the same breeds in Kenya all year long – this means that even in February they can supply them. Their series of Roses for Romance bouquets includes rose petals.

Carnations, it seems, are the flowers for mothers (note to son and daughter – please no) while amaryllis are associated with pride, daffodils with chivalry and heather with admiration. Daisies stand for innocence, crocuses for foresight and hyacinths for sincerity. Orchids signify delicate beauty, while tulips, like roses, have a complicated colour code – pink is for caring, red signals a declaration of love, white is for forgiveness, yellow is for being hopelessly in love.

Here are fifteen chrysanthemums, twelve for your twelve when they are faded, three to round out your twelve; I hope the stems will be extremely long as I requested. And that these flowers – proud and sad, like you, proud of being beautiful, and sad that everything is so stupid – will please you.

Marcel Proust to Laure Hayman

HOW TO MAKE FLOWERS LAST

* Cut the stems off shop-bought flowers at an angle as soon as you get them home.
* Always use a very clean vase.
* Keep the water clean. A drop of bleach will help keep the water sterilised and so stop the stems from rotting.
* An ice cube in the vase helps revive flowers that are wilting.
* Use the plant food the florist provides, but if you're cutting your own, add some sugar instead.

They spoil every romance by trying to make it last forever. Oscar Wilde

Dinner for Two

You're not giving a party. You're dining *à deux*. So you can do all those truly delicious things that really can't be done for large numbers, such as fresh Dover sole (grilled or meunière), calf's liver (serve with mashed potato, which should be ready and kept warm while you just lightly sauté the liver in a little butter and oil to serve it crisp on the outside and slightly pink inside), trout with almonds, or steak with a wonderful Béarnaise sauce (and don't stint on the tarragon).

As a starter, you could buy in a really good borscht (Waitrose makes a good one or find one in a local delicatessen), do some asparagus (supermarkets sell it all year round now) either hot with a little melted butter and perhaps some Parmesan flakes, or you could wrap some parma ham round some lightly cooked stems and then grill lightly. If smoked salmon is your starter of choice, it has to be wonderful (see pages 25–29), and prawns have to be the freshest you can find. Toss them in some chopped garlic, ginger and chilli until they turn a pretty pink. Swill in a little white wine, amalgamate all the juices, add lots of parsley and serve with some crusty bread.

Scallops could be a starter or a main course. There's something about them that gives them an amazing affinity with bacon, so I like to serve scallops (they just need about two minutes a side in very hot butter spiked with oil) on a bed of cooked new potatoes crushed up with some crispy bacon and lightly sautéed leeks.

Rack of lamb, if you're in the mood for meat, makes an elegant meal – I like to cook a small rack each and serve on a bed of small new potatoes mixed with artichoke hearts (you can now buy them frozen or in jars) and broad beans (which aren't in season in February but you could, for once, use frozen) and lots of rosemary. You could do noisettes of lamb, if you have time. Marinade first in a mixture of oil, garlic and rosemary. Brown lightly on either side, and leave in the pan until they're cooked as you like them. Put them to one side, stir some red wine into the meat juices and pour over the noisettes. Serve with mashed potato and creamed spinach. A duck breast each is another option. Score the skin several times, stuff some ground star anise, lemon juice and other herbs, or a combination of fresh ginger slices and honey, into the cracks, and roast in a very hot oven for just twenty minutes if you like it slightly pink.

Then – if you're still hungry – go on to cheese with a green salad, followed by a delicious but light pud.

Pudding

If you aren't usually into cooking puds, there are certain things you can buy in that won't give the game away unless he/she is unduly percipient. Marks & Spencer, for instance, do delicious little lemon soufflés, which come in china pots and so look for all the world as if you'd made them. They also do divine little *pots au chocolat* and panna cotta, either plain or topped with fruit – I prefer them plain, but both are good. Then again, the chocolate pudding from Gü would make a perfect ending to a St Valentine's Day meal.

Trying your hand at producing a home-made pudding need not be an ordeal. An easily made coeur à la crème (see page 264) served with some poached pears, or other winter fruit, is impressive. If you believe in eating seasonally, you'll have to stick to winter fruits, but you might, just for once, consider buying out-of-season strawberries and dipping them in melted chocolate, or poaching peaches in champagne and serving them with crumbled Amaretti biscuits and crème fraiche. Alternatively, bake the peaches by halving them, removing the stone and filling the gap with crumbled Amaretti biscuits mixed with some butter and honey.

HEART SHAPES

If you're in a jokey mood, you could have a lot of fun with heart shapes. Avocado mousse, smoked haddock mousse, pounded Arbroath smokies mixed with some crème fraiche and tabasco, avocado and crab mix all lend themselves to being presented in the shape of a heart – jellies, too, of course. Moulds can be bought from cookshops or from the ever-obliging www.lakeland.co.uk.

Heart-shaped cake tins are also available. Make a sponge cake, vanilla or chocolate if you like, from the best Victoria sponge recipe you know (see page 318) and cover it with a truly delicious chocolate icing – mix 5fl oz/150ml of double cream with 5oz/150g of melted chocolate and add a spoonful of golden syrup to give it a gloss. You can, if you like, add raspberries, which go brilliantly with chocolate.

✳ It probably doesn't need saying, but if you have serious romantic intentions, I think you'd be wise to keep the whole dinner on the light side and lay off the heavy dishes of potatoes, pastas, cakes and cream.

Oysters

Oysters are a bit of a cliché come St Valentine's Day. Rumour has it that they act as an aphrodisiac (Casanova is alleged to have eaten fifty for breakfast) but even if that were to be true, it would seem to me a bit obvious, not to mention vulgar, to start wooing one's best beloved with such an obvious ploy – as if true love needed any artificial stimulus. What *is* true is that oysters are rich in the amino acids that scientists tell us trigger increased levels of sex hormones. They also have a high zinc content, a mineral that is known to encourage the production of testosterone. So there may be something in the old wives' tale after all.

Personally, I never eat them – something about my South African upbringing has made me dislike raw fish and bleeding meat. However, I love the *idea* of them – clean, fresh, ineffably simple and sophisticated and – oh, bliss – wonderfully low in calories. They're also full of useful trace elements and minerals – calcium, iron, copper, iodine, magnesium and selenium as well as zinc. As a rough guide to the difference between our native oysters and Pacific oysters, I remember that John Pawson, in his and Annie Bell's splendid book *Living and Eating*, tells us that natives are smaller, less fleshy but have a more complex, bitter, metallic taste that connoisseurs love – which isn't to say they don't also love the saline fleshiness of the Pacifics.

It's odd to think that oysters were once eaten by the poorest in the land. They were cheap, plentiful and brilliantly nutritious. The despoiling of the oyster beds due to overfishing and pollution brought this bonanza to an end, but the good news is that, with careful control, the oyster beds are recovering, and oysters are once again on the menu, if not in the same quantities at least as fresh and nutritious as ever. For most of us, they're definitely a celebratory food, and choosing them takes a little nous. So I've asked Chris Dines, head chef at the St Pancras Grand Restaurant, which has an Oyster Bar, to let us into a few secrets. People thinking of taking the Eurostar to Paris for a St Valentine's Day treat might like to know that they could keep up the celebrations on the way back by heading for the St Pancras Grand Champagne and Oyster Bar – between 5 and 7 p.m. you get free oysters with your champagne or white wine.

MORE ROMANTIC FOODS

* The mere smell of almonds is thought to induce passionate thoughts in women, and so Samson chose almonds with which to woo Delilah, while author Alexander Dumas courted his mistress with a bowl of nutty soup.
* The ancient Aztecs named the avocado tree 'Ahuacuati', which literally translates to 'testicle tree'. Avocadoes are rich in vitamin B, essential for the well-being of our hormones.
* Mead, made from honey, was used by medieval seducers to send their conquests into romantic rapture. Newlyweds used to drink mead during the marriage feast – hence the word 'honeymoon'.

Chris Dines' Guide to Buying Oysters

Forget the old adage about eating oysters only when there is an 'r' in the month. Oysters can now be found throughout the year, but are usually better outside of their spawning period, when the waters are colder. At St Pancras Grand Oyster Bar, we use rock oysters from the Pacific during our native oysters' spawning season, and start serving native oysters in September.

Rock, or Pacific, and native oysters look and taste quite different. Rock oysters have the familiar crenellated shell, while the natives are smaller with a smoother shell, and their flavour is subtler than the strong, sea-salty flavour of the rock oysters. Raw oysters have complex flavours that vary greatly among varieties and regions. Some taste sweet, others salty, or with a mineral flavour. The texture is soft and fleshy, but crisp to the tooth. This is often influenced by the water that they are grown in, with variations in salinity, minerals and nutrients. The best from British and Irish waters are considered to be those from Colchester, Whitstable, the Helford and Galway. Natives are pricier than Pacifics, and are generally regarded as the superior oyster. If you aren't near a good supplier, you can buy them from Colchester Oyster Fishery (www.colchesteroysterfishery.com). Loch Fyne rock oysters are available from www.lochfyne.com.

* STORING: oysters should be stored at a low temperature and smell briny fresh. The shells should be clean, bright, tightly closed and unbroken. Unopened (live) oysters can be kept in the fridge for up to one week if stored correctly – deep shell down and covered with a damp cloth to

prevent dehydration. Never store in an airtight container or water because this will cause them to die.

A live oyster uses its muscle to hold the shells tightly closed. When the muscles weaken, the shell gapes open and, if it will not close when tapped, the oyster should be discarded.

Shucked oysters can be kept refrigerated in a sealed container for four or five days. They can also be frozen for up to three months (previously frozen oysters are better for cooking than eating raw). The shell will open on thawing but the oyster must be eaten (or cooked) straightaway.

* PREPARING: ask your fishmonger to open the oysters, retaining the shells (if required) and liquor. If you really want to shuck your own, you will need an oyster knife, which is a special blunted knife made for the purpose. First clean the outside of the oyster under running water to remove loose grit or barnacles. Wear gloves to protect your hands and rub the shell with your fingers, or use a stiff brush.

Hold the oyster (deep shell down) in a towel or oven mitt in the palm of your hand with the hinge (pointed side) sticking out. This will protect your hand if the oyster knife slips. With the flat side of the oyster up, insert the tip of the oyster knife near the hinge to a depth of about 12mm/^{1}/$_{2}$in. Gently work the oyster knife between the shell halves, and then twist it back and forth to open the shell, saving as much liquor as possible. Once the shell is opened, slide the knife across the top to cut the muscle and then run it under the body of the oyster. Discard the top shell, and discard any oysters that are dry or do not smell fresh.

* SERVING: the best way to serve raw oysters is on a platter of crushed ice, or sometimes you see them presented on a bed of seaweed, accompanied by a wedge of lemon or shallot vinaigrette. At the Oyster Bar, as an accompaniment, we serve a choice of garnishes that includes lemon juice, mignonette, green and red Tabasco, or, if you prefer, au naturel. Some people like to add a dash of horseradish or Worcestershire sauce. For a dinner party, allow six oysters per person for a starter.

It is not true that oysters are alive when you eat them, because as soon as the shell is prised apart and oxygen enters, the oyster will die.

Cooking oysters can temper the salty tang and intensify the creaminess of the flavour. Either grilling or poaching produces great results.

Easter

Easter is joyful for lots of reasons. If we're religious, it signals the end of Lent and the forty days of fasting, the risen Christ, new hope, new beginning. If we're not, the bluebells and cherry blossom are (usually) out, making even city streets great places to be, the evenings are lighter and, with any luck, it's a bit warmer. We also get four whole days to spend with family and friends. Some people like to go away and head for ski slopes or sunny shores, but I think Easter is a great time to be in Britain and take part in some of the wonderfully traditional set-piece events that are put on up and down the land. The countryside is seldom more beautiful, and think of all those euros you'll save. Hardy types, of course, love the glitter of winter frosts and nothing keeps them indoors, but Easter marks the beginning of being able to enjoy the great outdoors more languorously, of not having to walk at a route-march pace to keep frostbite at bay. It's a time for picnics, point-to-points, rambling and visiting splendid gardens, museums, galleries, churches. For children it's a special time, a glorious mish-mash of celebration, with some poignant church services for the religiously inclined, whilst the high point is usually being allowed to guzzle chocolate in quantities that are otherwise strictly forbidden.

Out and About

Don't just sit there. Do something. Get walking. Get a guidebook, map, or look to the internet for inspiration

(www.walkingbritain.co.uk). For serious walkers there's
nothing to beat Ordnance Survey maps, which are available in
most bookshops that have a travel section. Many pubs and
hotels are good at giving instructions about local walks and
often have printed leaflets.

A good friend who is a walking addict tells me that the
Time Out Country Walking Guides are brilliant for tougher
walks for adults. They cover an area stretching down to the
south coast, west to the Chilterns and north through Essex
and up to Hertfordshire. The directions are very detailed and
walks are rated on a 1–10 scale of difficulty, with notes on
how long they are, how to get to the starting point and
things of interest to look out for along the way. Suggestions
for lunch and tea stops are included together with reviews of
pubs on the route. Also check out www.visitbritain.co.uk and
start planning a trip to the Lake District or perhaps Wales.

For pubs to visit when you're all walked out, or just want a
refreshing stop, there's *The Good Pub Guide* (www.goodpub
guide.co.uk). It now offers a service that allows you to text
for advice on the nearest good pubs.

For those who live in London, have small children and
want some uplifting excursions, let me recommend *Adventure
Walks for Families In and Around London*, a book co-written
by my daughter-in-law Becky Jones and Clare Lewis. It's
filled with all sorts of heavenly walks, each one of which is
themed – there's the Darwin walk, Kipling's walk, Dick
Turpin, Beatrix Potter and loads more. Along with directions,
the book tells the story of the person whom the walk
features, and takes in a whole host of ancillary fun things to
do – flowers to collect, catapults to make, sights to look out

for, where to picnic. Even quite small children will be able to negotiate each walk within a day, setting out from London.

Bluebells

Visit bluebell woods if you possibly can. Did you know our native bluebell woodlands hold some 25 per cent of the world's entire population of bluebells? A mass of them is an uplifting, joyful sight, and although some years are more wonderful than others, I've never known a bluebell wood to disappoint. The Woodland Trust (www.woodlandtrust.org.uk/bluebells) will keep you up to date on all woody matters but here are a few fantastic places to visit.

* Bovey Valley Woods, Lustleigh, Bovey Tracey, Devon – part of Dartmoor National Park

* Brede High Woods, Sedlescombe, East Sussex – ten ancient woodlands, which are also good for bird-watching

* Bunkers Hill, Stourbridge, Staffs

* Letah Wood, Hexham, Northumberland

* Credenhill Park, Herefordshire

* Glen Finglas, 'Brig o' Turk', Stirling

Other Ways to Enjoy the Great Outdoors

* Go bat-spotting at Ickworth House, Bury St Edmunds (www.suffolktouristguide.com).

THE CHITTY CHITTY BANG BANG WALK

Turville, The Chilterns, Buckinghamshire
This is the place where the children's classic *Chitty Chitty Bang Bang* was filmed, complete with the windmill on the hill where Caractacus, Jemima, Jeremy and Grandpa Potts lived. Sing the songs, tell stories of pirates, spies, castles and child catchers. Keep on the lookout for the Vulgarian Baron Bombast and his child-hating wife. Watch out for flying cars.

Map Ordnance Survey Explorer Map 171
Distance 4 km/2½ miles
Terrain Rolling fields, clear paths, one mild uphill at the start of the walk. The last stretch is gently downhill all the way.

What will I need?
* The words to all the songs from the movie
* A bag of toot sweets
* Fudge
* Binoculars for bird-watching, looking out for pirates and to see the windmill in close-up

How to get there
Take the M40 out of London and come off at Junction 5. Turn left off the motorway towards Ibstone. Soon after Ibstone village is the County primary school. Turn right here, on a narrow lane down to Turville. Take the signposted left into the village. Park by the village green, between the church and the pub.

What can we listen to on the way?
The *Chitty Chitty Bang Bang* soundtrack.

Walk the Walk

1 Walk past the telephone box, towards the church, and take the left turning up the lane, past Sleepy Cottage and the village nursery school. The tarmac lane soon becomes a footpath shaded by trees.

2 Go through the gate at the open field and carry straight on for 90 m/100 yards, before turning right through a wooden gate in the hedgerow. Follow a clear path up the hill through the open field, passing a conveniently placed resting bench at the top.

3 Look back at the view of the windmill behind you. Look out, too, for pairs of circling red kites as we are close to the area where these elegant birds were recently reintroduced to Britain. Head on to the gate at the very top. Walk straight on through the gate and along the hedgerow.

4 At the tarmac lane, follow the road left, past the big gates of Turville Court (the place to sing 'POSH'). Then turn immediately left on to the marked footpath and into a field. Walk down, over the stile, heading straight through the field, steeply down to the bottom of the hill.

5 Cross over the lane and climb the stile opposite into the next field. *Make a Catapult to Defend Yourself against the Wicked Baron and Baroness Bombast or Vulgaria's Evil Child Snatcher:* Find a stick with a y-shaped fork. Shorten the top branches of the y to about 8 cm/3 inches and the handle to a manageable size for small hands. About 3 cm/1 inch down, cut a notch in the bark and tie a length of rubber (a thick rubber band will work well) to both sides of the y. Give yourself just enough length to pull back slightly. Find some ammunition and fire, well away from others.

6 Head across this field in a perfectly straight line up to a five-bar

gate at the top. Climb over two stiles into an arable field, looking out for the views of the windmill to your left.

7 Halfway through this field, there is a fingerpost in the hedgerow pointing left. Bear left here, on a well-defined path cut through the wheat crop, towards some cottages.

8 Turn left on to a tarmac lane and past Southend Farm. You are now on the Chiltern Way, a well-marked footpath that takes you in a more or less straight line, downhill all the way back to Turville. Aim for the windmill directly ahead of you. Once back in the village, it is worth popping up to the windmill for a closer look, but it is a very steep climb. Bear in mind that it is on private land, on the other side of the fence. You get the best view of the windmill from the walk but the views of the valley from the hillside are well worth the scramble.

Eat Me, Drink Me

* The Bull and Butcher Pub, Turville, Henley-on-Thames (www.thebullandbutcher.com). Lunch is served on Sundays and bank holidays from 12 p.m. to 4 p.m. and from 12 p.m. to 2.30 p.m. the rest of the week. Just what you want from a pub. Good food as well as a children's menu that serves Chitty Chitty Bangers and chips, and a beer garden. Ales from the Wychwood Brewery. Very busy so worth booking.

Useful Information

* For information about the Chiltern hills and events in the area, contact The Chilterns Area of Outstanding Natural Beauty online at www.chilternsaonb.org.
* For places to stay or general tourist information visit www.visitbuckinghamshire.org.

Did you know?

* The *Chitty Chitty Bang Bang* film script was written by Roald Dahl, and the book by Ian Fleming of James Bond fame.
  (Taken from *Adventure Walks for Families In and Around London* by Clare Lewis and Becky Jones, £8.99, published by Frances Lincoln. Further information from www.adventurewalksforfamilies.co.uk. Clare and Becky's next book will be published in Spring 2010.)

* Take the children to see the Cerne Abbas Giant in Dorset, where the Wessex Morris Men usually dance at sunrise.

* Jousting competitions with knights in armour, and various other historical dramas, are often staged around the country (www.english-heritage.org.uk).

* Join up with a party of friends at a point-to-point meeting. Take a picnic (see picnic food page 91). These are great social occasions and you can have a mild punt on who'll win. It's worth checking fixtures (www.pointtopoint.co.uk) if you're visiting an area, or are new to it.

* Visit a church. Even if you're not religious, English churches are an architectural and aesthetic glory. Prince Charles regularly takes Sandringham guests on guided tours of the churches of Norfolk. So can you. Norfolk was a hugely prosperous county in the Middle Ages and about

1,000 churches were built of which some 659 remain, many with glorious rood screens, decorated ceilings and glorious works of medieval art (www.norfolkchurches.co.uk).

* Listen for a cuckoo. The arrival of the first cuckoo traditionally heralds the start of spring, and Marsden in West Yorkshire sometimes puts on a special celebration to mark the occasion, with special activities for children (www.marsdencuckooday.synthasite.com).

* Check what the National Trust is up to (www.nationaltrust.org.uk). Fairs and special events are often held at their properties around the country.

* Try camping. Don't buy the kit until you've tried it first. Featherdown Farms rent out gorgeously comfortable but retro tents on a series of proper working farms to enable urban families to see what camping and the countryside are really like (www.featherdown farms.co.uk).

* Follow a 3km/2 mile trail through Low Sizergh Barn near Kendal in Cumbria (www.lowsizerghbarn.co.uk) to see 400-year-old hedgerows and ancient woodlands as well as cows and free-ranging hens. For urban children who've never seen a farm, here's a chance to see cows being milked and hens roaming – and to follow it up with a cream tea. You can also buy artisan cheeses and home-made ice creams.

* Plant seeds. If the weather is good and you have a garden, it's a good time to get the children involved in growing summer vegetables. Hugh Fearnley-Whittingstall says you

can grow a lettuce in less than five weeks. Try radishes, lettuces, tomatoes (Gardener's Delight is a good variety but it needs regular watering) and various herbs. Children living in cities grow strawberries in hanging baskets. The National Trust launched a scheme in the summer of 2009 to encourage children to grow their own food to eat, and their very jolly website has lots of advice (www.foodgloriousfood.org.uk).

Indoors

I f the weather is dire think of it as a good opportunity to encourage the children to be creative.

CARDS: grandparents and relations love getting home-made Easter cards and not much more than some card, paper and colouring or painting materials are needed. Old magazines are useful, too, so that the children can cut out images and stick them in their masterpieces. Baker Ross have cute packs for making wooden eggs, cards, chicken-shaped baskets, Easter decorations, divine little angels – you name it, Baker Ross sells it (www.bakerross.co.uk).

DECORATED EGGS: blowing eggs in order to paint and decorate them is fun, and used to be a part of the Easter ritual. It's not difficult but needs a little care. Firstly, the eggs should be at room temperature – they're harder to do if they're cold. You need to get hold of a sharp but fine needle and pierce a hole at either end of the egg. Make sure to break the yolk – wiggle the needle round inside if you can.

Then put the more pointed end of the egg to your mouth
and blow the contents out into a strategically placed bowl
through the other end. That makes it sound pretty easy – in
fact, it takes a bit of patience.

After that, you're all set to paint or decorate the eggs,
which is where your child's imagination can be let loose.
Using anything from crayons and paints to glitter and
sequins, feathers and strips of ribbon, each egg can be wildly
different. The empty egg shell can also be filled with melted
chocolate – you will need to work the needle a little to make
one of the holes slightly bigger and, if necessary, you could
block the other end temporarily with some kitchen paper.
Simply melt the chocolate over some hot water and then
pour it through the hole. Put the filled eggs in the fridge to
chill but remember to keep them upright.

DYED EGGS: a tradition in many houses is to dye the eggs
for Easter breakfast. You get a wonderfully delicate effect if
you use natural dyes (see below). Use white-shelled eggs and
simply add the dye to the water when boiling them. Use as
much of the dye as you can.

* Yellow: add saffron, turmeric or cumin, or orange or
  lemon peel

* Red or pink: use cranberry juice or frozen raspberries, or
  red onion skins

* Orange: use yellow onion skins

* Green: add spinach or carrot tops

* Brown: use grape juice or coffee

* Blue: red cabbage leaves will dye eggs a beautiful blue

* Burgundy: red wine will turn them a rich burgundy

* Speckly: dip an old toothbrush into some contrasting paint colour and then run your finger over the bristles to spatter the eggs with spots of the paint.

You could ask each member of the household to paint an individual egg (or two) with coloured pens that use permanent dyes. Then they're easy to identify at breakfast, each with its own funny design.

＊ If your children are addicted to bunny-related matters, a very useful website is www.allfreecrafts.com/easter, which will give all the instructions needed to turn two round cakes into a bunny-shaped cake. Strictly for the kids.

EASTER BONNETS: once they were, we're told, an integral part of the Easter parade but I've never been to one and nor has anybody I know. Nobody wears them and if you had one or – worse – went to the trouble of making one, what on earth would you do with it and where would you wear it? However, having said all that, if you have craft-loving children who would find it fun, you could turn to www.mumsnet.com, which has lots of creative suggestions for making Easter bonnets.

DECORATIONS

It's easy to fill the house with flowers – daffodils and other spring bulbs are usually coming out. Plant them in the autumn in bowls, window-boxes and tubs. If you've got trees in the garden, cut some branches that are full of blossom and put them in big jugs (you don't need fancy vases). Cherry blossom is particularly lovely. Easter trees are a new and nice idea. Buy a twisted willow tree in a pot (almost all garden centres have them) and from it hang little eggs, either ones you've blown and painted, or wooden ones or other decorations. Afterwards, you can plant the willow in the garden.

Chocolate

Chocolate is the indispensable, non-negotiable part of Easter, certainly as far as children are concerned. Their tastes vary. Some become quite the little connoisseur early on, while others go for sugary, cheapish mass-produced bars. Why not let them have their way for once?

Easter Egg Hunt

Easter Egg hunts are part of every child's birthright and they can be organised almost anywhere – best in a garden if you have one, but if the weather is truly dire, inside the house is fine. What matters is quantity. There have to be lots of eggs, but you can keep them small, and they have to be hidden judiciously – reasonably hard to find but not so hard as to be impossible. Some families give each child a basket, let them hunt for the eggs and then pile them all together and dole them out equally. In other families, it's finders keepers. You decide. If you do make it slightly competitive (the emphasis is on slightly – adults will need to make sure the smaller ones don't miss out), cut a ribbon to start the chase.

At one Easter egg hunt I know of, each child was given a different silly hat, first to wear, and then to use to collect eggs. Eggs were hidden in all sorts of extraordinary places with some placed in very easy spots, for the small ones who were sent off first, and some in very difficult places for the older children to have to search for.

If you can't face doing the Easter egg hunt yourself, or there wouldn't be enough children to make it fun, egg hunts are often organised in various houses and grounds around the country. In London, for instance, Battersea Park Children's Zoo (www.batterseaparkzoo.co.uk) often has an Easter egg hunt as well as card-making sessions (they charge for entry).

Sutton House, a grand Tudor mansion in the middle of East London, built in 1535, usually holds an Easter egg hunt with prizes, courtesy of Cadbury, as well as offering face-painting. Again, there's an entry charge.

More cultural is an outing to the Handel House Museum (www.handelhouse.org) where you can combine wonderful music, including the Messiah, with an Easter egg trail. Other places worth checking to see what's on offer include Kenwood House, Ham House and Garden, Osterley Park and House and the Red House, Bexleyheath. All charge something, which seems fair enough. Children with an interest in military history might like the Imperial War Museum (www.iwm.org.uk), which has what it calls an Easter Eggsploration hunt around the museum with a chocolate as a prize.

Check out www.nationaltrust.org.uk for details of Easter egg hunts happening at their properties over the Easter weekend. Chatsworth (www.chatsworth.org) and Castle Howard (www.castlehoward.co.uk) are well-established favourites.

Real chocolate is low in sugar and has a low glycaemic index, meaning it keeps you feeling full for longer and helps keep your blood glucose levels steady. It contains a multitude of vitamins, and cocoa butter acts to lower blood cholesterol levels. On top of that, it increases levels of serotonin in the brain (serotonin is what makes us feel happy) and it also contains phenylethylamine, which is very similar to the chemicals released in our bodies when we fall in love. Chantal Coady, founder of Rococo Chocolate

Sophisticated Chocolate

For adults – who have been known to indulge in an egg or two – chocolate has become awfully complicated of late, with a vocabulary and a mystique of its own. Choosing chocolate has become nearly as sophisticated a matter as choosing wine. Connoisseurs track down little-known makes, the smaller, more tucked-away the better. Serious chocaholics, that is those who mind about quality as opposed to quantity, want something exclusive, something where the bean, the making, the centre, the coating have all had serious attention paid to them. They are after brands so exquisite, so tiny, hardly anybody else has heard of them.

The fashionable word in chocolate circles is 'artisanale', which means hand-made to you and me. Hang on to the word. It counts in chocolatey circles. Some of the terminology connected with wine has begun to creep in, too. Words such as 'varietal' (meaning a chocolate made from a single named bean as opposed to ones made from a standard mix of cocoa beans), 'estate' and 'vintage', 'terroir' and 'cru' are appearing more and more often. Indeed, the Scharffenberger behind the chocolate of that name from San Francisco, which Selfridges' food departments sells, actually used to be a wine-maker and turned to making chocolate as it required much the same sort of sensitive palate.

ROCOCO CHOCOLATE (www.rococochocolates. com). Chantal Coady, of Rococo Chocolate, has, I think, to be credited with first making most of us aware of the sophisticated and subtle heights that fine chocolate can reach. When she opened her shop twenty-eight years ago, she opened up a whole new chocolate world, and still today her artisan bars of organic chocolate, esoterically flavoured with black pepper, pink pepper, Earl Grey tea, sea salt, cardamom and much more, are cult buys among those in the know. At £3.75 for 70 grams they're not cheap but they're certainly different. She taught us all a lot about chocolate. We learned that her chocolates, made from high-quality cocoa solids, were a million miles from the usual candy-bar stuff, which is made mostly from sugar, vegetable fat and powdered milk with cocoa accounting for as little as 20 per cent of the final product. Real chocolate, the kind that melts in the mouth with a deep, intense flavour that is almost like an endorphin charge, has very high amounts of cocoa solids but very little sugar. Valrhona's Guanaha Noir, for example, has 70 per cent cocoa solids and a mere one-tenth of the sugar content of the cheaper-end chocolate bars.

GREEN & BLACK'S (www.greenandblacks.com). These days, there's much more chocolate choice than there ever used to be with some wonderful niche players. For those who care about provenance and the quality of the beans, Green & Black's dark organic bars, now sold in most good supermarkets, were a breakthrough. Since then, the brand has branched out and offer all manner of flavours (including fantastic chocolatey ice creams), Easter eggs and sumptuous variations on a theme.

LA MAISON DU CHOCOLAT (www.lamaisonduchocolat.co.uk). Robert Linxe opened his first establishment in the rue du Faubourg Saint-Honoré in Paris in 1977, and the recently opened London branch attracted a huge welcome from its British fans. The chocolates, all made by hand, come in a range of pure chocolate flavours, but the shop is probably best known for its ganaches – these are the fillings that harbour the flavours, which are then coated with a fine layer of chocolate. Raspberry, lemon and provençal herbs are probably the most well known, but I like the dark plain Caracas best.

PIERRE MARCOLINI (www.marcolini.be). Belgian chocolatier
Pierre Marcolini claims to be the only chocolatier still making
his own chocolate base – almost all of even the very best
chocolatiers buy them from people such as Valrhona, who
make it in bulk. He buys his beans from single plantations.
Most, but not all, makers use a Forastero bean but Marcolini
maintains that the finest flavour of all comes from the Criollo
bean, which is the most expensive to buy and can't be grown
in vast quantities. He can even tell the difference in taste
between a Criollo from Venezuela (a floral taste), one from
Ecuador (spicy) and one from Madagascar (fruitier). His
chocolates certainly look and taste divine and a handbag-
shaped dark-brown box of five little drawers, each packed with
different sorts of Marcolini delights, doesn't come cheap (£80)
but would make a fantastic present. A slim box of little plain
chocolate slabs is £15 – perfect for after dinner or on a picnic.

COCO MAYA (www.cocomaya.co.uk). All the chocolate is
made on the premises, using the finest beans, in a range of
tastes and flavours you won't find anywhere else, including
pomegranate. Try the crisp lemon peel dipped in chocolate.
Others to sample include ginger-paste chocolate and
chocolate flavoured with cinnamon, cloves and ginger. The
chocolates don't keep very long because no preservatives are
used. The shop is deliciously pretty and the chocolates so
moreish that one Middle Eastern princess sent her private
plane simply to pick up a bigger fix. Some of the more
expensive shops are beginning to pick up on its wares –
Liberty, Harrods, Melrose & Morgan.

L'ARTISAN DU CHOCOLAT (www.artisanduchocolat.com). Gerard Coleman is another great chocolate maker who is also famous for his ganache – he has some fifty different varieties, including red wine, lavender, mint, tobacco, banana with thyme, a fragrant orange blossom and Bramley apple, but the real connoisseurs go for his sea-salted caramels.

Department stores are beginning to cotton on that chocolates need artisanale names attached to them, not just pretty boxes. Selfridges, for instance, sell not only Scharffenberger's chocolates (he also selects his own beans, roasts them himself and produces his chocolates in very small batches – they're renowned for a cocoa fruitiness) but also have the exclusive rights to sell the chocolates of niche Spanish producer, Xocoa. Besides wonderfully graphic packaging, Xocoa have esoteric flavours of their own, such as tandoori, green tea and thyme. They're also developing such concepts as chocolate beer and chocolate tea. While you're browsing in the chocolate department, try some of the Italian maker Venchi's extra dark bars and blocks of plain chocolate made from a fine blend of Ecuador and Ghana beans. How does an artisanale slab of hazelnut chocolate sound? Try comparing each maker with the others and your palate will soon begin to discover just what a rich and diverse place the world of chocolate is.

Drinking Chocolate

Most of these makers offer drinking chocolate that is a million miles away from the varieties to be found on most supermarket shelves. Pierre Marcolini, for instance, sells dark chocolate flakes to turn into a fantastic drink at £15 for 200 grams and £35 for 500 grams. Since we're talking serious quality here, and the potent words flung about by the makers include 'hand-made', 'bespoke' and 'couture', you will not be surprised to discover that they are far from cheap.

In New York, chocolate-lovers should visit Marie-Belle in SoHo's Broome Street, which has an amazing chilli-flavoured drinking chocolate. Back in the UK, the Chocolate Society's drinking chocolate has flakes of pure Valrhona chocolate and comes in boxes, bags or a very smart caddy, at £10.99 for 300 grams (www.chocolate.co.uk). Green & Black's drinking chocolate is also fabulous – no cheap added sugar, pure chocolate heaven.

CHOCOLATE FOUNTAIN

If you're having a big lunch (or dinner come to that) over Easter, you could hire a chocolate fountain – £59.95 for two days – from the Chocolate Fondue Company (www.chocolate fonduecompany.co.uk). It comes with instructions. You melt the chocolate separately and then put it into the fountain where it pours down and everybody dips pieces of fruit or biscuits into it. Lots of fun.

Make Your Own Easter Eggs

If you have children – for without them I can't think that anybody would dream of embarking on such a messy venture – you all might like to spend an afternoon making some chocolate eggs. They're not difficult (I'm told). To make around 12 mini-eggs you'd need about 4oz/110g of good-quality chocolate, Belgian couverture for choice (Selfridges, Fortnum & Mason and good kitchen departments sell it). The only piece of equipment you'll need to buy are some egg moulds, which once again you can find in good kitchen departments and the ever fabulous www.lakeland.co.uk. It helps to have a cooking thermometer and to remember never to let the chocolate boil. Otherwise follow the instructions that come with the chocolate egg mould and be prepared for lots of fun and some serious mess.

You could also make a chocolate-egg base by combining melted chocolate with crushed Shredded Wheat and shaping the mixture into half an egg. Then fill it with little eggs.

Betsy's Chocolate Cake

My friend Betsy, who is one of the best cooks I know, gave me this recipe years ago and it's a firm family favourite.

8oz/225g bitter chocolate (Belgian or Green & Black's)
4 eggs, separated
3oz/75g self-raising flour
8oz/225g caster sugar
8oz/225g butter

In a pan, melt the chocolate and butter together over a low heat – do not let it boil. Beat the egg yolks and sugar until they are very light and fluffy. Add the chocolate and butter mixture. Fold in the flour. Beat the egg whites until stiff and fold into the chocolate mixture. Bake in a greased cake tin for 35 minutes at 400°F/200°C/gas mark 6.

Spring Picnics

What, Mole wanted to know, was inside the contents of the fat, wicker luncheon-basket? 'There's cold chicken inside it,' replied the Rat briefly, 'coldtonguecoldhamcoldbeefpickled gherkinssaladfrenchrollscressandwichespotted meatgingerbeerlemonadesodawater – it's only what I always take on these little excursions.'

Wind in the Willows by Kenneth Grahame

Easter, as anybody who has spent more than a couple of years in Britain will know, is not known for its reliable weather. It likes to keep us on our toes. You could be greeted by the most delightful of spring days, sunny but fresh. It could – yup, really, it's happened – be blisteringly hot, or yet again, you could be back in full-on winter mode with wind, rain and even snow. So flexibility has to be the watchword, but if you're an ardent picnicker, you can adapt the picnic to the day.

I love all picnics – except, it has to be said, in driving rain. Even wintry ones up in the Scottish highlands, in the lee of sand-dunes on the Suffolk coast or in protected hollows on Hadrian's Wall have, in their time, provided magical experiences. It's the carrying of the stuff that is the problem. I used to be in thrall to the old-fashioned notion of the picnic – the wicker basket, the china, the cutlery, the glasses – but really that only works if you're tottering from the car to an extremely nearby site. It's great where distances are small, but since the main point of a picnic, it seems to me, is to be in glorious countryside, that sort of grand affair is hard to achieve if you haven't a full flotilla of staff to carry it all. Fortunately, technology has come to our rescue and these days all the usual suspects – John Lewis, Habitat, Lakeland, Sainsbury's, Argos – have an extraordinary range of attractive, lightweight melamine and plastic plates, containers, glasses and cutlery. Gone is the utilitarian, make-do air that plastic ware used to have. Even such places as the Victoria and Albert Museum have got in on the act – DeBeauty's plastic cutlery set is enchanting (www.vandashop.com). Yes, I know, it doesn't have quite the allure of crystal, silver and wicker but it does make it all so much easier to picnic in wilder, more remote places.

All the companies that specialise in the rugged, outdoor life, such as Blacks and Snow + Rock, sell lightweight rucksacks, which for those who love rambling or hiking and want to picnic on the tops of mountains are fabulously practical without having, it has to be said, much aesthetic appeal. You will need a rug to sit on and the Glyndebourne

shop (www.glyndebourne.com/shop) has a brilliant one in
dark green tartan with a dark green mackintosh backing
(essential in this 'temperate' climate of ours). It measures 72 x
54 inches (183 x 137cm) and costs £60. Otherwise, Picnic
Ware (www.picnicware.co.uk) has one for under £12. This is
a brilliant website. As well as the rug, it has a range of
lightweight picnic backpacks, including cutlery, glasses, plates
and space for the food, all for under £40.

A picnic should be held among green things
. . . Green turf is absolutely an essential.
There should be trees, broken ground, small
paths, thickets, and hidden recesses. There
should, if possible, be rocks, old timber,
moss, and brambles. There should certainly
be hills and dales – on a small scale; and
above all, there should be running water.

Anthony Trollope in *Can You Forgive Her?*

Picnic Food

For Easter, when the weather is usually what the stoics like
to call 'fresh' and I call downright chilly, I think sturdy fare
is what's needed.

PIES: I love game or chicken pies and these days good ones
can often be bought at local markets. If you can't get to one,

have a look at www.foodfullstop.com and www.fortnumand
mason.com. Fortnum & Mason's traditional game pies are
wonderful and are available online. If you're up for some
home cooking, Rick Stein has a fabulous recipe for a good
old-fashioned raised pork pie that you can access online
(http://cooksforcooks.com).

SOUPS: if it's particularly nippy, I adore hot soups. My
current favourite is courgette soup made with an intensely
flavoured chicken stock, but minestrone, leek and potato, and
mushroom are also dead easy to make, and goulash soup is
delicious (see page 94). If you really, really don't have the
time or the inclination to make your own, it's worth knowing
about Rod and Ben's soups (www.rodandbenssoups.com),
which are made from organically grown vegetables and
proper broth on Bickham Farm in Kenn, near Exeter, in
Devon – Selfridges and Wholefoods both sell them. Heat
them up, put them in the Thermos and off you go.

HOT FOOD: goulash or chilli con carne can be kept hot in
wide-mouthed Thermos flasks (Lakeland has a very sturdy
wide-mouthed stainless steel flask for £11.73). Other
contenders for the wide-mouthed Thermos are hot potatoes,
either baked or boiled. Small new ones usually come in
around this time, delicious boiled and tossed in butter and
herbs. Little spicy sausages are another alternative – so much
nicer hot than cold.

FRITTATA: this is a favourite for slightly warmer weather –
dead easy to make and little different from a slow-cooked
omelette or a Spanish omelette. I love a spinach frittata but

you could do the Spanish version (with sliced potatoes). Courgettes work very well – gently sauté some finely sliced courgettes until soft, then add the beaten eggs and lots of chopped herbs and cook very slowly until the consistency is as you like it. You may need to finish it off under the grill. When it's cool, slice it like a cake. Broad beans and roasted pepper salad or a Greek salad go well with it (pack the dressings separately in a jar with a tight lid).

✳ If you're on the coast, you can often buy wonderful freshly cooked crab or lobster for your picnic, or indulge in hot fish and chips eaten traditional style out of newspaper and on the hoof or in the shelter of dunes.

If you're stuck and can't find the time to cook, Marks & Spencer's quiches make great picnic food. It has also started doing some more enterprising take-away dishes that are ideal for picnics – small balls of mozarella tossed in pesto, salads of various mixed beans and roasted peppers. Snacks featuring chicken satay, edamame bean dip, prosciutto, artichoke and parmesan tartlets are all good standbys if you're in a hurry. Incidentally, they also sell lightweight picnic gear, including rugs, cool boxes and disposable plates and champagne flutes.

Don't forget, there's nothing wrong with some crusty bread, good smoked sausage, delicious cheeses, sweet tomatoes, fresh fruit and some fruitcake or shortbread. Add in some ginger beer, wine, hot tea and coffee and it couldn't be simpler. What matters is that all the ingredients are the best of their kind – you can't do 'simple' otherwise. Some good fruitcake (I happen to love Fortnum & Mason's Gamekeeper's Fruitcake but there are lots of nice rich, dark versions around), a fine cheese and a piece of dark chocolate make a terrific finish to a meal after a long walk or a couple of hours spent in the bracing British weather.

✳ Ginger beer is very traditional picnic fare. These days it's available in most supermarkets. I'm particularly fond of Luscombe's version (www.luscombe.co.uk). Home-made lemonade is brilliant, too, and it's incredibly easy to make your own (see page 273).

Goulash Soup

1 lb/450g onions, chopped
2 tbsp vegetable oil
1½lb/680g shin of beef, cubed
2 tbsp sweet paprika (Hungarian)
4 small tomatoes, peeled and chopped
2 peppers (red or green), cut into strips
½ tsp caraway seeds
salt to taste
3 pints/1.75 litres hot water
3 medium potatoes, peeled and cubed
smoked sausage

Sauté the chopped onions in the oil until they are golden brown. Add the shin of beef and paprika. Sauté for about ten minutes, turning the pieces of meat often. Add the tomatoes, peppers and caraway seeds. Season with salt and simmer gently for about 45 minutes. Add the hot water and simmer

for another one and a half hours. Add the potatoes and
continue simmering until they are tender. Ten minutes before
serving – or ladling into a wide-mouthed Thermos flask –
add some slices of very good smoked sausage. You'll need to
find a really good delicatessen for this – I buy mine at
Wholefoods in London's Kensington High Street. Selfridges
and Harrods food halls also stock them.
Fabulously warming!

Easter Menu

Easter is when most of us like to see our families, and if
not family then friends tend to gather, so food and the
providing thereof looms rather large. My view is that I love
delicious food – I'm inherently greedy – but not at the cost
of causing tension or stress, and not if preparing it doesn't
leave enough time for the things that really matter, such as
spending time with the people you care about. So buy in
the things that shops do well – why would anyone sweat to
make their own hot-cross buns, unless (admittedly, a very
big unless) you find it fun and can, say, involve your
children? Otherwise get them from the supermarket. Ditto
the simnel cake. My motto is – if I can't do it better than
the supermarket or the deli (although for my sense of
amour propre, I'm happy to say that there are still some
things that I can do better) then there's no point in
sweating over it.

✻ Easter brunch is a nice idea – masses of coloured hard-boiled eggs, or a huge platter of scrambled eggs and smoked salmon, jugs of fresh orange or other fruit juices, a cold ham, salads, lovely breads and croissants, and the obligatory cake – simnel, chocolate, hot-cross buns, Victoria sponge – decorated if you like with small chicks and baby eggs.

For lunch or dinner, the classic notion is that you should roast a leg of lamb. I'm in some kind of minority here for I seldom have a roast leg of lamb that I really, really love. I like the notion but the reality is usually disappointing – two rather bland slices and a bit of mint sauce. Not a feast in my view. I like it done the Greek way – cooked slowly, tenderly, until it's almost falling off the bone. I quite often add aubergine, red peppers and some skinned and peeled tomatoes about halfway through the cooking to provide some richer flavours.

I also love it prepared the French way, with flageolet beans cooking in all the juices surrounding the lamb. If you look on www.deliaonline.com you will find a gorgeous recipe. The blessed Delia also suggests using pieces of neck fillet, but I simply take a leg of lamb and cook it in much the same way.

If you have a really good grill (this works brilliantly on a barbecue), a butterflied leg of lamb is fantastic. A butterflied leg is nothing more nor less than a leg of lamb that has been boned and flattened. My local butcher (Lidgate's in London's Holland Park Avenue) sells a butterflied leg all sealed up in a plastic bag where it should be left to marinade for at least 24 hours. All you have to do then is to lift it out of the marinade (use that to cook the potatoes in the oven) and cook it under a very hot grill for about 10 to 12 minutes each side, depending how you like it. (Ask your local butcher to do something similar.) Carve long thin slices so that they are crusty on the outside, pink inside. Then all you need is a green watercress and rocket salad.

Another thing to do with lamb is to make a Moroccan tagine (see below) – it makes the lamb deliciously tender and flavoursome.

Lamb Tagine

4½lb/2kg lamb (from the leg), diced
3 tbsp olive oil
1 large onion, finely chopped
2 garlic cloves, thinly sliced
1 tsp ground cumin
1 tsp ground coriander
1 tsp ground cinnamon
14oz/400g canned tomatoes
½ pint/300ml tub lamb stock
pinch saffron threads
salt to taste
3 tbsp ground almonds
3½oz/100g dried apricots, halved
4 large courgettes, cut into large pieces
4 tomatoes, skinned and quartered
2 tsp harissa (a North African hot red paste, available at big
    supermarkets)
2 tbsp fresh parsley, chopped
1lb 2oz/500g couscous, prepared as directed on the packet

Soak the apricots in a small amount of boiling water until soft. Preheat the oven to 350°F/180°C/gas mark 4. Brown the lamb in the olive oil in batches (if you do it all at once, it lowers the temperature too much and the meat stews instead of being sealed). Use the same oil to cook the onion gently until golden but not burnt. Add the garlic and spices and cook for a couple of minutes. Add the lamb, the soaked apricots and their liquid, the canned tomatoes and the stock to the casserole, along with the saffron threads and the ground almonds. Bring to boiling point and then put the covered casserole in the oven to cook. After an hour, add the courgettes, fresh skinned tomatoes and the harissa. Check for liquid – if too dry add some more water. Cook until the lamb is tender – about another 45 minutes.

Lamb tagine is traditionally served with couscous. Add parsley for decoration.

A ham is another great standby. You could serve it hot on Easter Sunday, and cold with brunch on Easter Monday. I like it hot with a sauce I was once given in America, which was very spicy and fruity – a mixture of dried raisins and sultanas, simmered in cider, spiced up with cinnamon and slightly thickened with a little cornflour.

Plenty of fresh spring vegetables are around, so it's worth thinking of new asparagus, baby peas and carrots and doing interesting things with young leeks. In fact, my favourite spring starter is a mixture of cold cooked baby peas, mange-tout and broad beans (you might have to use frozen broad beans as it's a little too early for fresh ones) dressed with a mustardy vinaigrette, masses (and masses is key) of chopped mint and basil and crumbled goats' cheese. I served it last Easter Monday and followed it up with chicken pieces browned, then braised in sherry with lots of shallots and tarragon and the sauce thickened at the end with some crème fraiche. New potatoes (the Jersey Royals were just in) were all it needed as an accompaniment. I followed this up with a rhubarb fool and a clear rhubarb jelly. (I copied this idea from the St Alban restaurant, using the excess juice that cooking rhubarb always produces and gelatine leaves to set it – divine.)

My Favourite Cheesecake

This makes a terrific pudding after lamb, and incidentally packs up well for a picnic. You will need an 8½ inch round tin with a loose bottom.

For the crust:
5oz/150g digestive biscuits
2oz/50g caster sugar
3oz/75g butter, melted

For the filling:
12oz/350g Philadelphia cream cheese
2 eggs, beaten
4½oz/125g caster sugar
1 tsp vanilla essence
1 tsp lemon juice

For the topping:
½ pint/300ml sour cream
1½oz/40g caster sugar
1 tsp vanilla essence

Put the biscuits in a plastic bag and crush with a rolling pin until they are crumbs. Transfer to a bowl and stir in the sugar and melted butter. Then press into the base of the lightly greased cake tin to form the crust.

Beat the cream cheese to an even creamier consistency, and then add the rest of the filling ingredients, continuing to beat until the mixture is smooth. Pour over the crust and bake for 30 minutes at 350°F/180°C/gas mark 4. Remove from the oven and allow it to cool for five minutes. Prepare the topping by mixing all the ingredients together, then pour it over the cheesecake and bake for a further 10 minutes.

Christenings, Bar Mitzrahs and Naming Ceremonies

Speaking as somebody who had to get herself christened (when in my religious phase, aged about thirteen) and find godparents of my own, I feel very strongly that christenings and godparents are wonderful institutions. As a child, I minded terribly that everybody else had gone through the ritual and had these generous beings called godparents and I didn't. Now I'm very well aware that christenings and godparenting have their roots in deep religious convictions, being after all an essential step to becoming an adult member of the Christian faith and that religion is not part of many people's mainstream lives these days. So to embark on that first step simply because it would be nice for one's child to have all those extra presents at Christmas just doesn't seem right. I do think, though, that being linked in a warm, close way to other adults is a great gift to give children. So many long-established traditions, like this one, fulfil a deep psychological need. Families and close friends need to mark the baby's arrival, and a christening, surrounded as it is with ritual and a bit of religious drama, gives the event gravitas and shape.

Of course, christenings are just one way to celebrate the birth of a child. All over the world, every religion, culture and society has its own form of ritual to mark the event. A Muslim father recites the call to prayer in his newborn's right ear. After seven days the baby is named and, if a boy, circumcised. In Jewish circles, circumcision takes place on the eighth day of a baby boy's life, and both boys and girls are named. In Sikhism, a special prayer is read, holy water placed on the baby's tongue and a name chosen from the holy scriptures, while in Hindi families, Jatakarma is performed to welcome the baby into the world. Some honey is put in the child's mouth and the name of God whispered in his or her ear. The naming ceremony, Namakarna, is another big day. These ceremonies bring families together to celebrate the miracle of a new life – which is a wondrous thing and needs to be given due weight.

Church Service

Those wanting to have their children christened in a church and wanting them to belong to the wider world the church embraces should start thinking about it quite early on. If you were married in church, and still go to services there, you will probably already have a good relationship with the vicar, which you should nurture. You should start discussions about dates and timings as early as possible. While some vicars are relaxed about the parents' church attendance, others will expect to see you and your child on a regular basis before and after the christening. There does seem to me something unattractively opportunistic about merely using a church for the set-pieces in one's life and giving it no attention at all in between. A baptism, after all, involves making promises about bringing the child up as a Christian, and it doesn't seem decent not to share these values before asking for a religious ceremony. Increasingly, christenings are performed during a service attended by the whole congregation, and it seems to me there ought to be some commitment to this wider community if you are having your baby christened. For practical, spiritual and pastoral information on baptism, visit www.baptism.org.uk or www.mybaby celebration.co.uk/Catholic-christening.

Secular Naming Ceremonies

For the large numbers of non-believers who feel it would be hypocritical to go in for a religious service but still want to acknowledge in some important way what the arrival of a new human being means to them, a civil christening or humanist naming ceremony are possibilities. Parents can devise their own agenda. Friends and family may be asked to speak or read from poems or books, letters are read out and special music chosen. A ceremony such as this can be held anywhere that seems appropriate – outside in a garden or field, in the woods, on a beach, in a village hall, at home. Supporters, rather than godparents, are nominated to fulfil that vital role of other caring adults in the child's life.

As one atheist, writing on the www.friendlyatheist.com website, put it: 'Atheists like me also have values and aspirations, family and friends. So after my twin daughters Lyra and Sophia were born, my wife Shannon and I decided to create a humanist "Welcome to the World" ceremony. The ceremony focused on our commitment to raise our daughters to be creative, compassionate, critical thinkers. There was no commitment to encourage them to be atheists or humanists: while they will be raised in an openly humanist family, we want them to work out their beliefs and values for themselves. A central purpose of the ceremony was to appoint Mentors. These supporting adults, from outside the family circle, promised to take a special interest in our daughters' welfare and happiness.'

Also check www.humanism.org.uk and www.civilceremonies.co.uk for advice on secular naming ceremonies.

Godparents

The notion of godparents came about because converts to the early Christian church were usually adults whose parents were not Christians. The role of godparent was to provide a Christian mentor to help them on their journey as they embraced their new faith.

Choosing godparents these days is a tricky manoeuvre. In fancy, celeb circles, the tendency is to choose equally rich and famous friends as godparents, which makes sense because they probably all feel at ease with each other. In some circles, well-off bachelors are much-favoured since not only might they take more interest in the newly born, having no children of their own, but also (ahem!) not have too many conflicting claims on their assets when they eventually leave this world. Others choose their most important friends, bearing in mind how useful they might be to the growing child.

FAMOUS GODPARENTS

* Model Kate Moss chose actress-turned-designer Sadie Frost and actor Jude Law as godparents for her daughter, Lila Grace, while she, in turn, is godmother to Sadie and Jude's daughter, Iris.
* Nicole Richie, daughter of Lionel, is the goddaughter of none other than the late Michael Jackson, while 'The Thriller' singer's son, Prince Michael Joseph Junior, and his daughter, Paris Michael Katherine, reportedly have Macaulay Culkin as their godfather.
* Drew Barrymore's godmother is famous actress Sophia Loren, and her godfather is director Steven Spielberg.
* Madonna and Guy Ritchie's son, Rocco, has Sting as his godfather.
* Liz Hurley is godmother to Patsy Kensit and Liam Gallagher's son, Lennon, while her young son, Damian, has no fewer than six godfathers, including her ex, Hugh Grant, Sir Elton John and his partner David Furnish, and US comedian Denis Leary.

In what I like to think are more down-to-earth circles, it is customary to call on one's closest friends. In the Anglican tradition, it is usual to have three godparents – two of the same sex as the baby and one of the opposite sex. In recent times, though, this seems to have gone by the by. A recent issue of *Vogue* featured the glitzy baptism of one Sasha Filgueiras de Castilho Blow, all swaddled up in posh

christening clothes and surrounded by his nine (!)
godparents.

The idea is for godparents to help in the child's religious
upbringing, but these days most parents hope that they will
provide some outside adult support and succour, and will
perhaps introduce the child to interests that he or she might
not otherwise discover. Godparents with a keen passion for
sailing, modern dance, stamp collecting or whatever it may be,
can open their godchildren's eyes to all these different worlds.

My son says that he and his wife chose godparents for his
three sons firstly because they are close friends, and secondly
because each of them has different passions and hobbies, and
he hoped that some of these would be passed on to the boys.
One is a passionate walker who has followed the Robert
Louis Stevenson trail in the Cevennes, near to where my son
has a house. Another has introduced the whole family to a
series of games they knew nothing about – Memoir '44, Ra
and Citadel, to name but three. He is also, incidentally, a lot
of fun, endlessly turning up at birthday parties and playing
the role of the professional entertainer. Another is a sports-
mad medic, who has the inside track on all sorts of special
sporting events, and yet another is very musical and an opera
fanatic. For his part, my son is busy introducing his
godchildren to his own passions, which include certain sorts
of music and theatre. He took one of his godsons to a jazz
club recently – the boy was just at that age when he was too
young and insecure to go on his own, but it would have been
a bit naff to have gone with his dad.

Godparents play an important role during the early
teenage years, when the relationship with parents may be

tricky. A calm, affectionate adult outside the family can be a great support. Ideally, the godparent is a wonderfully concerned friend, wiser and older, to whom the young one can turn when he or she needs advice, help or a bit of a confidence boost. In the unlikely event of some ghastly family tragedy occurring, a godparent may be named as the child's legal guardian, but it's more usual for that role to devolve on a family member than a godparent.

Some people seem to feel that being asked to become a godparent is a burden. I guess, if you are asked too many times, there must come a point when you might feel you can take on no more of the emotional commitment, but I've never felt less than flattered when asked to be a godparent and am, indeed, rather envious of those of my friends who have been asked many times over. One of my friends has something like fifteen godchildren and she spoils all of them rotten, taking them on outings, giving them imaginative presents and bringing them all together for great lunch parties from time to time. They are like one big extended family, and recently they all clubbed together and gave her a tremendous lunch as a thank you.

As godchildren grow older they can become great friends. One very glamorous friend of mine has a godson who is now a successful actor, and she gets invited by this extraordinarily charming and handsome young man to be his companion for all manner of interesting events.

✳ Godparents should be there for the important landmark events in a child's life, and turn up to sports days, school plays or concert performances as he or she grows up. The closer the relationship the more rewarding it is for both sides.

Christening Clothes

I n some circles, the baby's outfit plays almost as big a role in the proceedings as the bride's does on her wedding day. In some families, an ancient garment is handed down the generations and worn by every baby in turn, which seems to me a rather charming custom. It connects the generations, becomes a symbol, like a precious thread running through the history of the family. If you don't have an heirloom christening robe but have always dreamed of dressing your own offspring in one of these old-fashioned garments, plenty are to be found in shops that specialise in antique or vintage linens. Some of the best seem to be in the US (check www.antiquelinen.com and christeningbabyangel.com) but most ship to the UK. In the UK, www.designerchristenings.co.uk has some charming clothing (not to mention a very practical checklist for anyone going in for a rather grand, highly organised christening). In this way, you can initiate your own tradition and hand the robe on to your children when they start producing babies of their own.

However, these days most babies aren't kitted out in olde worlde garb just because they're being christened – simple, modern, white and cream outfits can be stunning; or dress the baby in his or her smartest clothes. If the child is a toddler, or older, rules are even more relaxed, but obviously it is a day of some importance, so the youngster's smartest gear, or at least something other than jeans and trainers, should be worn. For girls, it's a chance to wear their prettiest dresses.

✳ Wait until the last possible moment to dress your baby in christening
clothes (for obvious reasons) and get the photographs taken as soon as
possible. For the same reason, it makes sense for you to wear
something that doesn't stain too easily – probably a dark colour.

Presents

C hristening presents aren't like other presents. They should
be designed, I think, not for ephemeral pleasure (so
nothing jokey, too glitzy or showy) but to be treasured all
through life – fine editions of classic books, a piece of
jewellery or silver, a picture or something that will add a
dimension to the child's world.

The Book of Common Prayer is an obvious choice for
a christening. Shakespeare, Dickens, Jane Austen and
T.S. Eliot ('The Wasteland' or 'The Four Quartets') are
authors to consider, but the list is long and distinguished. If
you are particularly keen on a certain writer or subject (say,
wilderness, in which case let me recommend two amazing
contemporary writers on the subject – Robert McFarlane and
Jay Griffiths), a book to reflect that can be a good idea. If
later the child responds to your encouragement, you could
keep adding to the collection as he or she grows. Speaking
personally, I have a passionate interest in Africa and its
multifarious peoples, so I would hope to nurture those
interests in my godchildren with books, trips and presents.

Since being a godparent involves years of close involvement,
it is nice to start collections so that present-giving forms a
pattern, and if not books, why not the old established one of

wine? If you don't feel up to choosing it yourself, or storing it, many wine merchants will do it for you. Berry Bros and Rudd (www.bbr.com) have been doing it for generations for grand-, god- and other parents. Other collections to start for godchildren include lithographs, antique glass, silver cutlery, mugs or beakers and egg-cups. I'd skip the traditional napkin ring, since all they do these days is sit in drawers.

For girls, a charm bracelet is lovely, and you can add to it every Christmas and birthday. Otherwise, Tiffany or antique crosses, if you can find them, little strings of pearls or coral beads are items to be cherished. Scouring the antique shops or auction houses is fun and can yield up some fantastic bargains.

For more ideas, check www.direct-uk.net (member log-in required) and www.celebration-books.com.

✳ Most unusual christening present I've ever heard of? The small daughter of some friends was allowed to name a foal born to one of her godparent's horses. She thinks it's the most fab present she's ever had.

After the Service

Much the nicest christenings I've been to are those followed by an informal lunch or tea back at the parents' house. If you prefer, though, small hotels or village or church halls are just as suitable.

If the christening is in summer, a buffet lunch or tea in the garden is lovely. Offer different teas (include lapsang souchong and Earl Grey or more exotic brews that you fancy), fresh lemonade (see page 273), orange or apple juice and ginger beer, and maybe some nicely chilled champagne at the ready to wet the baby's head.

Good traditional egg and cress sandwiches, and smoked salmon and cucumber, followed by cakes of various kinds, are all you need, although if there are many children present – and one of the nicest things about christenings is that they involve all the generations from grandparents down to the new arrival – it's good to offer a few treats, such as meringues, jellies, ice creams, brownies, or even old-fashioned sandwiches made from hundreds and thousands – that sort of thing.

Some people like to keep the top tier of the wedding cake for the christening, which is a lovely idea. If that's long gone, though, there's no need to go to a grand cake-maker. Make your own, or order an iced fruit cake from Marks & Spencer or Waitrose. I'd probably also have a traditional Victoria sponge and a chocolate one (see pages 318 and 88), to cover all tastes.

Whether the party is to be held indoors or out, I'd go to some trouble to make sure the table or dining-room looks a bit special. Lay a beautiful cloth – use antique embroidered sheets, or Cabbages and Roses (www.cabbagesandroses.com) has some gorgeous, faded, antique-looking fabric, which you could buy by the metre to make a terrific tablecloth – and put out your prettiest things. Line up china jugs filled with flowers or foliage, depending on the season. Use vintage china for the table, if you've got it. Or you can buy charming chintzy cups and saucers from www.joannawood.co.uk. They are mismatched to give a thrift store feel. I love old-fashioned cake-stands, and you can always find a selection of them along with compote bowls and sundae glasses at www.re-foundobjects.com. Several cake-stands of different heights look terrific – and bear in mind that, although buying a few of them might seem like an extravagance, they'll be doing their wonderfully decorative bit at masses of other celebrations through the years.

If it's winter, and tea-time is going to run into the gloaming, candlesticks add to the magic. The Conran Shop (www.conranshop.co.uk) has a lovely selection of not very expensive glass candlesticks of varying heights and decorative styles – buy some of them and your table will look fabulous. Try Ikea (www.ikea.com) for a wide range of candles.

Suggestions for a summer lunch are to be found in The Grand Picnic chapter, and for chillier times, you'll find them in the Christmas and Thanksgiving chapters.

✳ Don't forget to invite the vicar as a way of saying thank you for the service.

My father always wanted to be the corpse at every funeral, the bride at every wedding and the baby at every christening. Alice Roosevelt Longworth

Bar Mitzvahs

The bar mitzvah ceremony is a formal recognition of the coming of age of Jewish boys. At thirteen, a boy becomes obligated to observe the commandments, and from then on is allowed to take part in leading religious services, to form binding contracts, to testify before religious courts and to marry. During Shabbat services on a Saturday shortly after the boy's thirteenth birthday, the celebrant is required, at the very least, to recite a blessing over the weekly reading from the Torah (or holy text). These days, he is often called upon to learn much longer portions of text, including a traditional chant, and recite that in the synagogue, while in some places, the celebrant undertakes the entire weekly reading or leads the congregation in certain important prayers. He is also required to make a speech, which traditionally begins with the phrase, 'Today, I am a man.' The father recites a blessing, thanking God for removing the burden of being responsible for his son's sins, the boy now being old enough to be held responsible for himself.

The equivalent ceremony for Jewish girls, a bat mitzvah, is held when they reach twelve years of age, and since women are not usually allowed to participate in religious services, is usually little more than a party.

Rabbi and synagogue are the chief sources of information for all formal religious aspects of both bar mitzvah and bat mitzvah.

How to Celebrate

In affluent Jewish communities, bar mitzvah celebrations are exuberant. They're as lavish as weddings, often taking place in grand hotels. Gladrags are the order of the day and mothers, particularly, always find something new and special to wear (again, bearing in mind the analogy of a wedding). Food, obviously, needs to be kosher and there are lots of specialist caterers – in London, the most-often quoted appears to be Tony Page (www.tonypage.com) – along with planners who will take over the whole thing, finding the venue, organising the food, the music, the decorations and the dancing, which is an important part of it.

It doesn't have to be done that way, though. What is essential is the celebratory element, the sense of generosity over food, the fun, the laughter, the dancing. All these things can be done at small hotels or at home, and frequently are. Celebrations often go on for several days taking in, say, a dinner for close family on the Friday night, a biggish dinner and dance on the Saturday after the ceremony itself, followed by a Sunday brunch-type 'do' for all those who have travelled from afar. Wonderful puddings are an established part of the ritual, including dishes such as profiteroles, chocolate mousse, cheesecakes and gateaux. Dancing often follows.

As with all celebrations, there's something about the warmth and intimacy of having friends in your own house that makes it that much more special. Cook your favourite dishes, ask friends and family to help, put on the music system and celebrate.

SPEECHES

Speeches are an inextricable part of both bar and bat mitzvahs. The boy or girl who has come of age thanks parents, relations, friends, rabbis and anyone else it seems appropriate to mention. Often there are special readings by others present. If anyone needs a little help with ideas, www.speech-writers.com has suggestions for speeches and toasts.

PRESENTS

There's no need to be unduly original. The most frequently given present is money, and the amount deemed suitable varies, depending upon the circles in which you move. In relatively prosperous circles, £100 or £150 is ample. Otherwise, gift certificates or savings bonds are popular, and for girls, close family might give keepsake jewellery.

For interest's sake, Philip Green, according to press reports, didn't give his son, Brandon, a present at all on his bar mitzvah, but he did spend some £4 million on it! The event took the form of a three-day party on the Riviera and included building a giant temporary synagogue at the Hotel Cap Ferrat – and guests were entertained by Andrea Bocelli, the blind Italian tenor, as well as Beyoncé and Destiny's Child.

The House Party

Ⱨ ouse parties – the very word sounds rather grand – but they are one of the all-time great ways to spend time with friends and you don't have to have a grand house to hold one. It can be as splendid or as informal as you and your guests care to make it and it's perfectly possible for a single host or a group of friends to rent somewhere suitable, whether at home or abroad.

Of course, grand houses are wonderful and literature tells us that in their Victorian, Edwardian and pre-war heyday, house parties were sumptuous affairs. Those were the heady days when people who sashayed from one house party to another seldom had any necessity to engage in gainful employment. The weekend started on Saturday morning rather than the Friday evening that is more common today. Expeditions to the races, chances to stalk or shoot, all in grand style with plenty of staff to look after the large numbers of guests, were all par for the course. It finished on Mondays when the party dispersed, often heading to London for more jollifications. Some of this way of life still goes on with busy, relatively wealthy, people buying into it for a few days or a week at a time. An article in the *Spectator* in 1994, for instance, featured the writer's (one Dominic Prince) invitation to join a house party in Scotland for a week's stalking. The house had been rented by a politician and a journalist, and he described how trunks of food were flown up as excess baggage and crates of booze arrived by car. What is rather diverting, though, is to learn that the host picked one of the guests – a certain David Cameron – as a future prime minister, 'not least because he was the only one to help with the washing-up'. 'The dinners were magnificent affairs,' Mr Prince informs us, but the salutary sting in the tale is that 'the hangovers were horrific and had to be walked off by hours spent on the hill.'

But one doesn't have to go in for this sort of grandeur. All over the country all sorts of much less formal but just as jolly get-togethers happen all the time. Whether you own a cottage or a barn, whether you get together with friends to hire a yacht, a Tuscan villa, a Scottish shooting lodge, a simple Cotswold cottage or a chalet in the Alps you, too, can make your very own house party. The real appeal is the conviviality, the pleasure of sharing an experience, having an adventure, which binds friends together, gives them memories that linger on long after the snow has melted, the fires gone out or the sea grown cold. They offer the participants a better chance to get to know each other than a dinner or theatre outing ever allows. There's nothing nicer, at the end of a hectic week, than arriving at a peaceful house, fires lit on a winter evening, the smell of something delicious wafting from the kitchen – a boeuf en daube, say, or a saffron-scented fish soup. Then there's the pleasure of looking forward to all the weekend's activities – the trip to the local farmers' market perhaps on the Saturday morning, picking up provisions for a casual lunch (a home-made soup or some pâté, the freshest of salad ingredients, fruit and vegetables in season), walks in the surrounding hills or on the local beaches, visits to antique shops, reading books, playing games, just catching up with friends. It doesn't happen, though, without somebody putting in some effort. If you've all hired a place together, everybody is equally responsible for the fun and games and everybody should muck in. If you've done all the inviting, responsibility for making it all happen and for your guests' comfort is up to you.

How to Be a Good Host or Hostess

This isn't anything like as difficult as it sounds. Whether you're inviting people for a weekend, or even week, of carefully orchestrated entertainments or for tea in the afternoon, all that really matters is that you try to treat your guests as you would like to be treated if the positions were reversed. You like to be warm, don't you? So don't put them in freezing bedrooms. You like a hot bath with nice fluffy towels – so make sure hot water and clean towels are in plentiful supply. You know what it's like to feel a little peckish so make sure your guests know that they can help themselves to fruit, biscuits, tea, coffee or a drink whenever they like.

When people arrive, whacked after a long journey, the best hosts thrust a drink (or a cup of tea or coffee) into their hands, usher them to their rooms and let them be for a little while. Alex Polizzi, former owner of Endsleigh Hotel (www.hotelendsleigh.com), likes to give her guests vodka and ginger ale with a touch of cucumber.

Let guests know what's happening next and when they should come down. Have lots of newspapers to hand – it's one of the treats of the weekend – and don't bully people who hate the great outdoors into a huge yomp up the nearby hills.

Giuliano Morandin's Perfect Gin Martini

Giuliano Morandin is the Dorchester's well-known bar man and before he worked there he was at Duke's Hotel, which is a famous gin Martini spot. This is his recipe and he always uses Tanqueray No. 10 as well as bespoke grapefruit bitters to bring out its flavour.

1. Fill a mixing glass with ice.
2. Take a Martini glass from the freezer and chill further with crushed ice.
3. Stir the ice in the mixing glass to remove edges. Strain away the excess water.
4. Pour 50 ml Tanqueray No. 10 gin at room temperature into the mixing glass.
5. Add 5 ml French vermouth.
6. Add two drops of grapefruit bitters.
7. Stir everything briskly.
8. Discard the ice from the Martini glass and pour the drink into it.
9. Pare a white grapefruit zest and snap so the oil sprays over the drink.
10. Wipe the rim of the glass with the grapefruit zest for the scent. Serve.

Bedroom and Bathroom

The question of whether to offer double or single beds is a delicate matter, to be negotiated tactfully. One friend we stay with in the summer in Aldeburgh tells me that some of what she calls her more 'mature' friends ask specifically for single beds. It goes without saying that they should be comfortable and the sheets should be of pure cotton. You can buy inexpensive pure cotton ones at Zara Home (www.zarahome.com) or Ikea (www.ikea.com).

I always think that spare bedrooms should be tested out. Look at them with the critical eye of a Michelin inspector. Make sure the curtains keep the light out and that the reading light is adequate, and check for draughts. Once you've sorted out the basics, you can add some welcoming touches – a few magazines or biographies to read, a tin of biscuits, a bottle of water, a little flask of whisky in case your guests feel like a nightcap, and, if there's room, maybe a television to watch the late-night news.

In the bathroom, as well as the big fluffy towels (not expensive in the scale of things – Zara Home again, Marks & Spencer or John Lewis www.johnlewis.com), some nice unguents, shampoos and body lotions are another way of making your guests feel pampered.

* You should let guests know roughly what to expect beforehand – whether the weekend is going to be casual with cosy suppers and country walks, whether they'll need tennis racquets, swimming costumes, walking boots, some gladrags. It's not done to be the sort of hostess who says, 'Oh, just come as you are, it's all very casual,' and then dresses up like a peacock – very bad manners in my book.

Food

Rather a worry if one is the host or hostess with very little help. Now that we are older many of our friends are richer and staff tend to turn up for the Saturday night dinner and sometimes for Sunday lunch. too. But when we were all young and impecunious (but having just as much fun) it was all hands to the deck. Meals for those without help needn't be grand affairs – casseroles and other dishes prepared in advance are fine and nobody has yet turned up their nose at a roast lunch. Once, when we were staying on a Highland estate for a walking and stalking holiday, our hosts had a well-developed routine – breakfasts were hot and hearty but lunch was a self-service affair. In the kitchen you picked up as many rolls as you fancied and filled them yourself from whatever was on offer – usually avocado, cheese, tomato, chicken, tuna, but it varied every day – put in a piece of fruit and a bar of chocolate and off we all went. Dinners were cooked by a chef from Edinburgh.

If you have no help – and most of us don't – the good news is that there are all sorts of ways of making the weekend easier. Wild Rose (www.wildrosefood.co.uk) is a catering service which delivers home-cooked meals to your house so that all you have to do is put them in the oven or microwave. Starters are priced from £2.95, main courses from £4.95 and puddings from £2.50. They cater for the London area.

All the great comfort dishes that are mentioned elsewhere in this book – lasagne, moussaka, cottage pie (see page 349), fish pie, boeuf en daube – are very much back in fashion. They can all be made in advance, brought out and reheated. I've often thought back to some splendid hosts in Dorset who don't go in for intensive cooking but provide delicious food by dint of careful shopping – fresh crab for Saturday lunch with tomato and other salads, radishes in season to dip in rock salt and some unsalted butter, gorgeous fillets of beef tossed on the barbie or quick-roasted in the oven (I think they work best if sealed and browned in a casserole first) served with new potatoes and salads and followed by some judiciously chosen cheeses.

If you're going to do a Saturday night dinner party, don't go for anything too elaborate. First course could be charcuterie, asparagus in season, antipasti, for which you don't have to cook everything yourself – a good delicatessen should supply almost everything from marinated olives and mushrooms, to grilled artichokes and aubergines. The charcuterie should include some pata negra ham, if possible, and some fine salamis, and make it look pretty by adding herbs and breadsticks.

Main course could be roast fillet of beef (though not, of course, if you are doing it for Sunday lunch) – roll beef in some crushed coriander seeds and peppercorns, brown the meat all over then put in a high oven (425°F/220°C/gas mark 7) for 15–20 minutes. Take it out, wrap it tightly in cling-film, twisting the ends, and leave it to rest for 20 minutes. You can do that in advance, then take it out of the cling-film and put it back in the oven for 8–10 minutes just to heat through. Serve with fresh watercress and a sauce, either made from the juices with some wine swilled through (it must come to the boil to get rid of the alcohol), or I like one made with a mixture of some cream of horseradish mixed with crème fraiche and a little lemon juice.

Another easy dish is to stuff a whole fish (salmon trout is the most delicate) with butter, lots of herbs and lemon juice, wrap it loosely in foil and cook it in the oven at 400°F/200°C/gas mark 6 for 40 minutes (this is the timing for a fish weighing about 4½lb/2kg – adjust according to size). Serve with new potatoes and vegetables in season, or a big salad.

✳ For lunch or dinner, you could roast lots of chickens, but they must be the best free range. Good sources are www.abelandcole.co.uk and www.exmoor-organic.co.uk, or get to know your local butcher.

Puddings these days are dead easy, too – buy a tarte tatin or some patisserie and offer lots of fruit. In summer, berries with coeur à la crème (see page 264), baked peaches or grape brulée are all fabulous. In winter, a bread and butter pudding is divine (try Delia Smith's version at www.deliaonline.com) or a winter fruit salad of poached mixed dried fruits topped with toasted almonds. If possible, finish with a runny Vacherin or Stinking Bishop cheese, served with a spoon and a salad of green leaves drizzled with olive oil.

Sprinkled throughout this book are suggestions for easy food. These days it can be done – caterers, delicatessens, patisseries and supermarkets have all got a million times better since I was a housewife struggling to do all these things and more. Suss them out, cultivate them and you'll find that looking after your friends isn't the slog it used to be. And don't be afraid to ask your guests to help.

Breakfasts

I think there's an awful lot to be said for giving your house guests a socking great breakfast. 'Breakfast like a king' has entered the nation's phrase book for a good reason, and the great thing about it is that you don't have to rack your brains to be original – just do the traditional dishes as well as you can. That lets you off the hook at lunchtime, when no one will be completely starving, and gets the day off to a good start.

Clarissa Dickson Wright, in her splendid book *Clarissa's Comfort Food*, is big on breakfasts. She recalls that cold curry used to be a feature of breakfasts after hunt balls, while during shooting weekends, devilled pheasant legs were usually on offer. I certainly remember that on South African farms breakfasts always included meat, such as steaks and lamb chops, mostly for the men who had been up since dawn and had come back for breakfast after some hours out on the veldt. At the balls I used to go to when I was young and newly arrived in England, the great early morning dish was always kedgeree – fabulous – and sometimes there were tables manned by people cooking eggs to order, which is the only way to serve eggs in my view.

PORRIDGE: for a British house party, this is a must. It's quick, nutritious, warming and, if well done, delicious. Clarissa Dickson Wright is a purist and says it must be made with water – but me, I'm a soft South African and I like it made with milk and finished off with a dollop of cream and a dab of honey. Buy a packet of Scottish oats and read the instructions – it isn't difficult but you must on no account let it burn.

KIPPERS: I love kippers and the best ones I've ever had were at Olga Polizzi's wonderful hotel, Tresanton (www.tresanton.com), in Cornwall. Find a good source, usually a proper fishmonger, or check www.kipper.co.uk, which sells what it calls Craster kippers, either whole or ready filleted, in easy-to-cook packs. Selfridges sells terrific kippers and wonderful Arbroath Smokies. If you're feeling lazy, Marks & Spencer also has kippers in easy-to-cook packs. You just grill the fish for 6 to 8 minutes.

EGGS: some people like eggs fried, others like them scrambled or boiled. Nigella Lawson reminds us of some good advice about boiling eggs. If you're going to plunge them into boiling water, it's best to start with them at room temperature. If you're taking them straight from the fridge, put them into a pan of cold water and bring it to the boil slowly.

Scrambled eggs are delicious when good and awful when milk is added and they taste more like custard. Whisk however many eggs you think you need in a little bowl with some salt and pepper. Melt a little butter in a pan and add the egg mixture over a low heat. 'Stir constantly and cook slowly' should be your mantra. If you want them to be ultra luxurious, add a touch of butter or cream to the mixture just before it's ready to serve, when it should be soft and creamy. Add smoked salmon pieces to the mix if you like it, or to make a change.

Souffléd omelettes look quite fancy, as if somebody has made an effort, and are easy to do. Simply separate the whites from the yolks. Beat the whites until stiff and then fold them gently into the beaten yolks and make the omelette in the usual way. You can add herbs, smoked salmon or any other filling you fancy.

BACON: buy only the best because the sort that oozes white gunk is horrid. I like Duchy Originals bacon (www.duchy originals.com), and the bacon sold by www.formanandfield.com is wonderful, too. My husband is addicted to George Foreman's grill (most kitchen departments sell it) and cooks his bacon on that. It's just as good for hamburgers or steaks.

MUESLI: some really good brands are available. I particularly like Dorset Cereals mueslis (www.dorsetcereals.co.uk), which

you can buy in supermarkets. Check the many varieties
online. Of course, you can always make your own. I found a
recipe years ago – I can't remember where but it is delicious.
Take 7oz/200g of mixed nuts, coarsely ground in a food
processor, the same amount of organic oats, 3oz/75g of
sunflower seeds and 5oz/150g of sultanas, spread them all on
a baking sheet and toast for 20 minutes – yum!

ORANGE JUICE: a jugful of freshly squeezed orange juice is a
cheering sight on the breakfast table, packed as it is with the
vitamin C that those with slight hangovers crave (always a
threat after a convivial dinner).

TOAST AND MARMALADE: toast made with good-quality
bread, brown and white, spread with great marmalade –
Cooper's Oxford Chunky Marmalade is the one I like best
after my son's home-made – is the traditional finish to a
hearty breakfast. Croissants, if you like them, make a change.

✳ Some people prefer not to eat a huge cooked breakfast, and plain yogurt
with berries in summer and a compote of dried fruit in winter makes a
lovely alternative. In any case, if you're somewhere hot and sunny,
possibly surrounded by delicious fruit of the spoiling variety, a selection of
that, coupled with yogurt, toast or croissants, fruit juices and coffee is
about all that most people want. So you don't need to overdo it.

Coffee

There's nothing like coming down in the morning to the smell
of freshly brewed coffee to make one feel that all is well with
the world. It's worth doing a bit of research to get your coffee

right. Some people believe that you must use freshly ground beans to make the best cup in the world, but in fact the ground coffee sold in supermarkets stands up extraordinarily well in blind tastings. Waitrose's Kenya AA coffee beans get the best reports of all the supermarket brands.

If you like some eco credentials, Cafédirect (www.cafedirect.co.uk) produces lovely coffee and the company is endorsed by the Fairtrade Foundation. Their Rich Roast is strong and black as night. For something more medium bodied, Daylesford's Union Coffee is 100 per cent organic and also Fairtrade approved. Among the ground coffees, Taylors of Harrogate's Columbia Supremo, roasted medium dark, is rich and velvety.

There's a good reason why Jamaican Blue Mountain coffee is regularly cited as the best in the world. Its Arabica beans are grown at high altitude, some 5,000 feet above sea level, and everything in the natural world conspires to make the location perfect for the cultivation of coffee beans. The resulting coffee is distinct and delicious in a way that is unequalled by coffee from any other region anywhere. It has an intense aroma and is perfectly balanced with a full-bodied flavour that develops on the palate.

Coffee on the Web

* www.coffeecompass.co.uk is a supplier of gourmet coffee, specialising in fresh roasted as well as green coffee beans. They import beans from all the major growing areas and hand-roast them using traditional slow-roast methods, which they say gives a fuller flavour. It's a good place to start if you want to move away from supermarket coffee to

something more adventurous – single origins, rare estates and special blends. The language becomes more esoteric, as if discussing whisky blends. These are Coffee Compass's most popular coffees, in order:

> Jamaica Blue Mountain 'Wallenford'
> Kenya Gethumbwini
> Philippine Alamid Kopi Luwak
> Red Roast Blend
> Miniature Jamaica Blue Mountain Barrels
> Mocha Italia
> Kenya AA Blue Mountain
> Mediterranean Mocha Espresso
> Mexican Altura Chiapas (Liquid Amber))

* www.monmouthcoffee.co.uk is a London legend and has for years guided generations of customers to coffee nirvana.

* www.thebeanshop.com not only sells a fantastic variety of beans but has instructions on how to make the best coffee.

HOW TO MAKE GREAT COFFEE

Use 6fl oz/175ml of cold fresh water to 2 tablespoons of whole beans for each cup. Coffee made using paper filters is generally strong and without residue at the bottom of the cup but I find either a jug or a cafetière is simple and easy to use and makes terrific coffee – the only problem is that they don't, like their electrical counterparts, keep coffee constantly hot. Here is what the Beanshop has to say: 'The key to a really good cup of coffee can be summed up in one word: freshness. It is critical to use freshly roasted, freshly ground beans. The quality of the coffee-making equipment, and even the coffee itself, will be irrelevant if it is stale. The next step is to use clean equipment because grounds and coffee oils can become rancid. Use good water freshly drawn, and the purer and softer the better. Water should be used at the proper temperature – not boiling, but approximately 190°F/88°C, and cups and utensils should be warmed beforehand. It is also important that the correct grind of coffee is used for each method of making. Never re-use coffee grounds and drink the coffee as soon as possible after it is made.'

The House Party Abroad

If you've rented somewhere divine and are inviting friends to join you, rather than everyone sharing, it's vital to make it absolutely crystal clear what you are paying for and what you expect them to pay for. As the world got richer some of the very rich threw in all sorts of treats, such as air-fares, gala dinners, invitations to stay on yachts. But it isn't done to present guests with bills afterwards. For instance, some friends of ours who were celebrating a wedding anniversary in the South of France at the utterly divine Hotel Crillon le Brave (www.crillonlebrave.com) let us know well in advance what they were providing, when we would be left to our own

CULT COFFEE-MAKING MACHINES

Plenty of people I know have a deep and ongoing love affair with their coffee machines, stroking them as if they were pets. Most recommend going for the Italian effect.

* The Bialetti Mukka Electrical (www.bialettishop.com) is a no-fuss cappuccino maker that makes one mug at a time. It's easy to clean and, at £50.43, not a bad price. It comes in two versions – a crazy 'fun' design, known as the 'cow', or a more classic and elegant polished aluminium. In my experience one tires of 'fun' almost as soon as the wrapping is off.

* The Bosch Tassimo (www.bosch-home.co.uk) is more sophisticated, making a range of different coffees at different strengths – espressos, latte macchiatos, cappuccinos. It's very speedy and somewhat more expensive at £98.50.

* The Gaggia Espresso machine (www.gaggia.uk.com) has a devoted following. Some fans will brook no other make. Expensive at £279.95, it has a capacity of nearly 4 pints/ 2 litres and does the job to perfection, making a superior espresso in a couple of seconds flat.

* Coming up fast on the inside lane is the Nespresso Coffee Capsule Machine (www.nespresso.com), starting at £99. In a few seconds you have a cup of Arabica or cappuccino or a latte, depending upon the capsule you've put in the machine, but the capsules are quite expensive to buy.

devices (with suggestions for how we might spend that time) and what we would be expected to fund for ourselves. We all knew exactly where we were and a grand time was had by all.

Sensitivity is required for these arrangements. The last decades have thrown up huge changes in the disposition of wealth. In the old days, whatever class you were born into most people had roughly the same lifestyle with more or less the same sort of income. These days, the same family, let alone circles of friends, can incorporate huge disparities in wealth. I mean, it's lovely if you have your own island, private jet, dog-walker, chef and hand-holder, but you should not issue the sort of invitations that are going to cripple your less-well-off guests financially – that is ones requiring enormously exclusive chartered flights, outfits or tips (have you checked the tips expected on yachts? Grab a gin and tonic and sit down before you do). House parties where large bills are run up as everybody heads off to expensive restaurants every night are lovely if you can afford it, but a nightmare if you can't. So make sure you are inclusive and cater for everyone's needs.

✳ As well as being clear about what financial contributions are expected, matters concerning dogs and children should be settled in advance – are they invited, to start with, then what provisions will be made for them and what should guests arrange themselves. If you're a family and you're asking other families with children you probably need to make sure your guests think as you do over meal-times, not to mention discipline. It's fine, indeed lovely, to have all the children around at lunch but rather nice if they're fed before the evening meal (bribe the children with promises of a bit of TV-watching, some games or a good DVD) so the adults can have some grown-up time together

SMOKING

If you're a non-smoker, and you really hate it, what do you say to smoking guests? A tricky one this. I tend to let them smoke as I take the view that, if they're in my house, I want them to be happy, but I have friends who so dislike it that it makes them think very carefully about whom they ask to stay in their Venetian apartment. If you hate smoking that much, you should make it clear in advance – nothing worse for an addict than to arrive for something that's supposed to be a treat and find nicotine has been banned. (Of course, good guests go outside to smoke anyway, or at least always ask permission to smoke in the house.)

Things to Do

* In the country, walks are the obvious activity. It's a good idea to have some local maps available so guests can plan a route. If anyone's interested, you could provide a list of birds and plants to look out for. (See the Easter chapter for walking suggestions.)

* Get tickets for a concert or a show if there's a good theatre or concert hall nearby. Often, house parties are centred round festivals – the Bath Festival, the Aldeburgh Music Festival, the Edinburgh Festival – which makes entertaining guests a doddle.

* Visits to craft centres, local artists' studios, galleries, churches and museums are often a good idea. Consult local guidebooks for inspiration and check opening times. Visits to National Trust and English Heritage properties and gardens are always interesting.

* Indoor games are a necessity, in case it pours with rain – Mahjong, backgammon, chess and several packs of cards should see you through. (See pages 34–35 for more ideas.)

* Jigsaws are the perfect wet weekend entertainment. Theatre producer Michael Codron has, it seems, done a jigsaw a day for more than thirty years. You can do as, apparently, the Queen does and borrow them from the British Jigsaw Puzzle Library (www.britishjigsawpuzzlelibrary.co.uk). The pictures feature art subjects, murder mysteries and maps among other things. Join the library for three or six months or for a year, and exchange the puzzles by post. Personalised puzzles of your own photographs are fun, especially if they include several of the house-party guests (www.jigsaws.co.uk will make them – £23.95 for 140 pieces). Postcode puzzles are another idea, jigsaws that feature the area around any named address (from www.firebox.com), while most museums and galleries sell puzzles based on their exhibits. You could get the Rokeby Venus, for instance, from the National Gallery – £10 for a 1,000-piece puzzle. Children's puzzles, such as a Noah's Ark, can be bought from www.woodentoys-uk.co.uk, while www.alljigsawpuzzles.co.uk has an enormous selection of jigsaws of all sorts.

I have often been surprised at the fantastic discomfort and deprivation the grand English are prepared to put their friends (and total strangers) through, particularly in my youth. I've been shown into bathrooms that could just about manage a cold squirt of brown water, bedrooms with doors that don't shut, blankets like tissue, and pillows like rocks. I have driven an hour cross-country to lunch with some grand relations of my father, who gave me one sausage, two small potatoes and twenty-eight peas. Once, during a house-party for a ball in Hampshire, I was so cold that I ended up piling all my clothes, with two threadbare towels, onto the bed and then holding all this together with a worn square of Turkish carpet – the only bit of floor-covering in the room. Julian Fellowes in *Snobs*

How to Be a Good House Guest

First, it scarcely needs saying, you should reply to any invitation as soon as possible. If your hostess is going to some trouble to put together a group of friends for your mutual delectation, you should also put in some effort. Secondly, you should try to be punctual at all times throughout your stay. Remember Uncle Matthew in Nancy Mitford's *The Pursuit of Love*, who was driven to such fury by guests whom he knew to be unpunctual that he'd start fretting ahead of time – 'In precisely six and three-quarter minutes the damned fella will be late.'

✱ Good guests don't drink their way through their hosts' cellar, certainly not without lifting a finger to help. They always leave when they're supposed to (outstaying your welcome is a serious solipsism) and show some eagerness to do something helpful about the beds.

TACT

Good guests are always tactful. The awful story of travel writer Patrick Leigh Fermor's famous faux pas when invited to stay with Somerset Maugham at Cap Ferrat is salutary. His big mistake was drawing attention to his host's stammer at dinner. Leigh Fermor, who had initially been invited to stay for a week, was approached by Somerset Maugham at the end of the evening, and offered 'a hand as cold as a toad, with the words, "W-w-well I'll s-s-say g-good-b-b-bye now in c-case I'm not up b-by the t-time y-you l-leave."'

You should try to do your bit to make the weekend jolly for everyone, and take some interest in your host's affairs. Here are some more specific tips.

* The matter of offering help requires sensitivity. While some people hate their kitchen being invaded, others love to chat and are pleased to have some help. If cooking isn't

your bag, you're best not to rattle the pans – you can at least be a sous-chef and peel, chop or wash. You could also wash up. Suss it out tactfully and act accordingly.

* If you have any food allergies or preferences – if you're vegetarian or vegan, for instance – it's only polite to let your hosts know well in advance and, if possible, try not to put them to any trouble. Otherwise you'll just have to pick your way round the problem.

* It's not polite to stay in bed until lunchtime. If you need the sleep, at least ask your hosts if they mind you getting up late, and make it clear you don't expect any breakfast. One friend was kept hovering most of the morning, waiting to serve up breakfast for guests who didn't appear until noon. If a house party includes drowsy teenagers, or the over-worked, exhausted drones that our society seems to have nurtured, hosts can make it easier for themselves by putting everything out, telling people to help themselves, and instituting a rule that everybody washes up and puts away their own breakfast things.

* Try to find some ways of amusing yourself – don't make your hosts feel they have to dream up some form of entertainment for every minute of the day. If they're a bit harassed over shopping/cooking/laying the table, either help or get out of the way – hanging about is the worst of all worlds.

* Be enthusiastic about treats – join in the shopping expeditions, visits to galleries or whatever else your host

has planned. Nobody likes a wet blanket. Try to contribute in a way that helps – one friend who isn't mad on skiing, nevertheless joins a Swiss chalet party when invited, and always makes it her job to sort the lunch rendezvous by finding a new place to eat, sussing out the best table and booking it. If you're a guest in a swish holiday villa, you could organise a treat for everybody – say hiring a magician to perform tricks at dinner, or (a friend did this in Goa) asking a local trader to bring a selection of finest pashminas to the villa.

* Guests usually club together to take the hosts out to a good local restaurant at least once during their stay.

* If there is help or, even more grandly, servants, tips should always be left for them on the dressing-room table.

The House Present

Since we don't ourselves have a country house I've much more often been on the giving than the receiving end of the house present conundrum. If you're giving them to polite people it's quite hard to gauge which ones have really given pleasure as all are greeted with effusive thanks. By dint of serious questioning I have arrived at some kind of consensus of what makes a good house present. The list will not surprise you for it's astonishingly conventional. They all love fine versions of everyday commodities.

UNCOMFORTABLE TIMES

Oddly enough, it's in the grandest houses that you can feel the least at ease. You sense there are rules but don't always know what they. How to get a cup of tea, what time to gather, what expeditions, walks or other entertainments are on offer and which ones you are expected to take part in – all these things should be explained but are not always clear.

Dress codes can be a nightmare. One of my most embarrassing moments was the time we were invited to stay in one of England's grandest and most beautiful houses, an architectural gem. I bought what I thought was an amazing nightdress, especially to impress the valet, whom I knew would be there to unpack our bags. When I came up to bed that night, he'd laid out a pink gingham shirt-dress – my new nightdress was clearly not a garment he recognised as such at all.

One of my least relaxed stays ever was in an embassy a long way from home when we had no idea how to get any refreshments, or indeed how to find our host and hostess when it wasn't a meal time, and worried endlessly about who or what we might be disturbing. The dinners were delightful – the great thing about embassies is they can rustle up the most diverting guests – but the days that didn't have planned outings were weirdly disconcerting. Weekends with close friends are much less fraught, when there's no formality and everybody just mucks in.

THINGS NOT TO DO

* Flood the bathroom by letting the bath over-run.
* Arrive with previously unmentioned boyfriends/girlfriends/ hangers-on.
* Run around and pocket all the tips for the staff.
* Wear jeans when specifically asked to dress up a bit in the evening.
* Let your dog get out of control – in fact, you should always ask before you arrive if your dog is welcome. A sad story here is of a friend whose pug committed suicide at Haddon Hall. As she strolled around the gardens with the host on a dreamy summer day, her much-loved pug was sniffing and panting around the house, and climbed to the top turret where it was stung on the bottom by a bee, dived out of the window with the shock and landed at her feet, stone-dead. It was too much to cope with and she deemed it proper to leave straight after lunch.
* Arrive empty-handed (see page 142).
* Forget to write thank-you letters – though *not* on the host's writing-paper (it's been known!)
* Overstay your welcome. Leave when you're supposed to leave.

* A fine Bordeaux or Burgundy (better than champagne), a great cheese, caviar, delicious oils and fine vinegars, wonderful chocolates (see pages 82–86 for the low-down on what makes good chocolate). You could also go for a big chunk of proper Parmigiano, some bottarga (that fabulous dried cod's roe that is ambrosia spread over pasta) or truffle oil, or even, in season, a truffle itself. The big

kilner jars of potted brown shrimps sold through www.effortless-eating.com always go down a treat.

* A selection of teas that are not run-of-the-mill. Postcard Teas (www.postcardteas.com/) have the most amazing list of teas you've never heard of (ever tried Monsoon Flush Goomtee?) and some you know well (English Breakfast). Their website tells you more about tea than you ever suspected there was to know.

* Luxurious versions of everyday things – a new or particularly gorgeous bath oil and plush soaps. The Conran Shop and Liberty are two excellent sources of lovely smelly things, often from very small niche suppliers. I like Jo Woods Organic bath oils, Ren's wonderful Moroccan Rose Otto or Lavender bath oil, Designers' Guild soaps and almost anything from Farmacia Santa Maria Novella in London's Walton Sreet. But I also love the collection of soaps and bath and body lotions from Brown & Harris (www.brownandharris.co.uk) – all are perfumed with traditional English flowers such as rose, lavender and lily of the valley. Perfumed drawer liners, wardrobe and drawer sachets are also available, and all make great house presents, as do beautiful hangers, softly padded in a pretty fabric.

* An antique doorstop, a beautiful pair of pillow-cases (antique if possible, and only in white), a pair of salad servers or a single exquisite spoon.

* For gardeners, a trug, glass lanterns, a croquet set, a linen tool bag. Find them at Sarah Raven's Cutting Garden (www.sarahraven.com).

* Lovely scented candles. These may have become a bit of a cliché in giftland, but I think that when they're good, they're divine, and when they're bad, they're horrid. Try True Grace's scented grass (www.truegrace.co.uk) – it's subtle, late summery and elegant. All True Grace's candles are made from natural wax with 10 per cent fragrance, and they burn for about fifty hours. The ones from Rigaud, Cire Trudon, Diptyque (www.diptyqueparis.com) and Ormonde Jayne (www.ormondejayne.com) are all fabulous.

* If you've been invited on a rather grand house party – a week in a villa in Tuscany for instance, or on a yacht – something more substantial and imaginative is required, something bespoke perhaps. You could take photographs during your stay and afterwards present your friends with a beautifully bound album filled with images of the holiday you shared – www.55maxbespoke.com will transfer your pictures on to cushions, quilts, lampshades or canvas.

HOW TO RECIPROCATE

One of the better British traits is that we are, on the whole, more interested in being diverted and amused than in our friends' incomes – a point worth remembering for those who are endlessly worried about how to reciprocate the hospitality of their richer friends. My own view is that the whole point of being rich is that you can forget about money and be generous with your friends and family.

The best ways to reciprocate involve emotional effort – the

SOAP

I have a bit of a thing about soap. There's a world of difference between divine, lightly perfumed soap that keeps it shape and the sort that smells like a cheap brothel and goes all slimy and mushy. Look for triple-milled, which means it's been fed through heavy rollers, known as 'mills'. This gives the best soap fine consistency and lovely lather, and means it lasts and lasts.

* Soaps fragranced with pomegranate (Sapone al Melograno) from the Farmacia Santa Maria Novella are among my all-time favourites – they're beautifully wrapped in thick cream paper with black and gold lettering and make fabulous presents. A single bath-size bar costs £16 – so more expensive than Boots but not so expensive that you need a mortgage.

* Selfridges and the Conran Shop both sell Gianna Rose Atelier French triple-milled soap – the bars, bound in old-fashioned paper, look and smell divine (£8.50 for a big bar of honey and aloe).

* The Conran Shop also has Portugal's answer to the Farmacia's range – Claus Porto's hand-milled, fabulously perfumed (almond oil, verveine, citron, wild pansy, red poppy or honeysuckle) and traditionally wrapped soaps (£29.50 for a box of five).

* Selfridge's Fig and Almond Husk Soap (£12) comes wrapped in beautiful Japanese floral paper.

* A friend with amazing taste tells me she likes nothing better than the soaps from Brissi (www.brissi.co.uk), which are hand-made in small workshops in Provence. They come in a variety of scents and all are £5 a bar.

carefully chosen book, the thoughtfully put-together photograph album after the event, organised treats for your host's children. I remember clearly some enormously rich friends feeling sad and left out at not being included in a small dinner when I knew the reason they hadn't been asked was that the host, who actually really cared for them, had been too embarrassed to ask them, thinking her do couldn't match their own stupendous hospitality. In fact, they didn't give a hoot about that – what they wanted was the conversation, warmth and friendship.

The Shared House Party

This is obviously a more relaxed affair where a group of friends all share in renting a cottage, a villa, a yacht, a chalet – or even a castle. No one person has to take responsibility for everything and everyone should pull their weight in terms of finances and effort. It makes a lot of sense to join up for a skiing or summer holiday so that there is companionship for all and the cost of renting is halved or quartered. Which doesn't mean to say that it isn't without tensions of its own. I remember some close friends falling out while sharing a holiday villa – there was a joint kitty to pay for the food and each couple had very different notions of the amount that should be spent on foodie treats and wines. It all ended badly with one lot feeling they had been prevented from really enjoying themselves by their friends' parsimony and the other couple disgruntled because they'd had to spend more than they wanted on food and wine.

Then there are children – the biggest minefield of all. Sharing houses during early child-rearing days can ruin many a friendship. Bedtimes, pickiness over food and drink (are Cokes or fizzy drinks allowed?), the degree of discipline deemed necessary – these are all areas where it's almost impossible to have identical habits. I'd advise spending some time with any other family you're thinking of joining on holiday. First of all, it would be good to know if your kids get on with theirs, and secondly, you need to share roughly the same ideas and values if nuclear fall-out is not to follow.

A shared house party doesn't have to be a full-blown holiday, of course. Weekends away often do everyone a power of good. You can rent cottages pretty cheaply, and make it very democratic by arranging for everyone to chip in with the provisions. Some people bring booze, some bring food. It doesn't have to be elaborate. Local pubs often serve good food, which is not only fun but saves work, and other meals can be had in the form of picnics. People can take it in turns to cook while those who can't cook can be detailed to do the washing-up.

How you organise the cooking when you're away for longer than a weekend depends on temperament – you can either all muck in for each and every meal, or you can organise a rota so that everyone has some evenings entirely free of domestic chores. The important thing is that nobody should feel like a skivvy.

Where to Stay

Holiday cottages, shooting lodges, grand houses and everything in between can be found on the web. For instance, the wonderful www.breconcottages.com has all sorts of properties from a barn to a large house, all within reach of those magical Welsh mountains, and www.leebay.co.uk has at least one property I can think of by a beautiful bay in Devon. (See pages 134 and 148 for more suggestions.) Depending how many of you there are, it can work out very cheaply.

One thing to bear in mind is how many drivers there are in the group. One summer, when our children were about twenty and seventeen, we took a large villa in Tuscany, just outside Sienna, and invited lots of friends, ours and theirs, but keeping it supplied with water, wine and food was almost a full-time job as none of the young were allowed to drive hired cars. We spent hours taking relays of young to and from railway stations.

These many villas and chalets come with staff, which alleviates the shopping and cooking burden but, of course, costs more and you lose part of the fun. I still remember the conviviality of the evenings as, glass of wine in the hand, we all got together to prepare the evening meal.

Another popular thing to do is to hire a boat. Sailing around the Greek islands can be fun, so long as one or two in the party are experienced sailors. A friend has just got back from a holiday on a boat through the Moorings (www.moorings.com). Lunch was usually a picnic on board and they ate ashore in the evenings. And though it had some downsides – cabins are small, privacy is non-existent and there's the possibility of being seasick – it was a jolly and not very expensive holiday.

Quite a lot of country house hotels try to make their venue more alluring by putting together a sort of house party. At www.scorevalley.co.uk, for instance, you and your friends could take over a whole hotel and they organise mystery and murder weekends, which are a lot of fun.

If – sob, sob – you can't face organising a house party of your own you can tune into social websites (Facebook and MySpace), where house parties are often advertised. But it would be a matter of pot luck.

The Wedding

When two people are under the influence of the most violent, the most insane, most delusive and most transient of passions, they are required to swear that they will remain in that excited, abnormal and exhausting condition continuously until death do they part. George Bernard Shaw

Weddings aren't what they were. Apart from the fact that there are fewer of them – from the department of useless information comes the statistic that in 1850 there were 27 marriages per 1,000 unmarried individuals while in 2005 there were just 12 – those pledging their troth are mostly infinitely older than in years gone by. As well as that, a goodly number of brides may well be pregnant and other couples may already have children together before they tie the knot. A recent survey by the Office for National Statistics predicts that by 2031 only 41 per cent of those over sixteen will be married. Nevertheless, the wedding business is still a £5.5 billion industry and the average wedding in the UK costs twice as much as it did some ten years ago – which is to say, some £21,000. Many, of course, cost a great deal more. Also, since the credit crunch began, loans for weddings have become harder to come by and more expensive to pay off with typical interest rates running at between 10 and 12 per cent for a five-year period. Thinking back to the shenanigans of the Hurley/Nayar nuptials (was it eight days in heaven knows how many different exotic Indian palaces?) and the Beckham celebrations, where bride and groom ordered bespoke thrones for themselves, it all seems like a phantasmagoria from another distant, preposterously exotic age.

The overtly opulent is clearly no longer the way to go, so the challenge will be to find ingenious ways of marking the day, of making it special without spending obscene amounts of money. It's perfectly possible and it is, after all, what most of the population has been doing even through the boom years. Bargains are being struck every day with caterers, florists, suppliers of marquees, and of food and wine, who are all having to revise their erstwhile grand ideas. Pomp and ceremony can, in a curious way, spoil the day. Many of the most charming weddings I've been to were simple country affairs, with long tables charmingly decorated with flowers and greenery from hedgerows. Friends and family can be recruited to help with everything from the food and flowers to the photographs and discoing. The true indispensables are poetry, magic, love, family, friends and joy.

Now I know that weddings can also be fraught – *you* want an intimate little affair while your mother dreams of seeing you waft down the aisle in front of five hundred of her closest friends and family. *You* fancy a romantic reception down in the country, but your father-in-law wants a posh do so all his business connections can be awe-struck. Every wedding is different. Each requires tact, no doubt a compromise or two, a willingness not to hurt and an acknowledgement that weddings, although primarily about the bride and groom, are also about the bringing together of

OLD FOLKLORE RHYME

January: Marry when the year is new, he'll be loving, kind and true.

February: When February birds do mate, you wed nor dread your fate.

March: If you wed when March winds blow, joy and sorrow both you'll know.

April: Marry in April if you can, joy for maiden and for man.

May: Marry in the month of May, you will romance the day.

June: Marry when June roses grow and over land and sea you'll go.

July: Those who in July do wed must labour for their daily bread.

August: Whoever wed in August be, many a change is sure to see.

September: Marry in September's shine so that your life is rich and fine.

October: If in October you do marry, love will come but riches tarry.

November: If you wed in bleak November, only joys will come, remember!

December: When December's snows fall fast, marry and your love will last.

friends and family from their two different worlds. Above all, they're to be enjoyed, not just on the day, wonderful though that is, but also in the remembering, in the lingering memories that will echo down the years.

The Ring

This is where it usually starts – with the engagement, and with the engagement comes the expectation of a ring. It was Zsa Zsa Gabor who said, 'I never hated a man enough to give him diamonds back.' What she was talking about, of course, was 'the ring', the enormous whoppers given to Zsa Zsa by what seems like a steady stream of smitten lovers. There are other rings, of course, but it is the engagement ring that symbolises the fact that the union should be eternal – and the idea resonates potently in the minds of almost every woman, even those who spend most of their days jousting in the boardroom or handling million-dollar investment funds.

It was Miss Piggy, of course, who was in no doubt that, when it came to diamonds, big is better than small, but for those of you who are young (or even old) and poor let me assure you that it is the emotional significance of an engagement ring that means far more to most women than any notion of its value. My husband and I were very young and exceedingly poor when we got engaged (I had been in the UK for six months and had arrived straight out of university, while my husband was still 'eating dinners' as a wannabe barrister) and the little ring he bought me then is my most cherished piece of jewellery. We were staying with his parents in Edinburgh and a tray of what I imagine were the least expensive rings were sent up rather grandly from the family jeweller. We chose a tiny diamond with a little zircon on either side. I wore it for many years until the shaft gave out. Once, twice, I had it mended and then the jeweller said he could do it no more. Today it sits in a box, much loved but, sadly, little worn.

Conventional thinking in the UK has it that an appropriate amount to spend on this age-old symbol of love and commitment is about one month's salary. Americans, it seems, think in terms of two months while in Japan, where they're fanatical – and knowledgeable – about clarity and cut, anything less than three-months' worth of salary is considered cheapskate. Most jewellers I have spoken to said you could get a wonderful ring for between £3,000 and £5,000 but if that's too much, it's worth noting that De Beers' latest collection of engagement rings starts at £800.

The tricky part for any chap trying to get his head round this daunting new territory is where to go and what to buy. All depends, it scarcely needs saying, on the lady in question. Stones are what engagement rings are mostly about, usually, and conventional thinking has it that diamonds are the ones to have, but these days plenty of couples are turning to semi-precious stones and coloured stones, which often provide a lot more drama for your buck. If she's a boho sort of girl, who likes to dress at The Cross and little-known boutiques, I'd go the Pippa Small (www.pippasmall.com) or Marie-Helene de Taillac (www.brownsfashion.com) and Erickson Beamon (www.ericksonbeamon.com) route. Pippa Small does wonderful rough-cut stones – diamonds, sometimes featuring the Indian rose-cut or semi-precious ones – all slightly asymmetrical. She's even been known to set a pebble in white gold as an engagement ring for a romantic couple who wanted a reminder of the beach where they got engaged. Marie-Helene de Taillac sets a wide variety of stones in white or yellow gold.

Stephen Webster is the current darling of the showbiz set, and his great gift is to manage to imbue his rings with drama without making them vulgar. He knows how to do large with style. Madonna commissioned wedding rings for herself and Guy Ritchie from him and now that he's also creative diretor of Garrard's the expectation is that he'll add lots of zip to its collection.

None of these jewellers goes in for your conventional classically cut diamond. If that's what you're after, and you know that a gorgeous box from a recognisable name is what it will take to quicken her pulse, then Cartier, Tiffany, De Beers *et al* will take you by the hand, usher you into an intimate little room and talk you through the four Cs – cut, clarity, carat and colour. The fifth C, for conflict-free diamonds, is often thought of as more or less a given these days, but is still worth checking. Nearly everywhere, the word is that classic and simple, either the round brilliant cut, or the almost square Asscher cut, is what the newly engaged couple is looking for these days.

If what matters most is the amount of stone you get for your money, try buying online. At www.cooldiamonds.com and www.bluenile.co.uk you get all the proper certification and as big and plain a stone as you can afford. Alternatively, head to Hatton Garden (www.hatton-garden.net/designers) where a company like Hirsh, a combination of manufacturer, designer and retailer, offers high-quality stones in not too way-out designs. Cookson (www.cooksongold.com) is also worth a look.

Buying a loose stone is another option, so you can choose as good a quality as you can afford. Graham Tom (www.grahamtom.com) has no middlemen (so prices for what you get are good value), and his designer (ex-Cartier) will help devise a setting specifically for you.

Some men might like to think of buying a loose diamond to present with the proposal (nice to have something solid to mark the day), which then gives the bride-to-be the option of choosing a designer to make it up into a ring that she helps design.

If none of the above seems personal enough, many women love jewellery that comes with a romantic history. A family ring that has been handed down through the generations probably comes surrounded with meaning and a story that makes it infinitely more beloved than any store-bought bauble. If your grandmother neglected to leave you such a treasure, antique shops and auction houses are always worth a trawl – the value is often astonishing compared with the prices charged by smart jewellers, who add the high costs of retailing and marketing to the inherent value of the stone or ring. Sotheby's, Christie's, Bonhams and lots of smaller provincial auctioneers have regular jewellery sales. Ask for the catalogues and see if anything catches your eye.

The Wedding Ring

Obviously, this has to go well with the engagement ring. Lots of jewellers offer pairs that fit neatly, yin and yang like, into each other. The traditional engagement ring usually sports a stone or two, so the wedding band is kept plain, possibly with some engraving to mark the occasion. Since a wedding ring is the one ring that is worn all the time, it should be a) practical – no sharp edges and a good fit, and b) very personal. You could have one made from a material that has meaning – Welsh silver for a Welsh couple, gold from South Africa for a South African. You get the picture. My own is a slim band of white gold engraved with orange blossom.

I dreamed of a wedding of elaborate elegance, of a church filled with family and friends. I asked him what kind of a wedding he dreamed of and he said one that would make me his wife. Unknown

Invitations

You can do the conventional thing and order some standard stiff invitations from posh stationers – Smythson, the Wren Press, Leeming Brothers – or less expensively from some of the online operators (www.heritage-stationery.com will produce fine copper-engraved writing paper or a set of invitations in 48 hours). Or John Lewis always has a good selection. They'll look very proper, but with all the technology available on computers, you could devise your own, and make it personal and particular – I remember our son and his wife personalised the invitation by making a little booklet, including photographs of themselves at their engagement and a compilation of poems and memorable quotations that were meaningful to them. It made for an enchanting – and different – invitation.

A vast array of companies (too many to list here) operate online and, if you're at all techy-minded, will help you design your own invitation at a fraction of the cost of the established stationers. Some of the designs are, it has to be said, fairly naff, so my advice is keep it as simple and classical as you can. One brilliant website, though – www.theweddinggirl.co.uk – is filled with great offbeat ideas, and has discovered a great source of stationery. Mindy Weiss goes in for enchanting vintage designs, check www.finestationery.com to order.

If you're a perfectionist and can afford the fee, commission a professional calligrapher to do the invitations, place cards, menus and all the rest. Check www.paulantonioscribe.com to see what can be done.

If you're having to count every penny you could have post-cards printed up – instead of aping the classical and the traditional, make it a bit kitsch and fun.

If you don't want children at the reception, you should say so on the invitation – these days, though, now that so many couples are much older and some of their friends will already be parents, it's a nice touch, if you can run to it, to hire a child-minder and lay on some special food and entertainment (face painting, balloons, games) for children of the guests. My son and daughter-in-law did this at their wedding and it was a huge hit with parents who couldn't leave their children all day on a Saturday, which is still the most popular day for weddings.

✳ It's a good idea to include an RSVP card, already stamped, with the invitation.

WHAT TO DO IF THE WEDDING IS CALLED OFF

Forget Zsa Zsa Gabor – if the wedding is called off, you should return the engagement ring. Ditto the wedding presents and, it goes without saying, all guests should be informed immediately.

Expert Help

You can get professionals to find the venue, make suggestions about colour schemes, marquees, flowers, food, music, and organise the lot. This doesn't come cheap – swanky prices are quoted on page 165 – and quite apart from the cost, I feel that handing it over lock, stock and barrel to an outsider is a bit of a pity. Weddings are one of life's rarest, greatest celebrations and if you pay through the nose to get somebody to organise it, you may get rid of the hassle but you miss out on a lot of the fun.

On the plus side, professional organisers often have wonderfully original ideas and contacts. These days many are also open to a bit of bargaining on price. If you really are incredibly busy, or don't know where to start, you can buy-in selected help – you don't have to go for the full package. Many of the organisers who, in more prosperous days, would only do the full fandango are now selling their services in smaller packages. Isabella Weddings (www.isabella weddings.co.uk), for instance, have what they call a Snowdrop package – for £99 you get two hours of professional time during which incredibly useful pointers and contacts are passed on, while for £899, a very reasonable sum in this context, it offers a much fuller package. The Bespoke Wedding Company (www.thebespokeweddingco.com) offers a two-hour consultation package for £300, and Sophie Lillingston has a full consultancy day for £1,380. You come away from that with masses of ideas for everything from the invitations and the venue to flowers, seating cards and music.

For something more offbeat, visit www.utterlysexycafe.co.uk, which offers fabulous vintage-style catering for lunch, dinner or special old-fashioned teas, using proper cake-stands, vintage china, silver candelbra and lanterns. They take care of the marquee, decorations and everything else. Staff wear 1950s aprons and create a fantastic retro atmosphere – an idea to copy if you don't want the full catering service.

As well as stationery, www.theweddinggirl.co.uk offers advice on everything to do with weddings from suitable venues to where to have fun with make-up. That's where I discovered that the Berkeley Hotel offers a nine-week Cloud Nine package, including free membership of their spa and health club, to all brides having their reception at the hotel. That should be enough to get anybody into splendid shape.

Is marriage much ado about nothing or something much to do about everything.

Unknown

The Dress

Many a little girl starts dreaming of 'the dress' long before she's given even a passing thought to the sort of man to whom she might be pledging her troth. It's the centrepiece of the wedding drama and getting it right matters.

Although for most of us white (or cream) is the quintessential, traditional colour, it's interesting to note that this is a fairly recent tradition – until the 19th century, women used to marry in their best dress, with red being popular with Republican brides during the American Revolution, and Icelandic brides apparently favouring black velvet embroidered with gold and silver. These days, it's worth giving the matter a second thought.

If you're young and it's your first wedding, indulge yourself. If a Princess Diana meringue-like extravaganza is perfect for you, go for it. Then again, since white is so inextricably linked to the notion of virginity, you might feel just a tad odd doing the full meringue/white veil number if you're verging on forty, marrying a long-term live-in partner, or are pregnant, not to mention if it's a second wedding. In any of those circumstances, if you're set on wearing white, think in terms of something simple and sophisticated rather than frothy and pretty – a long slim Grecian column, a sculpted long dress, a beautifully fitted, subtly sexy cream two-piece tailored suit, that sort of thing. The Duchess of Cornwall managed to judge it perfectly. Yes, I know she went the couture route (Robinson Valentine designed the clothes – these days Anna Valentine operates on her own, www.annavalentine.com) but the general idea of a fitted, well-cut coat and dress in a pale but flattering fabric, is hard to beat. Anne Louise Roswald often does lovely coat dresses, as does Burberry and, less expensively, L.K. Bennett.

For some brides, nothing but couture and expensive will do. The dress is, after all, the external symbol of all the bride's hopes and dreams, and if you can afford it and your heart yearns for it, then go for a real couture number. All those who've experienced it think it worth every penny. The dress lingers on in all the photographs and in the memory and the right one can capture all the perfection of the day. If that's how you feel, Bruce Oldfield, Jasper Conran, Vivienne Westwood ('structured and sexy' is how one commentator described her take on the bridal number) and the great Parisian designers, Galliano, Chanel and Christian La Croix, create magical, fairytale concoctions. The price will be well into five figures, so before you indulge, do ask yourself why? A friend, after many tragic-sounding *affaires du coeur,* recently married for the first time in her late forties and although she wanted to keep it small (both fathers were dead, both mothers not very well), she did want the proper bridal dress – she bought an enchanting number from eBay for something like £100. She looked a dream.

Where to Buy

* Check the bridal boutique on www.net-a-porter.com
  (when a wedding dress by Vivienne Westwood appeared
  on the site, it was sold out in days) for some highly
  sophisticated examples – for really grown-up allure I loved
  a Bill Bass lurex silk crêpe gown for just over £3,000.

* Lanvin's Alber Elbaz has recently launched a capsule
  collection of bridal dresses, largely it seems because he
  recognised how much weddings themselves had changed
  and therefore how many people were after a different sort
  of 'look'. Some brides, he pointed out, get married in Bali,
  others are getting married for the umpteenth time, yet
  others are in their sixties or seventies, and there are plenty
  more who don't want to look like an ageing Cinderella.

* Liberty of Regent Street has the Rosa Clara couture
  collection for which Karl Lagerfeld designed a bridal
  range.

* Elizabeth Emanuel, who with her husband David made
  Princess Diana's wedding gown, has a four-piece wedding-
  dress collection for BhS (www.bhs.co.uk). All have full skirts,
  and each one costs £495. There's tulle with diamante, satin
  with a bustle back and corset, and two in organza.

* Vera Wang, generally acknowledged as the queen of the
  wedding dress, has recently reduced her prices by some 20
  to 30 per cent – partly in acknowledgement of these tricky
  times and partly because of her success. She's selling more
  so she can lower her prices.

* · Antique clothes shops can be brilliant. Long after I was married I came upon the most beautiful wedding dress I'd ever seen in a small antique dress shop in Holt for some £200 – I longed to do the whole thing all over again just so I could wear that dress.

* A young friend whose wedding I went to recently looked divinely ethereal in a vintage number from the Vintage Wedding Dress Company, owned and run by Charlie Breer (www.thevintageweddingdresscompany.com). The dresses are sourced from all over the world and mainly date back to the first half of the 20th century. Don't leave it to the last minute, though, because it may take several visits to find the one you really love and to get it properly fitted. The company also sells accessories.

* Vintage wedding dresses may also sometimes be found at www.vintageacademe.com – I spied a divine long cream embroidered lace dress with a train for £3,000.

* Vintage website www.atelier-mayer.com has some brilliant buys – for instance, a stylish Yves Saint Laurent cream suit for the older or second-time bride for £460. It's worth checking for jewellery, too.

* Browns Bride (www.brownsfashion.com/cm/bridalhome) is a good place for those who are no longer in the first flush of youth. It has some exclusive designers (Oscar de la Renta for one), but also takes suitable designs from mainstream collections and has them made up in bridal colours, so they are not too frothy or frou-frou.

* The Oxfam wedding shop in Eastbourne, East Sussex, for some bizarre reason appears to be a good place to find a bargain, but you'll need to hunt around.

* Finally, of course, there are sales. Bridal boutiques often have them, and if you can save money on a fabulous dress, why not? For young and beautiful brides to spend thousands of pounds on a single dress unnecessarily seems a bit crazy. Keep your eyes skinned.

ECONOMY CHIC

There are all sorts of ways of making your wedding day special on a shoestring budget (check www.cheap-wedding-success.co.uk for ideas). If you don't want to spend a fortune on a one-off dress, Milly Bridal (www.millybridal.com) and Landy Bridal (www.landybridal.com) make up copies of designer dresses, in China, starting at about £100 plus a shipping charge of about £25. The canny customer can try on the designer version, make a note of the model number and size and order a copy of it via the websites. So a dress that might cost anything from £700 to £1,500 (a Vera Wang can easily cost £5,000) in the UK can be had for a fraction of the money.

If you're not sentimental about it, you can always sell your wedding dress afterwards, wherever you bought it – recycling is good for the planet and good for your bank balance.

Great Expectations

If you're pregnant and have set your heart on the full traditional number, you might like to know there is a shop that caters especially for pregnant brides. Started by Tracey Wilkinson, who was seven months pregnant when she got married and found it almost impossible to find anything gorgeous, the Expectant Bride (www.expectantbride.com) has lovely dresses – mostly white and delicate – that have room at the sides to allow for growth as well as longer fronts, so the dress doesn't ride up over the bump. Prices range from £175 to £1,200.

Another source is www.bridesnbumps.com, which also has a good selection.

The other solution for the pregnant bride is to look for suitable dresses designed for slightly fuller figures – one friend found the perfect answer at a sample sale of dresses by Ann Louise Roswald. Blossom Mother and Child Store (www.blossommotherandchild.com) has a nice selection by designers such as Chloé and Marni that work well as non-white wedding dresses.

Hats

The matter of the hat seems to loom large for the wedding guest (one trauma the bride is spared). As a woman of a certain age for whom hats can be wonderfully accommodating, I certainly think it a pity in these informal days to pass up on the opportunity to wear one. My views, oft expressed, are that hats are there to make them beautiful. Perhaps for the very young, they're also there to make them look cute or foxy. There has been a fad in recent years for headgear to be no more than tiny little pieces of fabric and tulle, feathers or flowers. These need to be really well chosen if they're not to look rather daft. Just for the moment, the fashion is back to proper hats.

There are few rules to finding the right one – there's nothing for it but trying them on and seeing what suits – but it would be unwise to have a brim that is wider than your shoulders, and those with short necks should choose upturned or assymetrical brims. If you're under 5 foot 4 inches (which, sob, sob, includes me), you shouldn't really wear a big picture hat – you risk looking like a mushroom. If you have a nose you'd rather not draw attention to, choose a shallow crown. Experiment with the angle, particularly with berets where angle is all. And don't be snobbish – some of my young friends look awfully cute in numbers they've unearthed at Urban Outfitters and Diesel. Don't go for too matchy-matchy a look. Either pick up a colour from the outfit or be very bold and go for a colour clash. Don't go for plain black for a wedding (fine for a little cocktail number).

Some of my Favourite Milliners

PATRICIA UNDERWOOD has an elegant, refined, exquisite way with straw, which never ceases to charm me. Her sophisticated straws come as cloches, wide-brimmed beauties and trilbies, and they're to be found at Fenwick in London and Bergdorf Goodman in New York.

GABRIELA LIGENZA also does gorgeous straws, which are mostly pretty and flattering rather than highly sophisticated.

STEPHEN JONES not only makes hats for the house of Christian Dior as well as John Galliano's cute numbers, but also provided Carla Sarkozy with the demure little pillbox that wowed us all when she came to London on an official visit. His designs featured in a retrospective exhibition at the V&A.

PHILIP TREACY'S creations are likely to cost between £600 and £3,000, but you can find a good diffusion line at Fenwick for between £100 and £750.

MARIE MERCIE specialises in charming little cocktail hats, which can add a large touch of drama to a plain black dress. Many a society dresser goes to her for hats that don't look quite like anybody else's.

EMILY LONDON is new on the block. She uses only vintage materials, whether fabrics, feathers, lace or tulle, so each and every hat is different. They start at £120 and go on to £250. Find her at Fenwick.

VICTORIA GRANT, another newcomer, does stunningly glamorous hats – the sort that, if you dared (they seem to me to take a little courage), you'd don for a party or a first night. She has some wonderful little curved skull caps with sequins and glitter. Check her website – www.victoriagrant.co.uk – and you'll get some idea of the film-star glamour she brings to the matter of millinery. Find her also at Fenwick and at several other stores, including Harrods and Browns Bride.

KAT GOODISON used to be a lawyer and now does brilliantly innovative bespoke hats. She says people mostly come to her for wedding hats, because they realise that if you want a hat that really works with your face and your outfit, there's nothing for it but a couture milliner who will do it to order. (Telephone for appointments: 020 7828 6498.)

❄❄❄❄❄❄❄❄❄❄❄❄❄❄❄❄❄❄❄❄❄❄

DIY HATS

If you're nifty with your fingers, you can make an old straw hat look good as new. Barnet & Lawson (www.bltrimmings.com) and Ellis & Farrier (www.creativebeadcraft.co.uk) sell lots of traditional trims, including beads, buttons and glitter. VV Rouleaux (www.vvrouleaux.com) may be a bit more expensive but they have gorgeous fabric flowers, ribbons and often offer inspirational ideas.

If you can't do it yourself, Kat Goodison, although primarily a bespoke milliner, is wonderfully helpful and will not only retrim her own hats to give them a new look but will trim a little number from Accessorize or anywhere else.

You might like to make a hat yourself. Janie Lawson (www.janielawson.com) holds regular workshops, from £65 a time, to show you just how to do it. In Edinburgh, Yvette Jelfs holds masterclasses in the retrimming of hats, while if you want to do it in grand style, Dillon Wallwork holds occasional beginners' classes at the Chateau Dumas in France (www.chateaudumas.net).

❄❄❄❄❄❄❄❄❄❄❄❄❄❄❄❄❄❄❄❄❄❄

The Groom

These days weddings have become much more informal and most grooms wear rather smart suits rather than top hat and tails. The wedding may be used as an occasion to order their very first bespoke number. The other day I saw a photograph of a groom who thought his Armani suit didn't require even a tie. I learn that when David Bowie married Iman, he wore a tux by Thierry Mugler with a white bow tie.

Personally, I love to see a chap in morning suit, and while the gold standard is the one made in Savile Row, you might like to know that Marks & Spencer sell pukka morning dress – charcoal morning coat, black and grey pinstripe trousers and grey waistcoat all for under £200; and Jasper Conran (www.jasperconran.com) makes great wedding gear to order and to measure.

In the meantime, this is what Hugh Holland of Kilgour (www.kilgour.eu) Savile Row has to stay on the matter. He thinks that the groom should stick to the rather conservative, accepted dress code and shouldn't even THINK of complementing the bride's outfit. The bride should look gorgeous and the groom should not dream of upstaging her – he should stick to striped trousers, white shirt, beige double-breasted waistcoat and a black double-breasted morning coat. 'He should be a good arm-rest and make sure not to mess up his speech.' Furthermore, the best man shouldn't dress like the groom – 'Very naff,' says Hugh Holland, 'he's the spear, i.e. ring, carrier, and shouldn't confuse the bride.'

Accessories

Well, of course, you need 'something old, something new, something borrowed, something blue'. The old should have some sentimental connection – a grandmother's or mother's brooch or head-dress, or a piece of lace or a handkerchief. Something new – to symbolise the new life you're starting out on – isn't hard (the dress, the ring, the flowers), nor is something borrowed, which should come from a happily married woman (there are some). A piece of jewellery is often borrowed. For something blue – traditionally, the colour symbolised loyalty, faithfulness and purity – most brides incorporate some blue ribbon into the garter, but it could be in the flowers, jewellery or a small trim on the dress.

Otherwise, the best accessory is decent underwear. If you haven't got that sorted, it's time you did. Take yourself off to Rigby & Peller if you possibly can, or a good local department store, and get properly measured – you'll be amazed at the difference it makes (some hideous percentage of women, the professional corsetiers tell us, don't know their real size).

Shoes (bridally speaking) don't matter half as much as everybody thinks they do – unless you're wearing a short or cocktail dress. Buy something plain and classic in the height you need. Rainbow Club (www.rainbowclub.co.uk) does hand-made satin shoes – either classic courts, flatties (if, Tom and Katie style, the bride is taller than the groom), beaded or high-heeled. They'll do the bridesmaids' shoes, too. If you do want something funkier, check Freya Rose (www.freyarose.co.uk) who specialises in wedding shoes. She adorns them with silk flowers, Tahitian pearls and other wondrous bits of glitz – definitely delicious. She also dyes them any colour you choose.

The head-dress should be chosen bearing in mind your dress. Two niche jewellers who do enchanting head-dresses are Kirsten Goss (www.kirstengoss.com) and Isabel Kurtenbach (www.isabelkurtenbach.com). Kirsten Goss has all sorts of lovely jewellery, ear-rings, necklaces, headpieces, as well as what she calls 'back jewels' – very important given that for much of the time your back is on view to your guests – while Isabel Kurtenbach, as well as ravishing, unusual head-dresses, has other pieces for brides.

Basia Zarzycka has some fantastic vintage hairpieces as well as some wedding dresses.

Beauty

Get this sorted early – find a hairdresser and a beauty regime that you like. Your hair is going to matter hugely and whether you cut it or grow it to match the head-dress needs thinking about well in advance. You could start by discussing what you think would suit you best with your hairdresser (presuming you've got one you can trust) and then work out the sort of head-dress that suits your hair, your face and your dress. Not easy – which is why it needs some serious thought.

As to a beauty regime – it's worth remembering that you can get free make-up advice at every beauty counter in almost every good department store. They'll all devise a scheme that works for you. If you want serious advice from somebody not allied to a specific brand, loads of good make-up artists will teach you exactly how to get that professional finish – John Gustafson at Fenwick of New Bond Street is booked up for years but can sometimes be persuaded to fast-track brides. He's a master of the art. Attracta Courtney (www.attracta courtney.com) is a professional make-up artist who specialises in a very natural look and is a past master at providing a make-up to suit the face, rather than the one that is supposedly in fashion (although she's right up there in fashion terms, too). If you're still stuck, most good hair salons can recommend somebody. It's crucial to have a trial run before the big day – I didn't. I had my first professional make-up done on the day itself and ended up looking like a painted doll.

Keep it as natural as you can. If you haven't yet found the foundation that is absolutely the right colour for you (and that's about the most important thing), take yourself off to a Prescriptives counter (www.prescriptives.co.uk) and get one customised just for you. Ask for the Prescriptives Custom Blend (£38). Also, if you wear mascara – most women make it their number one desert-island beauty accessory – make sure you choose one that is waterproof (no bride worth her veil ever goes through the day without weeping a tear or two). Chanel's waterproof version famously survived the ordeals of childbirth in a birthing pool. At the cheaper end of the scale, people swear by Maybelline's Great Lash waterproof mascara.

Near the big day you'll need to book in for a manicure – go for pale pink, not a vampish dark red, and on no account ask for a French manicure – a pedicure and a massage if you can fit it in. Now that brides aren't as young as they used to be, lots of beauty salons offers special pre-wedding 'anti-aging booster facials'.

As far as the groom is concerned, usually his hands and feet, hair and complexion could do with a bit of attention. Nowadays there are wonderful men's grooming salons that will do everything from smoothing the skin, removing blackheads and blemishes and tweaking stray bristles to providing manicures and pedicures.

Hen and Stag Nights

When I got married way back when, nobody I knew had ever heard of hen nights. Custom had it that while the bride-to-be spent the night before the wedding with her parents, who might give a dinner for close friends and family, the groom had a last Bacchanalian celebration with his male friends. That was about it – and there are still those who consider the very notion of a hen night a rather uncivilised invention from across the water. As for those stag weekends that seem to involve long-haul flights and too much alcohol – perhaps the upside of these tricky times is that they'll have to come up with more civilised ways of spending the last few days of bachelordom.

However, both hen and stag nights seem to be here to stay, so it's worth deciding how best to do them. Get the event right and it's a great bonding experience and everybody has a lot of fun. You don't have to spend indecent amounts of money, most particularly the bride or groom shouldn't oblige their friends to get into debt simply to help celebrate their nuptials. A straw poll on the subject of hen nights reveals that almost every girl I know has at some time or another been embarrassed by being asked to spend more than she'd like by a friend about to get married. That seems like madness – you can have just as good a time in simpler ways. To start with, save the air fares and the carbon footprint. Stay in this country.

What to Do

WEEKEND IN A COUNTRY COTTAGE: if the cost is divided up between everybody, it shouldn't be too much. Add in walks, some terrific DVDs, lots of tea, cakes and champagne and it's just as much fun, if not quite as exotic, as sweating somewhere hot and fighting off the mosquitoes. Activities could be arranged for the adventurously inclined – camping, climbing, abseiling, hiking, treasure hunts, riding or punting in Oxford or Cambridge. Girly girls might prefer a spa hotel (but check the costs first) with an indoor pool and pampering sessions.

A DAY TRIP: anywhere with Eurostar is a treat for most people, although towns in the UK have plenty to offer – think of Bath, Brighton, York or Edinburgh.

A NIGHT ON THE TOWN: book tickets to Madame Jojos (www.madamejojos.com), a private room in a favourite restaurant or a table at a lovely bar.

A PICNIC: choose somewhere beautiful – Hampstead Heath, Primrose Hill or Hyde Park if you're a Londoner, or a beauty spot near to home. Take food you know everyone likes – cupcakes and champagne if that's your bag (never have been able to see the point of cupcakes myself but I realise I'm an oddity). Other suggestions are smoked salmon, fat prawns and gorgeous brown bread – just whatever takes your fancy.

One friend organised a weekend based in Oxford with a picnic at Blenheim on the day of a knights' jousting contest. They picnicked off strawberries dipped in chocolate and pink champagne, and the knights were a wow of a success. A word of warning, though – the evening descended into naffness when the little restaurant they thought they'd winkled out in their searches turned out to be the setting for several other hen and stag nights.

TEA IN A GRAND HOTEL: the Randolph in Oxford, the Balmoral in Edinburgh, the Athenaeum, Brown's or the Ritz in London are all possibilities.

A BEAUTY DAY: book one, two or even three beauty therapists, depending how many of you there are, to come to somebody's house, so everybody can have their manicures and pedicures, facials and massages, while gossiping and sipping their favourite wine. Alternatively, gorgeous spa hotels are to be found all over the country.

AN ACTIVITY DAY: choose something everyone likes doing, or fancies trying – having salsa lessons, learning pottery, making jewellery, playing crazy golf.

A CULTURAL DAY: take in a matinee at Stratford or book for a great concert. Outdoor theatre seems to be more and more popular all round the country. In and around urban areas, there's plenty to choose from – Regent's Park Open Air Theatre and Holland Park Opera in London. Or how about

the Stamford Shakespeare Company at Tolethorpe Hall
(www.stamfordshakespeare.co.uk) or Cornwall's theatre under
the stars, The Minack in Penzance (www.minack.com).

KARAOKE PARTY: you can have a lot of fun with karaoke – in
London, Manchester and Cardiff, Lucky Voice (check
www.luckyvoice.com and book a room) allows you to choose
your song list and sing away in private. If you prefer to party
at home, Singstar works off Playstations 2 and 3 and allows
you to sing along to your favourite artists. If you like, you
can get competitive and score points.

The Place

You can, of course, get married almost anywhere. Even
easyJet, I see, is trying to muscle in on the nuptials
business and proffer their customers the chance to get hitched
'floating on cloud nine', while circling around in medialand are
stories of people getting married in a New York public
lavatory, in the middle of the London marathon and even, yes,
really, while parachuting down to earth in a sky-dive. Me, I
think forget the wedding with a difference. Do it the
traditional way.

Most people, I think, want their weddings to have some
kind of connection with their real lives, be it a formal or less
formal occasion. Whether the ceremony is held in the village
church, the local registry office or the university or school
chapel, some kind of association matters. All the top caterers
have long lists of attractive venues that offer packages for the

wedding and reception, ranging from posh hotels and grand guildhalls to castles in Scotland and ancient cellars, but by far the most enjoyable weddings, I think, are those that are held near the family home of either the bride or groom, somewhere that is imbued with meaning and a sense of belonging.

Registry office weddings don't have to be soulless. Most councils go to considerable trouble to make their venues warm and attractive, and although as far as I'm concerned they can't match a church for atmosphere, being surrounded by close friends and family makes it just as memorable.

If you don't fancy a registry office and aren't connected to a church, there are lots of National Trust properties that make wonderful settings for a wedding. Turn to the website (www.nationaltrustweddings.co.uk) and there is everything you need to know.

Some people like to escape to foreign parts to tie the knot – the weather is better and you don't have to invite every last cousin three-times removed. Surprisingly, weddings abroad can often turn out to be less expensive than those held at home, the average cost being around £6,000 as opposed to the £20,000 to £25,000 that is seems to average out in the UK. It seems to have something to do with the fact that couples don't feel obliged to have all the extras that have come to seem almost obligatory at home, as well as with the lower cost of venues and labour abroad. Planet Holidays (www.planet-holidays.co.uk) organise package weddings in Greece and Mauritius, while Tuscan Dreams (www.tuscan-dreams.com) focuses on Italy. Both report that, these days, 'small is beautiful' and they are receiving a lot of requests for intimate weddings that cost as little as £2,000. Ionian

Weddings specialise in the Greek islands. Whether you want a bouzouki-serenaded ceremony at an historic town hall, or a civil marriage, Anglican, Catholic or Orthodox, or just a simple blessing, the Ionian Weddings people know the ropes and can make it happen.

For rather more money, all the professional organisers – The Admirable Crichton, Sophie Lillingston, Rhubarb – have tabs on fantastic settings whether in an Italian palazzo, a Mallorcan villa, a Moroccan riad or almost any other exotic destination you care to name where amazing celebrations can be organised.

CONFETTI

Many churches ban the use of paper confetti because it is so hard to clear up. Real petals are so much nicer anyway. The Real Flower Confetti Company (www.confettidirect.co.uk) – patronised by Madonna and Catherine Zeta-Jones – offers a range of petals from different flowers and of different colours. If you have lots of roses in your garden, you can make your own – just dry the petals on trays in the airing cupboard or any other warm spot inside.

The Reception

I've been to plenty of very jolly wedding receptions in village halls, boathouses and barns, none of which is expensive to hire. Friends and family can be enlisted to help make any venue look wonderful. Greenery, flowers from farmers' markets, bunting, lights, photographs perhaps of the happy couple's journey to the altar, can be judiciously arranged around the place – what matters is that it's joyful and personal.

Nicest of all, if space allows, is a reception in the garden of the family home. This doesn't have to be grand, although, admittedly, if you're thinking of asking more than the immediate family, it will need to be of a certain size. Marquees don't have to be expensive – simple ones can be decorated to suit the occasion and made to look special. They're better value in summer than in winter, when heating and a raised floor may be necessary.

Billie Piper and Laurence Fox hired tepees for their reception and so, too, can you – www.lpmbohemia.com has all sorts of romantic yurts, tepees and Rajasthani tents. For her own wedding reception, Sophie Lillingston, who's organised plenty of weddings and celebrations for other people, decided on a picnic. 'We hired a big unlined cotton canvas tent with colourful rugs and huge cushions for people to loll on. We put up plain wooden trestle tables, stood pots of lavender, sage and rosemary along the edges and served pig and lamb on a spit. There were cappuccino vans dispensing lattes, ice-cream vans for the children and everybody had a ball.'

When stylist Charlotte Stockdale married uber-designer Marc Newson, they had the reception in a barn on her parents' farm and much nicer it all sounded than an anonymous hotel.

Simple trestle tables set out French-style in a field make an enchanting setting for a summer reception – although given our climate, nearby barns or tents are a must in case of rain.

Should the bride or groom suddenly find themselves out of a job – a hazard in recent times – many couples are being forced to think more creatively. Take one bride who had originally planned to hire a medieval barn, fill it with massed Christmas trees and serve a Christmas banquet to some two hundred of their friends. Now they've both been 'let go', they're going to celebrate in the home of one set of parents. Although caterers are doing a buffet, it's all hands to the deck with flowers and decorations, and everyone is having a lot of fun.

❉❉❉❉❉❉❉❉❉❉❉❉❉❉❉❉❉❉❉❉❉❉

SPEECHES

I've been embarrassed more times than I care to remember by smutty jokes and a best man who ritually denigrates the groom – not good manners in my book. In fact, at one delightful wedding the bride was so incensed by the best man's character assassination of her new husband that she rose to her feet and gave a rousing speech of her own, dwelling on his virtues and all the many reasons she loved him. Terrific stuff. Some jokes are fine – but 'affectionate and charming' is the way to go. If

you have to give a wedding speech and are stuck for ideas,
the internet offers masses of website samples, including tips and
advice. Try www.hitched.co.uk for examples of real speeches
delivered in times gone by. At least it'll get you thinking.

❋ ❋

A Wedding Breakfast

If you have a registry office wedding, you may have to have
the ceremony in the morning although you want the real
celebration to be an evening affair. This provides the perfect
opportunity for a wedding breakfast, either at home or at a
nearby restaurant or pub. Gastropubs are usually happy to
cater for wedding celebrations – you could take over a
section of the pub or hire a private room if one is available.
Decorate it with greenery and flowers (again from farmers'
markets or from Nine Elms if you're a Londoner), tea lights
and strings of fairy lights, bought cheaply from Ikea or
Argos – all make magical versions. Float some tea lights in
bowls of water, put some in among the flowers, line halls and
stairways and light up tables with others. If you don't want
to buy the electric lights, you can hire them. Low-cost lights
can be hired from www.confetti.co.uk, disco-style glitter balls
from Table Dressers (http://tabledressers.com), and if you
can't manage the magic touches on your own,
www.sparklemyparty.co.uk will sprinkle a little fairy dust over
the proceedings for you.

   Alternatively, loads of restaurants would probably be more
than happy for you to boost their lunchtime trade. You could

try to negotiate a bargain at your favourite local trattoria and just take over the whole place.

FAVOURS

These increasingly are part of the wedding routine. Ever since the 16th century, in some cultures brides and grooms have been giving little presents – known as favours – to their guests. I think it's a charming idea but they should be kept small and inexpensive – bookmarks, unusual candles, a small photograph frame or personalised notebooks and CDs. These are by no means essential, though, and personally, I love the French custom of giving guests little bags of sugared almonds to take away.

Flowers

The days of the grand statement are over – not only do elaborate arrangements cost the earth, somehow they no longer seem right. Speak to all the expensive florists and they'll tell you that they've toned down what they do. They put single blooms to float in neat rows of glistening fishbowls, or make up concise posies of snow-white carnations in beakers. The idea is to let the flowers speak for themselves, and choose those that are in season – narcissi from the Scilly Isles in the spring, English sweet peas in the summer.

TOUCHES OF MAGIC

* In China, they often celebrate a wedding by releasing hundreds of butterflies. That's a lovely idea, so why not copy it? Rather than letting them go *en masse*, give each guest a little box (www.gribblybugs.com – £450 for 100 butterflies) and match the boxes to your colour scheme.
* Hire a mixed range of chandeliers (try www.chandelier rental.co.uk) and hang one above every table.
* Dream Screen (www.thedreamscreen.co.uk) provides a booth where guests are encouraged to record personal messages to the couple – a wonderful souvenir of the day.
* Professional opera singers can be hired to double as waiters. Midway through the meal they break into song (www.thethreewaiters.com).
* Boothnation's glitter photo booth comes with rave reviews – it allows guests to prance around inside the booth and be photographed in memorable, if daft, style. Make up an album yourself or get the company to do it for you (www.boothnation.com).
* Instead of fireworks, think about Chinese flying lanterns. Each guest writes good wishes on a lantern, lights the wick and sends it up into the sky – particularly magical at night if all the guests send their lanterns up together (www.wishesinthesky.com and www.dragonfireworks.co.uk).
* To amuse the children, give them little kits for blowing bubbles, which look charming. If you aren't having a special attendant to look after them, you could put together packs of colouring books, pencils and stickers to keep them occupied.

Since you can buy flowers by the lorry load from wholesalers for a fraction of what the grand florists charge, if you have the time and can enlist some help, it's more personal and rewarding to do the flowers yourself. Props such as candlesticks and mirrored plinths can add magic for not much expenditure. If the wedding is to be in a church, tie posies and ribbons round the ends of the pews. Herbs – lavender, rosemary and thyme – smell lovely and look romantic, while if the wedding is in the spring, huge branches of tree blossom in great big glass jars look wonderful. It's worth checking if there are any other weddings either before or after you in the church – you could suggest sharing the cost of the flowers.

Another good idea is to use plants and trees that can be replanted later. At one recent wedding, white square tubs were filled with bay trees, which were entwined with white roses and underplanted with white hydrangeas. The effect was enchanting. Both hydrangeas and bay trees, not to mention the square white tubs, could be transplanted into any garden, where they'd give years of pleasure. Tubs can also be transported to the reception afterwards, if some handy person has a van, so they do double-duty.

At the reception, you could group little pots of orchids in the centre of the tables and let every guest take one home – it always seems a waste otherwise. When Leah Wood, daughter of Rolling Stone Ronnie and former wife Jo, got married, jam jars filled with seasonal flowers lined the tables, a lovely idea that costs little.

Food

Too many weddings go in for so-called posh food that usually turns out to be completely unmemorable. One of the best formats I've ever come across was guests being greeted with a big oyster bar and glasses of champagne, which kept them fed and watered as they milled around waiting to be seated for the dinner and dancing. Then came divine cottage pie – so much more satisfying than itsy-bitsy fancy tarted-up food. Simple but perfect. If one is going to a lot of weddings, there's no doubt (and I realise this sounds spoiled but it's a fact) one gets tired of the usual poached salmon, pavlova and ice-cream scenario. I think gutsy English food, really beautifully done, is the way to go – fish and chips with mushy peas, fine hamburgers, fish pies, steak and kidney pie, all hit the spot. At a very smart Scottish wedding, at least two years before the recession came along and spoiled the fun, bangers (for brilliant ones see pages 288–9) and mash were the main dish and everybody loved them. There were Scottish reels and dancing in the evening and the whole thing was immensely enjoyable.

To keep your marriage brimming, with love in the wedding cup, whenever you're wrong, admit it; whenever you're right, shut up.

Ogden Nash

In a restaurant or pub, it's also important to have
something to eat with the drinks while waiting for the main
meal to start. Discuss the best options with the pub or
restaurant. If you're organising the catering on your own, it's
worth knowing that Waitrose, Marks & Spencer, Carluccios
or any of the caterers in your area will do big platters of
various canapés.

And speaking of drinks, can I make a plea for providing lots
of water and some delicious non-alcoholic drinks as well as a
variety of wines and beers – nothing but champagne gives most
people a raging thirst and makes even the most robust feel
slightly off-colour. If you'd like to run a bar with an array of
sophisticated cocktails, you could think of getting in some
professionals. Mixology Events (www.mixologyevents.co.uk), for
instance, set up and run mobile bars. Cheaper would be to
enlist some friends to do it for you.

If you're having a party that's likely to last late into the
night, you should offer some late-night nibbles – a big
cheeseboard, fruit, hot dogs, mini-hamburgers or bagels.
Kedgeree, I always think, is the most perfect late night/early
morning dish in the world.

Other notions to help the party go with a swing are
chocolate fountains (masses available through the internet,
such as from www.chocolatefonduecompany.co.uk), a hog
roast (www.spittingpig.co.uk), a vodka luge (www.vodka-
luge.co.uk), or a proper barbecue (Blistering Barbecues at
www.blistering.co.uk). Any of these could be fun if you can
afford them.

REFRESHING DRINKS WITHOUT ALCOHOL

Glasses of water poured from jugs spiked with lots of fresh mint, or with ice cubes made out of puréed fresh fruit, are delicious. To make another really refreshing drink, mix equal quantities of fresh lime and lemon juice, add five times the amount of sparkling mineral water and add a few drops of angostura bitters. Keeping it simple, fresh melon juice and fresh tomato juice (and I mean really fresh – not out of a tin) are wonderful refreshers.

For a summer wedding on a hot day, you could serve fruit frappés. Put chunks of fruit – watermelon, melon, strawberries, raspberries – into a food processor with some ice cubes (about a quarter of the weight of the fruit) and sugar syrup (about a fifth of the weight of the fruit). Sugar syrup is very simple to make – just put 15fl oz/426ml of water in a pan, bring to the boil, add 15oz/425g of sugar, simmer for five minutes and then cool. Whizz all the ingredients together in the food processor until the fruit is smooth.

(Find more recipes for non-alcoholic drinks on pages 273–274)

The Cake

I t isn't written in stone that you have to have the full, tiered, traditionally iced number. Have what you like. It's quite fun to order something special and personal. For our daughter's small (second) wedding, by which time she had two small sons, we ordered an amazing chocolate pyramid from Patisserie Valerie (www.patisserie-valerie.co.uk) for the family lunch afterwards, because we knew her boys and other small children would love it – and they did. When she later had a bigger reception for the wider group of friends, we ordered a gorgeous number from Rachel Mount (see the range of her designs on www.rachelmount.com) – she decorated a light fruit cake with icing-sugar creations of wild roses, berries and brambles. It was a work of art (and it cost the sort of sum a work of art costs – madness really).

The Little Venice Cake Company (www.lvcc.co.uk) has made cakes for the Queen, Madonna and the Beckhams, and will make something special for you, too. Bill's Produce Store, in Lewes and Brighton (www.billsproducestore.co.uk), make wonderful, bohemian cakes, decorated with flowers and fruit. Peggy Porschen (www.peggyporschen.com) sells her wedding cakes through Fortnum & Mason but she also takes special orders and loves to incorporate sentimental bits and pieces, such as little heirlooms or pieces of jewellery, in the decoration. She finds that men like marble cakes.

Mostly, this bespoke artistry doesn't come cheap (something like £600 a time I seem to remember), so if you need to save pennies, save some here and make your own. It's not difficult. Peggy Porschen's book *Cake Chic*, published by Quadrille, could be just the thing. Otherwise, do as one bride I know did, and involve the family – ask those who are willing to make batches of iced cupcakes. They cost almost nothing to make (flour, eggs, butter and sugar). Most cookery books have recipes for them, and www.janeasher.co.uk has lots of cupcake cases (as does www.lakeland.co.uk). Then build up a tiered tower. With this idea, you can customise colours and decorations, and top the cake with something personal. In this bride's case, her friends had a small model made of her and her husband-to-be in icing-sugar – brilliant!

ETIQUETTE

Traditionally, who pays for what, who gives speeches when, what the duties are for everybody from bride and groom to ushers, best man and attendants are all governed by long-established and quite elaborate rules of etiquette. Times have changed and these days, for instance, many couples, since they're older, pay for their own wedding and muddle through financially on their own, but if you want to know what the formal rules are, you can find them all at www.topweddinglinks.com.

Music

If you're having a party with dancing, hiring a band and a DJ can be very expensive. Keeping it down to one or two musicians who can jam with the DJ, or just a DJ, comes cheaper than a full-blown band, and if that's for you, find a DJ at www.uk-djs.net.

However, in these days of iPods, you could dispense with band and DJ altogether and make your own compilation – ask your friends to help – but first make sure the sound system is good at the venue. If you haven't the time or inclination to make your own, Music Guru (www.musicguru.co.uk) will compile a play list especially for you (from £95).

Music schools and colleges are packed with students only too eager to earn an extra crust and they can often be hired for not a great deal of money. If you fancy some baroque, Renaissance or any kind of classical music, just contact the nearest college and see who'd be interested.

Civil Partnerships

Now that civil partnerships are becoming increasingly familiar, all sorts of organisations have sprung up to help see the happy couples through these less traditional ceremonies. The website www.pinkweddingdays.co.uk has links to all manner of gay-friendly advice and organisers, and gives tips on etiquette for same-sex weddings – both partners should walk down the aisle together, wear something pink instead of something blue, you get the picture. For essential legal advice on how to proceed, check www.gro.gov.uk/gro/content/civilpartnerships.

ROB VAN HELDEN'S CIVIL CEREMONY

Internationally acclaimed florist Rob van Helden kept a diary of his own civil ceremony and the events leading up to it:

Seb (Sebastien Barbereau) and I met in September 2000 at a party in London. We hit it off straightaway and haven't been apart since. Having been together for six years, we started discussing the possibility of becoming legal partners. My lucky number has always been 7, so with 07/07/07 coming up, I suggested to Seb that could be our special day. During one of our summer trips to see Seb's parents in France, I asked for their permission – rather nervously as he's an only son, but I have been blessed with the best parents-in-law one could wish for. Then it was Seb's turn to go to Holland and ask my mum the same question. Both our families were very excited and pleased for us.

I have also been blessed with having the most organised sister in the world as my business partner, and will forever be grateful for all the hard work she put in to give us the most unforgettable day. We started organising it in January 2007 and as I have been doing the flowers for over twenty-two years in some of London's most prominent venues, working with the *crème de la crème* of party organisers, I wanted nothing less for our own ceremony. For instance, I was privileged to be asked to look after the flowers for Sir Elton John and David Furnish's civil partnership ceremony and celebrations on 21 December, 2005, the first day civil partnerships became legal in England.

So we decided on our favourite London hotel, Claridges, for its location, service and reputation. 'Save the dates' went out, after registering at our local council the registrar got booked and we starting organising our day like other 'about to be married'. Seb always said he would be happy with a small celebration but for me, having done so many amazing parties for so many amazing people, it was difficult to keep it to a small affair. 'If we do it, we do it properly' was my motto and fortunately Seb agreed. In mid April I was asked to organise the floral decorations for the 45th anniversary of Valentino in Rome on 07/07/07! There was no way I was going to say no to that. We discussed changing our date but I decided I could make Rome happen anyway – and we did.

Having rather a lot of god-daughters, nieces, friends' daughters and girlfriends between us, we ended up having twenty-three groomsmaids on our day as well as six pageboys. Seb and I chose the traditional morning suit option for the day and bespoke tailored blue suits for our evening party. As we had been wearing exchanged friendship rings for years, we decided on proper platinum wedding bands to be exchanged on the day, which were designed and crafted by one of our close friends.

Of the twenty-three groomsmaids, the sixteen adult ones, in every shape and size, were given a few metres of fabric chosen by us and told they could do whatever they wanted with it. The smaller flower girls were all in original white bridesmaids dresses by Ben de Lisi, and the pageboys were in white shorts and shirts by Ralph Lauren. All of the groomsmaids carried my all-time favourite flowers – Lily of the Valley – which fortunately I'd ordered well in advance as there were none left in Holland that weekend. As for the rest of the floral decor, my head florist, Jason, called me five days before the wedding from Rome, where he was organising Valentino's flowers, and asked me what I'd planned for the rest of our floral decorations. I told him, 'Think masculine, white, summer fragrance.' They didn't let us down. Upon arrival we were greeted by an avenue of gardenia trees, followed by a wave of glorious white-stock fragrance, white phalaenopsis orchids and blue hydrangeas.

We spent weeks putting together a guest list, which kept creeping up, as many of my clients have become friends over the years, and it's the same for Seb as he's the bar manager at Nobu.

We split our day into two parts – first, the ceremony, reception and lunch for 180. Then in the evening, because of the large guest list, we didn't do a sit-down dinner. Instead, we turned the ground-floor function rooms of Claridge's into a nightclub for 425 guests.

As neither Seb nor I is exactly a spring chicken – I'm 44, he's 37 – we asked our guests to buy 'a brick' towards our kitchen extension instead of having a wedding list, and donated 10 per cent of what they gave us to the Elton John Aids Foundation and Great Ormond Street Hospital.

Our day was beyond perfect, thanks to the help of so many dear friends and family. We were surrounded by our parents, brothers and sisters, families and friends, from France, Holland and all over the world. There was not a dry eye in the house during the ceremony and speeches. In the end 'the day' turned into a three-day affair with 120 people from abroad at our house the night before, the wedding on the Saturday and a barbecue at my sister Patrice's house on the Sunday for another 120.

For the ceremony and day itself, we kept everything in the best possible taste as neither of us wanted to turn it into a glitzy gay affair.

We partied at Claridge's until 5 a.m. only to find upon our arrival in the 'Honeymoon' suite that my staff had decorated the walls and the bed with balloons, 'pictures', sequins, feather boas, you name it. It 'only' took us over an hour to bring some normality back to the rooms, although the night housekeeper told us not to worry as they'd seen much worse before.

As for the honeymoon – that had to wait for fifteen months since two days after our special day we left with twenty-five assistants for Ireland to make someone else's dreams of a special day come true.

Presents

As so many couples are getting married much later in life, when they've often got two separate homes and therefore two complete sets of basic equipment, it isn't a surprise that the wedding list, the essential prop of the Sloane Ranger wedding, has had to change and evolve over the years. When I got married (long ago), most couples were, like us, poor and unencumbered by most of the things then considered essential for solid wedded life. Casseroles, wooden salad bowls, silver candlesticks, place mats (eeek!), complete sets of matching china and glass were what featured on the wedding lists of the day, and what a godsend the presents were. Few of the gifts we were given were luxuries but those that were – a Mary Potter painting, a gorgeous Georgian silver salt and pepper set, later stolen, and a fine set of suitcases – were memorable.

A look at Liberty's Gift Brochure of 1960, which many couples at the time consulted for their wedding lists, shows how much tastes have changed. The catalogue is littered with the sort of dinky bits of floral-spattered china none of us would give house room to these days, and there is a big section of austerely dull Danish stainless steel ware – servers, platters, strainers and all the things that put me off anything Danish for years – not to mention place mats portraying scenes of Olde London.

Fast-forward to the next century and what do we find? Prosperity on an infinitely greater scale. Some couples want for so little that they do as Lady Sarah Armstrong-Jones did and ask for nothing but books or nothing but wine. A few even ask for cash (not, in my book, a permissible thing to do). While we're on the subject of bad manners, I think taking presents back and asking the store for the cash (apparently normal in New York these days) is very bad behaviour. If you really want for nothing, ask guests to subscribe to charities.

Some people still object to information about a wedding list arriving with the invitation (i.e. the presumption that a present is due) – speaking personally, I find it immensely helpful. What I do think, though, is that greed has no place on a wedding list and some have got out of hand with almost nothing under £200 or £300 being included. As Rowan Pelling pointed out recently in a splendid diatribe on the subject: 'Contemporary lists are moving beyond parody as the affianced plump for iPods, plasma TVs and digital photograph fames.' John Lewis has revealed that the Nintendo Wii (a mere £179) is now the most desired present.

✳ A few couples these days ask for contributions to the honeymoon. If you think this is a good idea, you can set up a website where guests can pledge to pay for, say, scuba-diving lessons, champagne on arrival, a massage each (see www.thehoneymoon.com).

At the Wedding Shop in London's Chelsea (www.wedding shop.com), they report that their brides and bridegrooms have much more informal tastes today than ever before. While they still like to be given such things as cocktail jugs and hand-carved salad bowls (although the provenance and precise nature of the wood are important now) the complete dinner set or matching sets of glass no longer figure on the list. Instead of essentials, they ask for decorative or luxurious items to add a bit of lustre to the things they already own.

Wedding Present Suggestions

* Updated, luxurious versions of the essentials – finer linen, better china, more interesting glass, fantastic saucepans.

* For avant-garde, designery tastes, something from Liberty's Wedding and Gift list service. There is, for instance, David Mellor green Chinese cutlery (a fork £11.90, knife £13.90, spoon £9.50).

* www.notonthehighstreet.com is a good source for those looking for something unusual with a little charm attached. It has just started a wedding-list service – look out for hurricane lamps, silver and glass candlesticks, a wooden

storage bench, birdcage mirror; www.fairtradegiftlist.co.uk has objects made by small producers in poor countries who would otherwise have trouble reaching Western markets, and some of the items are gorgeous – mirrors, vases, chairs. Special one-off antique pieces may be tracked down at www.thevintageweddinglist.co.uk; www.whatidlove.com has some wide-ranging ideas for gifts that can be bought from boutiques and tiny producers who make just a few of each piece.

* First edition of a favourite book.

* An antique mirror.

* Headed writing paper or note cards with lovely tissue-lined envelopes.

* If you want to give something bigger – a commissioned portrait, or a painting of the couple's house, dog, favourite tree. Mark Frith (www.portraitsbymarkfrith.co.uk) – to declare an interest, he is my son-in-law – does beautiful pencil drawings of people – and especially lovely ones of children – and fine, detailed oil paintings of houses and trees. You could consult the Royal Society of Portrait Painters (www.therp.co.uk) to find an artist.

* A wine-tasting, gardening or cookery course.

* A pair of antique pillowcases or a vintage throw. The Conran Shop (www.conranshop.co.uk) and the Designers' Guild (www.designersguild.com) often have exquisite ones made from antique textiles.

* A set of perfectly plain good-sized linen napkins from the Volga Linen Company (www.volgalinen.co.uk).

* A fantastic reading light – an Anglepoise or a Best Light.

* Gorgeous towels, white unless you know they have a favourite colour scheme.

* An espresso coffee machine.

* A piece of Georgian silver – a beautiful pair of serving spoons, for example – from Bruford & Hemming.

* A fine atlas or set of reference books or dictionary.

* A set of Riedel wine glasses.

* A bicycle made for two.

* Plants, trees, planters (www.crocus.co.uk or www.wildatheart.com).

* Something suitable from an antique shop – a young friend gave another friend who was getting married and had not sent a wedding list ('People are so hard up at the moment that I don't want anybody to feel they must give us something,' is how she explained it away) a beautifully chosen 1930s tea set. Alfie's Antique Market (www.alfies antiques.com) is a good source, and sometimes charming pieces can be found at Felt (www.felt-london.com).

Presents given by the Bride and Groom

Then, of course, there's the matter of presents that the bride and groom traditionally give to the bridesmaids, the ushers

and the best man. I think these should be classy and classic
– something they'll love all their lives. For a bridesmaid, a
small piece of jewellery is ideal – a string of pearls, a darling
bracelet, a cute brooch, a finely wrought silver spoon – if
possible, engraved with either her name or the date of the
wedding to link it forever to the special occasion; for the best
man, something silver – a fine pen, a silver flask, a hand-
wrought silver mug from a special craftsman, some cufflinks
(please not jokey ones that he'll never wear). The Goldsmiths'
company website (www.whoswhoingoldandsilver.com) is an
illustrated directory of the work of some of the best
craftsmen and women working in silver and gold today.
Prices are often surprisingly reasonable, because many sell
directly from their workshops. These days, some couples give
tokens but I think that's a pity – what's the point? Practical
they may be, but tokens are nothing special or memorable.

Photography

Established wedding photographers costs thousands and
sometimes the results are disappointing. Ours turned up at
the church only, and since it was a city church without any
surrounding greenery (St Simon Zelotes in Chelsea), there was
precious little space to take photographs and we're left with just
a small and rather lame selection of mementoes of the big day.
Now that digital cameras are so easy to use, family and friends
can take photographs of the whole day, which makes a much
more vivid memento. Start from early in the morning – snap the
breakfast, getting ready, capture all the excitement. It's quite fun

to buy cheap disposable cameras (£4 each) and put one on each table so that guests can all take some photographs – this certainly gives scope for different perspectives. One mother of a society bride commissioned an artist (David Downton – www.daviddownton.com) to do drawings instead. Nominate somebody close to you to be in charge and make sure that every moment and person you wanted photographed is pictured. Plenty of companies will help you put the digital files into albums (www.digitalalbums.co.uk is just one).

A video recording of the big day is a wonderful keepsake – you could hire somebody to do it for you (go to www.weddingvideoslondon.co.uk) but again you could rope in a gadget-minded friend instead. Most would be flattered. Another idea is to organise a photo-booth (www.boothnation.com). Have an album to hand and ask guests to stick a photograph of themselves, plus an accompanying note, into the book as a memento of the day.

Saving the Planet

When it comes to weddings, green is the new white. All sorts of small organisations have sprung up to help those who don't want their big day spoiled by worrying about what it's doing to the planet. Needless to say, for those keen to go down this path, it's the web that has come to the rescue by pulling together in the most user-friendly way a host of small sites: www.greenunion.co.uk and www.eco-friendlyweddings.co.uk both have links to masses of suppliers of the classic ingredients that make up the happy day – marquees, eco-friendly bridesmaids' dresses, florists, bio-degradable tableware, recycled stationery, cake-makers, you name it, they're there; www.carbonfund.org/weddings has (relatively) easy methods of calculating the projected number of carbon emissions the event will generate, taking into account flights, car miles and all the rest, and then offers ways of off-setting them.

As far as the honeymoon is concerned, www.godifferently.com has loads of suggestions for alternative honeymoons. You could work on conservation projects, help save the langurs (a species of monkey) in Khao Sam Roi Yot National Park in Thailand, stay in a local fisherman's cottage or travel the slow gentle way through third-world countries. Whatever takes your fancy, Go Differently will help you plan it.

If you have friends who have a house abroad, you could ask to borrow it, or you could offer to house-swap. Best of all, you might think of staying at home. Think what you save on the air fares and carbon emissions and have a ball at home with smashing dinners, theatres and all manner of treats, ranging from massages (if that's your bag) to tickets for the opera.

If you want to honeymoon abroad but feel bad about the flying, www.carbonneutral.com will help you balance out the carbon emissions by contributing to forestry and climate-friendly energy projects.

More Green Tips

* Hold the reception during the day, or if you prefer to have it at night, do it by candlelight.

* Minimise the use of paper by setting up a wedding website to issue invitations, or send texts, or use old postcards bought from junk shops.

* Wear your mother's wedding dress, buy a second-hand one, or wear a dress that can be altered and worn again. Family jewellery could be the 'something borrowed'.

* Use antique engagement and wedding rings, available from antique shops or auctions.

* Use seasonal and local flowers. Centrepieces could include fruit and vegetables, or potted plants, which could be used later.

* Serve organic, locally sourced food, and if possible, wine.

* Ask for trees and plants for your garden as presents, or donations to a charity. Throw flower petals instead of paper (rice can be harmful to birds).

* Have the ceremony and reception at the same place, or nearby, to minimise travel for your guests.

The Anniversary Party

A wedding anniversary is the celebration of love, trust, partnership, tolerance and tenacity. The order varies for any given years. Paul Sweeney

Special anniversaries, significant birthdays (big 'Os', eighteenths, twenty-firsts) deserve to be celebrated, not just for those whose day it is but because they're also important milestones for the wider circle, a not-to-be-missed chance for family, friends, children, cousins and second cousins to meet when they no longer live in the close communities that were the custom long ago. It's only these sort of celebrations that bring friends and relations winging their way in from remote and faraway places. As families grow, generations spread and the circle of friends enlarges, chances for the wider connections to get together become fewer and fewer, so celebrating these landmark anniversaries matters more and more. On these occasions, friendships are renewed, and families are reminded of what they mean to each other. Sometimes people who perhaps didn't know each other very well make friendships that become precious. If boats are going to be pushed out, these are the occasions to do it, and maybe sizeable (but agreeable) waves will be formed in their wake.

What Sort of Party?

Talk to the party planners and it's quite interesting to discover how they're busy adapting to the changing times. British-themed events, locally and more ecologically sourced, are the way to go. Ethics are back. Mary Killen, agony aunt at the *Spectator*, who seems to know more about parties than is proper, says that people have realised you don't have to splash out at Le Caprice. You can have just as jolly a time at the local Indian restaurant or trattoria if you're with people you care about – and you can probably swing an amazing deal there. You don't have to have fireworks or complicated agendas – make the evening memorable and original with personal touches that don't cost a fortune. After all, it's the warmth, fun and attention to detail that most people remember – the party where the hostess writes a limerick to describe every guest or a poem for the occasion, the favourite music that unexpectedly wafts over the proceedings.

Whereas in the past, the well-heeled would think nothing of whisking their best (and not so best) friends to the world's most exclusive beaches, grandest palazzos, plushest yachts where an endless series of treats and surprises would be orchestrated with all the efficiency of a Montgomery battle plan, these days softly, softly is the mantra. Speak to the florists, the musicians, the party organisers and as one they will tell you that lavish is no longer the catch-word.

Party and events planner Sophie Lillingston, for instance, recently organised an austerity-themed party in a warehouse in West London. She served stew and cottage pie, and everybody was asked to dress in post-war mode. The women wore red lipstick and had their hair specially done. As she pointed out, '1948 was a bad year for port but the music was great – Glenn Miller and his Orchestra, Duke Ellington, Benny Goodman, Bing Crosby, Frank Sinatra, Billie Holiday and Ella Fitzgerald were all riding high.' The party was a wow and cost a fraction of the old swanky dos.

Another of her clients who had a big birthday coming up had originally wanted one big fantastic bash but, on reflection, decided that she wouldn't really get round to seeing everyone. So she decided to break it up into a series of special monthly dinner parties – the food and drink would be above average, a bit more trouble was taken with the table and decorations, but she would have twelve events to look forward to and would actually be able to talk to all her friends.

MAKE IT DIFFERENT

Themes are worth thinking about and often make the party more memorable. The internet is full of suggestions (check www.ehow.com) but whether you go for a Gatsby party, a roaring twenties party, a thousand-and-one nights, a French revolution or Versailles Court party, there's a lot of fun to be had. Opera themes give a lot of scope, and an Indian evening is great for brilliant colour and exotica. Gorgeous picnics (see pages 235–276) are a lovely thing to do in the summer, and fireworks (see pages 343–345) can add magic to the evening. If you want yet more fun – cabaret, singers, magicians – check www.bestartistsever.com, which has a vast roster of performers of many kinds.

✳ Speeches, I think, are important. They mark the day. Children often make some of the best speeches at their parents' wedding anniversary parties, giving a witty and tender view of their parents' lives. It's a moment to pay public tribute and to draw the wider circle into some of the family's myths and stories.

❊❊❊❊❊❊❊❊❊❊❊❊❊❊❊❊❊❊❊❊❊❊❊

DECK THE HALL

Create the right atmosphere with dramatic big branches collected from the garden or nearby woodland, or seasonal flowers in simple jars. In season, you could colour-theme roses and strew the table with rose petals. Balloons and some personal memorabilia, such as photographs of times gone by, all help.

❊❊❊❊❊❊❊❊❊❊❊❊❊❊❊❊❊❊❊❊❊❊❊

Music

Personal taste is all and the music needs to match the event. Contact the music schools to find a string quartet, if that would suit. For my father's ninetieth birthday a friend, knowing my father's love of Japan, hired a Japanese student to play on a Japanese flute (although, truth to tell, he got rather drowned out by the chatter).

If there's going to be dancing, you can spend weeks making your own music compilations – ask friends and children to help, to broaden the selection – or buy a few party discs from

Amazon (www.amazon.co.uk). If you need advice, try HMV (www.hmv.co.uk) – tell them what you want and ask them to give you a list of the best discs for what you have in mind (the big store in London has personal shopping advisors, so you can speak to them in person).

Alternatively, you could hire a DJ or a small live band – word of mouth is the best recommendation here. Decide what sort of music you want from the band, though – some do jazz, some rock 'n' roll, some old-fashioned sentimental numbers.

As far as the music goes, I always think the old classics are best, although my young friends tell me their feet start twitching to Girls Aloud and Daft Punk. You don't want anything too edgy – stick with the best-loved stuff to suit the age range at the party.

FOOD

This depends of course upon the format. If you want to do it yourself and you're having large numbers, you'll have to keep it simple and rope in friends and family. For hot food, stick to the old-fashioned simple dishes, such as bangers and mash, shepherd's pie, lasagne, moussaka and fish pie (Delia has a brilliant version, with a rosti topping instead of the usual mashed potato – it consists of grated potato mixed together with lots of finely chopped capers, some melted butter and cheese and then spread over the top of the fish mixture before baking). All these can be prepared ahead in bulk. Buy in puddings from patisseries and have platters of bread and cheeses, fruit and sweetmeats.

Tables, chairs, cutlery and all the rest can be hired but it's the labour of setting up, serving and clearing that makes it tough without help. If it's your party and you want to enjoy it, my advice is to get the caterers in!

The Swanky Party

Yes it still is what some people want – a once-in-a-lifetime amazing event. For a proper swanky party, you will need professional help. Party organisers not only remove all the headache from the event, but have an inside track on the best venues, and they don't all cost an arm and a leg. Again, word of mouth is the best source of advice, but these are the ones that I know from personal experience do it well.

* Alison Price (www.alisonprice.co.uk)

* The Admirable Crichton (www.admirable-crichton.co.uk)

* Deliciously Sorted – THE caterer should you be thinking of celebrating in Ibiza (www.deliciouslysortedibiza.com)

* Mustard (www.mustardcatering.com)

* Rhubarb – does Andrew Lloyd-Webber's annual Sydmonton Festival (www.rhubarb.net)

* Sophie Lillingston (www.lillingston.co.uk)

For events such as these, organisation is all, especially if the celebration is to be on foreign shores. Culture matters. You can't, after all, just invite people to Rome and leave them to mill around, waiting for their dinner. A whole new breed of travel agents and party planners have grown fat on their extraordinary ability to deliver the essential surprises with the military precision these celebrations require.

Everything starts with the invitations. The aim is to be different and inspiring. Sophie Lillingston has sent them out in the shape of an artist's palette (the reply had to be painted), flip-flops (for a beach party), miniature orange trees (a three-day bonanza in Mallorca) and olive trees (a Grecian idyll). A check on invitations ordered from a posh stationer, the Wren Press, gives another glimpse of the high jinks that have been on offer. An invitation to five days in Courchevel had an RSVP that required you to state the size of your ski boots. Everything from fancy chefs to lift tickets and private ski-guides will have been included. Weekends at Cliveden, Highclere or Blenheim invite the lucky guest to book spas or saunas, clay-pigeon shooting or quad biking. Skating boots were to be on hand for the specially installed ice-rink and the dress code was either 'Dress to kill', 'dress sexy' or 'fancy dress'.

Surprises and treats are usually built in all along the way. In the flushest of circles it usually starts with a private jet or the tabs for the air fares being picked up by the host, or guests might be asked to pay their own fares but once they've landed everything else is taken care of. The best of friends have been whisked to the world's most exclusive beaches where barbecues and grand picnics, concerts and dancing have all been laid on. Some have been taken to see the splendours

of St Petersburg, with private galleries and dachas opened up
to scenes of enchantment that even Catherine the Great
might have envied. Some have had the charms of Angkor
Wat laid before them, others have been ferried in vast yachts
to the world's most pristine beaches with butlers, spas, beach
picnics, dances and even lessons in astrology on the menu.
The more energetic have trekked in the mountains of Bhutan
or skied down the best black runs. The world's best musicians
– from string quartets, conductors and soloists to pop stars
have been paid a king's ransom to provide the guests with
something to remember. Marrakech has been a hot ticket. It's
only three hours away by air, there are some gorgeous riads to
hire and it feels like another, more exotic, more extravagant
world. For those who take villas in Goa, Florence, Rome or
Phuket, the days are not idle, although the canny host builds
in plenty of downtime. Visits to vineyards, girly bonding over
shopping, manicures, pedicures and massages are often on the
agenda. Clever hosts think of the different or the unusual.
Lucky guests at one Tuscan villa, for instance, found ignition
keys planted by Sophie Lillingston's team in the breakfast
cereals, so that after breakfast everybody drove around in
amazing vintage cars, following maps to the picnic rendezous
for lunch. In Goa, merchants are summoned with rare
embroideries or fine pashminas, in Florence they head to
Lorenzo Villoresi's eyrie above the Arno and have a perfume
specially made for them.

The big celebration has to be something requiring
sophistication, insider knowledge and serious contacts – balls
in private palaces, visits to special collections, talks from the
great curators or artists, access to what would otherwise be

inaccessible. Here's where the experienced party planner or events organiser really earns his or her stipend. Emily Fitzroy of Bellini Travel, whose beat is Italy, can organise a private organ recital in the Duomo or the Basilica of St Mark's, or fix a visit behind the scenes of La Fenice. In Rome, she could organise a fantastic banquet in the still privately owned Palazzo Colonna, where you dine in a room with frescoes on the vaulted ceiling and walls lined with Tintorettos, Piero della Francescas and Titians.

The Sixtieth Birthday

While all the big anniversaries matter, somehow the sixtieth birthday has become a particularly special cause for interesting celebrations. Since sixty became the new fifty, it's clear that the world – funds permitting – is still one's oyster. With average luck, nobody's yet in a wheelchair and, as Johnny Roxborough of party and events organiser the Admirable Crichton puts it, 'It's almost like the last hurrah. You're all still active enough to do something physical and you've also worked out who your friends are so you don't have to ask a whole lot of hangers-on, which is why sixtieth birthday parties are often smaller and more intimate than the fortieths and fiftieths.' The idea of ongoing celebrations seems to be key. Children are often grown-up and mortgages paid off, which lends an air of being demob happy to the proceedings, and friends can go off together, sharing the fun of a bash lasting several days.

People celebrate in very different ways, though. Nicky

Haslam celebrated with a face-lift. Stephen Hawking went for learned discussions on warping spacetime and wormholes with fellow cosmologists. Lady Annabel Astor (mother of Mrs David Cameron) sailed around the Aegean in three gulets with some thirty of her nearest and dearest while Andrew Lloyd Webber celebrated twice – once with a house party for forty of his closest friends at his home in Mallorca and more publicly with a star-studded concert in Hyde Park. The Prince of Wales had a banquet at Buckingham Palace (given by his mother) and a party (organised by his wife) for sixty family and friends at Highgrove.

Perhaps the classiest thing of all is what Lady Helen Hamlyn did when her late husband, Sir Paul Hamlyn, turned sixty. She took over the Royal Opera House for a night and filled it with people who had never ever seen an opera or a ballet before. He was so thrilled that he decided to go on funding special Hamlyn nights for the next twenty years, so that now over 200,000 people have had their eyes and ears opened to the wonders of music and dance.

When it comes to sixtieth birthday parties there are, it seems, no rules. You've made it this far, seems to be the mood, so it's to hell with convention – you've earned the right to do it your way.

✳ Invitations for sixtieth birthday parties should always say 'no presents'. Anything else is naff.

What If You Don't Want to Party?

There are many ways to celebrate, so just follow your fancy. When it comes to wedding anniversaries, many couples celebrate by developing a ritual that is utterly personal to them – every year going back to the restaurant where they had their first date, booking the same room where they spent their wedding night, that sort of thing. As the years roll by, children come along and life gets frantic, so simple things such as booking a baby-sitter for the weekend (or roping in the in-laws) is wonderful. A single day and night that can be spent alone somewhere special works a treat. One young couple I know celebrate every year by having a night-time picnic – they pack rugs and champagne and some delicious food of the sort they don't eat every day and head off for a spot they know on some hills near where they live.

Birthday or anniversary surprises for your partner don't have to be expensive – a great breakfast in bed, the said picnic (planned secretly), a special opera or theatre with dinner afterwards. For one of my big 'Os' my husband orchestrated a whole day with the family – it started with us all (grandchildren included) going on the London Eye, then on to lunch in a Chinese restaurant followed by a short visit to a fantastic exhibition at the National Portrait Gallery, then tea in a Soho tea-rooms where we'd had meaningful meetings. Finally, he and I went out to dinner on our own after the children and grandchildren had gone home.

Some families celebrate with a holiday – a cruise (don't groan . . .) can be brilliant because it takes care of the interests of so many generations. Onboard nurseries, climbing walls, teens-only discos, planetariums, ice-skating rinks and movies on giant screens under the stars are just a sample of the offerings available. The elderly can totter from meal to meal and deck-chair to deck-chair. The very young can take part in games, parties and fancy-dress competitions. Their parents can go to the gym and the spa, the library, the bridge room.

Here are some other ideas:

* Sailing-mad families could hire as many boats as they need and cruise around their favourite waters.

* For skiers, hire a chalet big enough to house the family.

* For walkers, rent accommodation in the Highlands or Cornwall and spend days hiking, away from it all; or take a weekend break in the Yorkshire Dales or the Lake District.

Presents

Let's start with wedding anniversaries. Through the centuries, these have gathered traditional symbols. Quite where they all come from nobody knows but the twenty-fifth and fiftieth can be traced back to medieval Germany. A silver wreath was placed on the head of the wife after twenty-five years of marriage, a golden one after fifty years. Earlier years seem to be more modern inventions, but wherever they came from they make a starting point for a little inventive thinking about how to give each other something to commemorate what are, after all, momentous days in most couples' lives.

1st – Paper: a love letter or, if the creative juices are really flowing, a poem, beautifully written, probably make the most romantic presents of all, but a first edition of a book that is meaningful to you both would be pretty good. Then think of all the other things that come on slips of paper – airline, theatre, opera or concert tickets; vouchers offering anything from a massage to a weekend for two in a country house; a piece by a paper artist (weburbanist.com/papercraft). Su Blackwell (www.sublackwell.co.uk) is a paper artist who creates fairytale sculptures out of paper from old books.

2nd – Cotton: an unusual (but *not* jokey) T-shirt each is a great present (I'm particularly keen on the Velvet brand, www.velvet-tees.com). Otherwise, for him, a divine shirt, jacket or trousers, or a piece of striking African cotton fabric that would look fabulous draped over a sofa or framed on a wall. For her, one of those gorgeous Indian bedspreads made from patches of antique hand-blocked cottons, or a special tablecloth hand-embroidered in Portugal or India. Plain napkins are tasteful, or a pair of cotton pillow-cases, edged with lace. If you know her tastes well enough, and feel like splashing out, she'd probably love a fabulous cotton blouse or jacket from her favourite designer.

3rd – Leather: most women love a beautiful real leather bag – www.bagladies.co.uk gets them made in little ateliers in Florence for a fraction of the cost of the big-name numbers, and several of them look very similar. Debenhams has some brilliant bags in its designer diffusion ranges – look especially at Jasper Conran's and Matthew Williamson's. A really beautiful belt is another idea, or one or two of Smythson's adorable leather-covered notebooks. For him, a leather belt, wallet, jacket (but only if you're feeling rich – cheap leather jackets are horrible) or a beautiful leather briefcase. Marks & Spencer do some amazingly good shoes for men and sometimes have brilliant belts.

4th – Linen or silk: for him, a linen shirt, handkerchiefs, trousers or jacket, or a silk dressing-gown. For her, a linen tablecloth or some delicious silk underwear (www.figleaves.com and www.phoebecarlyle.com). If you want to splash out, nobody to my mind does more beautiful underwear than Carine Gilson (www.carinegilson.com). She uses silk from Lyons and the most exquisite hand-made lace from Calais. For really good value, head for the shop beloved of chic young Italians – Intimissimi (www.intimissimi.it). Silk flowers, silken lampshades, linen shoe-bags and antique linen sheets are other ideas. For gorgeous flower-spattered linens, including tablecloths and duvet covers, try Cabbages and Roses (www.cabbagesandroses.com); the French House

(www.thefrenchhouse.net) has divine linen, mostly just
white, of the sort you could wish your grandmother
had left you; and for old-fashioned, flowery linens as
well as some chic ginghams and plain whites, register
with Peacock Blue (www.peacockblue-online.co.uk –
you need a user name and password).

5th – Wood: the best thing is to plant a tree
(www.tree4life.com). Otherwise, everybody loves boxes
– search for fine, old, beautifully made ones in antique
shops. Other ideas are hand-carved Welsh wooden
love spoons (www.welshlovespoons.co.uk); good-
quality bread boards, salad bowls or serving spoons in
solid wood; a small piece of furniture; wine in a
wooden crate; an antique carved wooden frame, either
for a picture or mirrored glass; an antique mirror in a
beautiful wooden frame.

6th – Iron: how about wrought-iron garden gates
(www.cannockgates.co.uk have truly beautiful designs),
garden furniture (maybe a bench from
www.tredecim.co.uk) if you have a garden, or a
wrought-iron lantern (www.grahamandgreen.co.uk
have lovely Moroccan ones)? Order a hand-made
house-name sign from www.castinstyle.co.uk (all
made in a foundry in Wolverhampton). A cast-iron
casserole dish is great for a keen cook, or a
camping griddle for lovers of the great outdoors.
A metal mirror is another idea (get one from
www.artofmetal.co.uk).

7th –   Copper: a great set of copper pans is a life-long
treasure for anybody interested in cooking, although
they need a bit of upkeep (from
www.divertimenti.co.uk or any good kitchen supplier).
A copper preserving pan imbues the making of jam
and preserves with so much retro glamour (£140 from
www.thefrenchhouse.net). These, and the French
House's fabulous hand-beaten copper lamps (£110), are
made by M. Vergnes and his team in the Languedoc,
which has to give some added charm to the matter.
Copper moulds for old-fashioned jellies and mousses,
bain-maries and sauté pans are also great for cooks.
Or how about a copper bracelet, which is meant to be
good for your health.

8th –   Bronze: a bronze head or sculpture could be ordered
from www.bronzesculpture.uk.com. Prices start at
about £80 for existing pieces – a set of hares by Paul
Jenkins, for instance, starts at £83 – and the choice is
wide, with work by a series of artists. For gardeners, a
small bronze birdbath costs £16.99 from
www.thegardenersfriend.net. Bronze jewellery –
bracelets and necklaces – can be found in most
department stores and can look stunning.

9th –   Pottery: not difficult this one if you're not going to be
pedantic about the differences between pottery and
china. The choice is endless and depends upon
personal taste – a new dinner service, a great big
antique tureen or platter, a series of cute china mugs,
a tea service, some colourful Italian or French pottery

to lay a summer table. Alternatively, even if you can't run to a piece by Rupert Spira or Edmund de Waal, some fabulous vases and other works of art are available from galleries all over the country.

10th – Aluminium: you could go searching for jewellery made of aluminium, but if you don't mind compromising a bit, some gorgeous vases are waiting to be found, or you could think about a watch (aluminium or metal case). I read of a matchbox made from part of a crashed aeroplane, which would make a memorable present, as would an old helmet, sword or dagger. Thinking laterally, metal, whether aluminium, steel or wrought-iron, works well in the garden, with tools or a plain barbecue. If you're buying for your own anniversary, you could perhaps think of a conservatory, one of those gorgeous ones with metal lace work. The Metal Gallery (www.themetalgallery.com) has pieces by a wide range of artists, some well-established, others new and emerging, all working in different metals, including aluminium, steel, pewter, titanium, copper, gold and platinum.

15th – Crystal: there's a wonderful choice for this year, and it really depends on taste and how much you want to spend. For the wine aficionado, an elegant Riedel glass (see page 389), or even a complete set, would be terrific. Crystal jewellery is modern and gorgeous (www.astley-clarke.com). Antique glass is always lovely. For our twenty-fifth wedding anniversary,

I found a most beautiful large glass jug with a silver lid, which we bring out on special occasions. Perfume comes encased in crystal, so, for her, a limited edition in a beautiful bottle would be special (Roja Dove's Haut Parfumerie, www.rojadove.com), or the entire collection of Frédéric Malle's Editions de Parfums, or a great big flagon of her favourite perfume if she has one. Other ideas are a set of beautiful decanters or a divine chandelier (trawl Alfie's Antique market, www.alfiesantiques.com).

20th – China: look at the pottery (year 9) – a big enough gap after all – and remember the antique shops. I've got a collection of gorgeous platters that are fantastic for setting out food at buffet suppers, all collected from antique or bric-a-brac stalls and shops. Other lovely presents are a special set of old plates for, say, cheese or fruit, and some gorgeous bowls for summer soups. The Dining Room Shop (www.thediningroomshop.com) has gorgeous vintage dinner sets and tea sets, while Vintage Heaven (www.vintageheaven.co.uk) is another great source. Ceramic lamp bases are a more modern option, or the exquisite work of Bodo Sperlein. Heal's (www.heals.co.uk) stocks some of it but you can find all sorts of interesting work in galleries all over the country. For interesting, modern, usable china, go to Few and Far (www.fewandfar.net) and Nicole Farhi Home (www.nicolefarhi.com).

25th – Silver: time perhaps to visit the Silver Vaults in London's Chancery Lane, or to scour the antique

shops again. A beautiful pair of silver serving spoons
makes a lovely present, or even a single exquisite
spoon for jam or marmalade. Prices outside London
are generally much cheaper, so start trawling early
when you know a big anniversary is coming up.
The Contemporary Applied Arts shop
(www.caa.org.uk/shop) has lovely modern pieces of
silver, as do lots of galleries around the country. Links
(www.linksoflondon.com) has made a point of
providing well-priced small silver presents –
everything from spoons and pens to jewellery of every
kind. Tiffany (www.tiffany.com) has silver galore, from
the famous silver bean to pens and spoons, rings and
pendants. William Phipps is, to my mind, one of
the finest living silversmiths – see his work at
www.whoswhoingoldandsilver.com – so plan ahead
and think of commissioning something special.
William Phipps spoons are especially lusted over. Egg
(www.eggtrading.eu) often has some of his work in
stock and, in any event, is a good place to track down
one-off gorgeous things.

30th – Pearls: a doddle really, but what does she give to him?
Pearl cuff-links? A pearl tie-pin? A pen with a pearl
at the end? Pearls light up every woman's face, but it
is amazing how different pearls suit different people.
My own pearls, for instance (bought from the lovely
Bob Reid in Broome, Australia), are quite large South
Sea pearls with a tinge of pale grey. I had wanted a
classic creamy double row but on me they didn't look

right. I tried them on several times but always came back to the single row of larger pale grey South Sea pearls. For classic pearls, Mikimoto (www.mikimoto.com) is a good place to go, but for something different try Coleman Douglas Pearls (www.pearls.co.uk). Christianne Coleman Douglas uses South Sea, freshwater and Japanese cultured pearls in all sorts of interesting ways. Dinny Hall (see her work at Selfridges or www.dinnyhall.co.uk) has some deliciously delicate strings of fine silver interspersed with pearls. Carolina Bucci (www.carolinabucci.com) has a delicately beautiful lariat of pearls on a gold thread – especially useful because you can tie the lariat at whatever height suits the neckline of the day. Remember, too, that pearls make great earrings (particularly when nicely surrounded by sparkling diamonds!) and some simple drop pearl earrings belong in every woman's wardrobe.

40th – Ruby: if you think of ruby as a colour, the choice widens immensely – scarves, shoes, bags, vases, lamps, bedspreads, you name it. My husband gave me a gorgeous set of antique ruby-coloured glasses, perfect for pudding wines. Carl Rotter's wonderful ruby-coloured water glasses would make a splendid present (www.artedona.com) but are very expensive. For jewellery, it's got to be rubies, and they don't tend to come cheap, either. At Astley Clarke (www.astley-clarke.com) rings, pendants and earrings sporting rubies start at £100.

50th – Gold: it doesn't have to be jewellery, although for such a special anniversary I think jewellery has the right touch of intimacy about it. For him, some super plain gold cuff-links (unless he's already got more than he knows what to do with), a gold pen or even a gold watch if he doesn't have a really pukka one (fine-rimmed, not too much bling). You could get one for the year of his birth, or the year of the marriage, from www.vintagewatchcompany.com. For women, there are some newer interesting ways of wearing gold – Carolina Bucci's woven gold bracelets are understated, utterly distinctive and oh, so elegant (www.carolinabucci.com). Fine chains, or gold interspersed with pearls (Carolina Bucci and Dinny Hall again, www.dinnyhall.co.uk), are also subtle and easy to wear, and as well as drop pearls, every woman needs one pair of great gold earrings.

55th – Emerald: once again, you could use emerald as a colour rather than a jewel – lights, glass, Moroccan lanterns, cashmere sweater, just think laterally – but if it's to be jewellery, as I keep saying, scour the antique shops first. Our old friend Astley Clarke (www.astley-clarke.com) has some well-priced pieces sporting emeralds.

60th – Diamond: there's no getting round the fact that diamonds are expensive, but small items, not necessarily jewellery, may be found in antique shops or auction houses. If you can't find what you want there, and it has to be jewellery, take a look at Erickson Beamon (www.ericksonbeamon.com). The diamond jewellery is divine, with some very pretty, wearable pieces, starting at around £1,000. William Welstead (www.williamwelstead.com) does wonderful things with rough uncut diamonds (so chic). Pippa Small puts great big rough diamonds into irregularly shaped fine gold settings. If it's the size and beauty of the stone that matters, it's worth thinking about buying just the stone online, where because the retailing costs are so much lower you get rather more stone for your money (try www.cooldiamonds.com and www.bluenile.co.uk), while Neil Duttson (wwww.duttsonrocks.com) will bring a selection of diamonds to the house. You choose the stone and he helps you decide on the design.

More Ideas for Other Special Occasions

For the eighteenth, the twenty-first and the big 'O' birthdays, classic presents are best for the very good reason that they are the ones that have stood the test of time, and prove to be true heirlooms, passed down from one generation to the next. Initially, they may sound a bit dull – a really good watch, fine camera, beautiful string of pearls, charm bracelet, leather-bound first edition, beginnings of a wine cellar, classic gold, silver or mother-of-pearl cuff-links – but they do somehow go on pleasing their owners all through the years.

* For a girl, a charm bracelet is lovely – Tiffany has some enchanting ones, as does Links of London – and they can be added to each year.

* Personal photographs and portraits always make great presents. A company called 55max (www.55max.com) will take holiday or family photographs and turn them into an art form by putting them into frames, behind Perspex, on to canvas or making a brilliant découpage. Commission professional photographs of the best beloved, the children, grandchildren or even the dog or horse, and have one blown up big, or think of a painting (www.portraitsbymarkfrith.co.uk). The Royal Society of Portrait Painters (www.therp.co.uk) has a list of artists.

* To commission jewellery, the Goldsmiths' Company has a website (www.whoswhoingoldandsilver.com) that leads you directly to the workshops of some 200 different craftspeople who can do gorgeous things.

* Specialist galleries and craft shops up and down the country are well worth checking because they do things you won't find in the average high-street shop or department store.

* Commission a special binding for a favourite book – get a first edition if you can, and consult www.designerbookbinders.org.uk for a bookbinder. The site has details of individual bookbinders with small pictures to give some idea of each craftsman's style, as well as sensible advice.

* Wine, champagne or whisky, bottled in the year you want to remember, makes a good present, as do newspapers from the archives. *The Times* issues back numbers for almost any date you care to name.

* You can order a customised song from www.give-a-song.com – choose from a sample list of singers and music, and dates and references are changed to personalise your choice, although they can compose something from scratch (£79.99 for a CD).

* A Book Box, or a bespoke book, makes a lovely present that the next generation will cherish. This is the brainwave of Penny Mischon. You have a private session with her, tell her about your life, what you cherish, what you want commemorated, and she puts it all together in a very special book-cum-box (www.thebookboxpress.co.uk).

* Monopoly is a classic game, and a special marital version – Monogamy – could achieve heirloom status (from www.anniversary-store.com).

The Grand Picnic

've always loved picnics and the notion of a *fête champêtre* sounds so splendidly celebratory. In reality, *fête champêtre* was an eighteenth-century invention and, put simply, is a rather de luxe version of what you and I would probably refer to as a garden party. In its grandest form, as refined by the French court at Versailles, it appears that it involved quite elaborate entertainment with whole orchestras being hidden in trees and the guests bidden to come in fancy dress. Versailles, of course, was well endowed with the sort of extras – follies, pavilions, temples, lakes, grand gardens and views – that lent a special air of enchantment to the occasion. In their Victorian heyday in Britain they continued on this merry way – grand outdoor parties, with lots of opportunities for introductions and a vast array of elaborate foods, including jellied moulds, both savoury and sweet, and a huge and varied selection of roasts. What Mrs Beeton considered essential for the well-victualled picnic (see 237) would take weeks for most of us to prepare.

For my purposes, I'm thinking of the *fête champêtre* as more than a picnic, slightly less than a full-blown party, reminiscent of country wedding scenes in films – long tables formed like the letter E without the middle small leg, all bowed under with white napery, fresh country flowers in jars and an abundance of gloriously seductive but charmingly rustic food and drink. Think of the scene when Emma Rouault marries Charles in *Madame Bovary* – the sirloins and fricassees of chicken and veal, the legs of mutton, the roast sucking-pig, the descriptions of bottles of sweet cider 'frothing round their corks', and the cake, above all, the cake, which was a castle surrounded by battlements of angelica, almonds, raisins and orange, topped by a green meadow and lakes made from jam and little boats of nut shells. Oh, what a seductive scene it paints! (Of course, we don't know then how badly it would all turn out.) Even if we can't hope to do all that on our own, something of the charm and magic can be achieved none the less. And for grand picnics, celebrating with family or friends, everybody can help.

✳ I'm always struck, when I've been lucky enough to go on safari, or stay in some out-of-the-way lodges, by how changing the dining spot can lend enchantment to the matter of simply eating a meal (I remember El Questro in Australia's Northern Territory with particular affection in this connection). On safari, breakfasts and dinners are often particularly magical experiences. You walk through the bush, the sun coming up as the night predators retreat to some shady spot where they can lie up during the day, and you suddenly come upon a table with a cloth and a little stove, bathed in glorious early morning light. Eggs and bacon will be cooked to order and there'll be croissants and fresh juices, and the fact that this is happening in the remote outdoors lends it an extra air of charm. At night, dinner is often served beside a lake or river, or under trees. Tea lights are everywhere. Lanterns hang from every bush, and sometimes candles are pushed into simple containers filled with sand. Flares light the way and with quite simple resources – quantity is the thing – the place is made to look as bewitching as any film set.

MRS BEETON'S BILL OF FARE
FOR A PICNIC FOR 40 PERSONS

A joint of cold roast beef, a joint of cold boiled beef, 2 ribs of lamb, 2 shoulders of lamb, 4 roast fowls, 2 roast ducks, 1 ham, 1 tongue, 2 veal-and-ham pies, 2 pigeon pies, 6 medium-sized lobsters, 1 piece of collared calf's head, 18 lettuces, 6 baskets of salad, 6 cucumbers.

Stewed fruit well sweetened, and put into glass bottles well corked, 3 or 4 dozen plain pastry biscuits to eat with the stewed fruit, 2 dozen fruit turnovers, 4 dozen cheesecakes, 2 cold cabinet puddings in moulds, 2 blancmanges in moulds, a few jam puffs, 1 large cold plum-pudding (this must be good), a few baskets of fresh fruit, 3 dozen plain biscuits, a piece of cheese, 6lb of butter (this, of course, includes the butter for tea), 4 quartern loaves of household bread, 3 dozen rolls, 6 loaves of tin bread (for tea), 2 plain plum cakes, 2 pound cakes, 2 sponge cakes, a tin of mixed biscuits, ½lb of tea. Coffee is not suitable for a picnic, being difficult to make.

Things not to be forgotten at a Picnic: A stick of horseradish, a bottle of mint-sauce well corked, a bottle of salad dressing, a bottle of vinegar, made mustard, pepper, salt, good oil, and pounded sugar. If it can be managed, take a little ice. It is scarcely necessary to say that plates, tumblers, wine-glasses, knives, forks and spoons must not be forgotten; as also teacups and saucers, 3 or 4 teapots, some lump sugar and milk. If this last-named article cannot be obtained in the neighbourhood, take 3 corkscrews.

Beverages: 3 dozen quart bottles of ale, packed in hampers; ginger-beer, soda-water and lemonade, of each 2 dozen bottles; 6 bottles of sherry, 6 bottles of claret, champagne at discretion, and any other light wine that may be preferred, and 2 bottles of brandy. Water can usually be obtained so it is useless to take it.

What You'll Need for a Grand Picnic at Home

It can all be done in one's own dear garden, no matter how small. In urban patios and on rooftops, as well as in large country gardens, magic can be conjured up.

Tables

Tables should be prettified. I love vintage cloths and, having something of a fetish for them, collect them wherever I go. The best sources I've found are provincial French fairs – though not the Isle-sur-la-Sorge, which is grossly overpriced – and the Sablon area of Brussels. Otherwise, search out Jane Sacchi on www.janesacchi.com for beautiful, though expensive, treasures. More practically, Cath Kidston (www.cath kidston.co.uk) has wonderfully pretty wipe-down oilcloths, or you can buy the same oilcloth by the metre. If you're hiring tables and trestles for a big party, you could just use masses of sheets to cover them. Once the tables are bedecked with platters of food, jugs of soft drinks, jars of flowers and candles (if at night), all the joins will be invisible.

Glasses and Tea Lights

Coloured glasses and tea lights all add to the air of romance. Once again, Cath Kidston comes to the rescue. (Her brochure-cum-magazine costs £1.50 and is a delight.) If pretty rather than grand or classic is what you're after, she has sweet, glass tumblers in pink, turquoise or lime green for just £3 each – it wouldn't be a disaster if you broke one. Tea lights in the same colours are £2.50 each and a set of six wine glasses, two of each colour, £24.

Cutlery and Crockery

Cath Kidston – again – has enchantingly pretty, flower-bedecked cutlery, napkins and plates in china or melamine, but if you're having a lot of people, it may be worth hiring these things. For a really special occasion, a mixed collection of gorgeous vintage tableware (www.vintagetableware.co.uk) may be the answer, themed by colour or designs. Vintage china would be particularly good if you were having an old-fashioned tea picnic – a boiling kettle, teapot, cucumber sandwiches, scones and sponge cake are the key essentials (see pages 318–320), although some would add no British picnic is complete without wasps.

Lanterns

Cheap but enchanting lanterns are to be found in many high-street chains – Next (www.next.co.uk) sells gorgeous paper lanterns at £10 for three, and brightly coloured glass ones with metal holders for hanging from a tree at £10 for two. Matalan (www.matalanonline.co.uk) has plenty of choice, including some very pretty crackle glass lanterns at £7 a time. TK Maxx (www.tkmaxx.com) has perpendicular

lanterns with brightly coloured glass that exude a Middle
Eastern air for £24.99 each.

Made in Design (www.madeindesign.co.uk) has some
brilliantly coloured (green, red, orange, blue, clear) glass balls
on long sticks – the idea is that you put a candle inside the
glass ball and push the stick into a flower pot or into the
ground (£11.20 each).

Marston and Langinger (www.marston-and-langinger.com)
has enchantingly pretty glass, tea lights, lanterns and other
picnic props.

Flares

For an evening party, it may be a good plan to illuminate
pathways and edges of flower-beds. Plenty of high-street
chains, including Argos and Homebase, sell flares. Heals has
some excellent copper ones in three different sizes.

For incense flares, I particularly like the ones from
Habitat, and the giant ones from Posh Hippo
(www.poshhippo.com) for £5 a time. If you're worried about
your guests being bitten by midges, candles suffused with
citronella oils will keep the bugs at bay. Lots of places sell
them. Posh Hippo has them in little tins for £5 a time and
they'll burn for 28 hours.

Protection from the Elements

Parasols keep off light rain as well as sun and are widely
available from garden centres, B&Q, Argos, Homebase and
many other department stores. For a biggish party with
several tables, you could buy them in different colours, or

borrow them from friends, in which case they're bound to be in different colours.

If you feel like splashing out, the Burford Garden Company (www.burford.co.uk) sells some gorgeous parasols with gold embroidery and decorative tassles for £180, and the India Garden Company (www.indiangardencompany.co.uk) has a wonderful selection, from delicate and creamy through to vibrant and tassled, from £135. Although these are not cheap, they should last for many years.

Alternatively, consider buying or hiring a gazebo. These are lightweight and not as sturdy as a marquee, but with a fabric roof and sides, offer more protection than a parasol. For £45.66, you can buy one in Argos big enough to provide cover for a largish dining table.

A picnic is the Englishman's grand gesture, his final defiance flung in the face of fate.
Georgina Battiscombe in *English Picnics*

Get Some Help

The traditional Victorian picnic typically involved everybody bringing along a contribution. For a *fête champêtre* at home, continuing this tradition makes the whole thing much more feasible and, often, grander because each person has merely one dish to concentrate on and tends to go to town a bit.

Otherwise, I'm a great believer in buying in help as

necessary. Full-blown caterers are great if you can afford them – trouble and stress free – but I can't help feeling that part of the fun lies in doing a lot of it oneself. You could, of course, do what a great grandmother of our acquaintance did for her eightieth birthday, held in a Gloucestershire garden with a rather makeshift marquee at the ready in case of rain. Some of the food (the poached salmon, I seem to remember) was ordered from a small local catering firm. Her two daughters-in-law made the puddings, and with help from those staying in the house, she did the salads herself. Everybody helped lay everything out on the day. There were great bowls of new potatoes turned in butter and herbs, gorgeous cheeses and the pavlovas and chocolate torte made by the daughters-in-law, all washed down with champagne and good wines. The occasion couldn't have been bettered.

STREET PARTIES

Everybody who remembers the Queen's jubilee celebrations, or the royal wedding when the Prince of Wales married Lady Diana Spencer, remembers the street parties held all over the land. They were fun and everybody joined in. Children in particular had a grand time. Don't wait for another jubilee or wedding to do it again – organise your street and get started. There's lottery money to be had for 100 London street parties, and plenty of local councils are encouraging them (see www.playengland.org.uk for more details).

Some outdoor summer events in London would be greatly enhanced by combining them with a terrific picnic.

Opera Holland Park, www.ohp.rbkc.gob.uk

Open Air Theatre Regents Park, www.openairtheatre.org

Kenwood Picnic Concerts, www.picnicconcerts.com

Proms in the Park, www.bbc.co.uk/proms

Jazz at the 606 Club, Regents Park, www.606club.co.uk

If not at Home, Where?

If you don't have ancestral swards or gardens of your own big enough for a re-enactment of Manet's 'Déjeuner sur l'herbe', you can still carve out a little bit of outdoor magic by holding your *fête champêtre* on the beach or at a National Trust property, at a music or some other sort of festival, during a cricket or tennis match, or in a city park. If you log on to the National Trust website (www.nationaltrust.co.uk) and type in 'hot picnic spots' up will come a list offering some wonderful choices – how about Corfe Castle in Dorset, Fountains Abbey in Yorkshire, Brownsea island in Dorset, Kedleston Hall in Derbyshire or Petworth in Sussex? Britain's domestic architectural heritage is one of its great glories, and we have access to many of the best houses and gardens via the National Trust.

I happen to live within a couple of minutes' walk of Hyde Park and in the summer months the park is filled with people having splendid picnics. Romantic twosomes indulge in champagne, lobster and some light salads followed by strawberries. Families who live nearby spend long, summer evenings lounging on a rug, eating their evening meal in the form of a picnic. Groups of young people eat and play games, and huge extended Middle-Eastern families lay out food that looks a million times more exotic than our usual standard fare.

Festivals of all kinds are splendid occasions to eat outside, in grungy style if that's your preference, or you could turn it into something much more joyful. All through the summer, festivals are staged all over the land. The Whitstable Oyster Festival, the Caerphilly Cheese festival, the Lynton and Lynmouth Musical Festival are just a few examples. There's music in parks, gigs in woods – you just have to keep your eyes skinned to see what grabs you. Camp Bestival (www.campbestival.co.uk) is a good family festival – each year there's a different theme, and it involves dressing up, if you like, and much fun and games, including a kid's garden, storytelling, toys and child-friendly activities. On a personal note, I remember well one Summer Music Festival in Aspen, Colorado, in America. Hordes of the young and impecunious, who either couldn't afford the tickets or simply had not been able to get hold of any, brought along great big picnics with deep-fried chicken and cheesecake, sat on the grass outside the music tent and enjoyed it all for free.

THE NATION'S FAVOURITE PICNIC SITES

In a nationwide survey to find the country's best picnic sites, these came out as the top ten.

1 Richmond Park, London
Largest royal park in the capital and home to more than 600 deer.

2 Southsea Common, Portsmouth
Vast open space near the seafront, perfect for picnics and kite-flying.

3 Uphill, Somerset
Stunning views across Brean Down to Weston, and the Bristol Channel to Wales.

4 Milton Country Park, Cambridge
A haven of tranquillity on the northern edge of the city.

5 Stanley Park, Blackpool
Supports extensive wildlife and flora, and has 22 acres of lake and 96 acres of golf course.

6 Tanfield Railway, Co. Durham
Take a ride past Causey Arch, the world's oldest surviving railway bridge, where there is a picnic site.

7 Loch an Eilein, Rothiemurchus estate, Cairngorms
Surrounded by spectacular mountains, the estate is home to roe deer and red squirrels.

8 Ironbridge Gorge, Shropshire
A glorious wooded gorge, spanned by the world's first iron bridge.

9 Rhossili Bay and Worm's Head from Rhossili Downs, Gower
Offers views across the five-mile bay.

10 Sewerby Hall and Gardens, Bridlington, East Yorkshire
Set within 50 acres of grounds, with views over Bridlington Bay.

These are just a few popular places. You may have your own favourite spot, but if not and you take to picnicking, you will undoubtedly find one, tucked away in a wood somewhere, or hidden among rolling hills or in a sheltered part of a beach. Even in winter, all these places have a very English charm.

Glamping

There's a new word in the camping lexicon – 'glamping' – and it's an indication that camping has moved upmarket. If you've never tried camping because you thought it involved anoraks, leaky tents, clumsy backpacks and tins of baked beans, think again – glamping, or glamorous camping, has arrived, and you have to wonder what took it so long.

Camping has, of course, always had its good points – it allows one to spend time in remote, wild, tranquil places and to move around as the spirit moves. African safari lodges, it seems to me, have led the way – they are adept at making you feel awfully adventurous by sleeping in a tent whereas, in fact, the tent is usually twice as luxurious as anything one's used to back home (adjoining bathrooms and loos, Ralph Lauren-style interiors with oil-lamps, Persian rugs, telescopes, four-poster beds, mosquito nets and all the other romantic props). Now the rest of the camping world has cottoned on and is trying to glam up the image – and, of course, being prepared to camp – or 'glamp' – gives you access to the sort of wondrous settings where you can have the most divine *fêtes champêtres*.

At Glastonbury's music festival, for instance, if you can't face camping old-fashioned style, especially if the weather's not likely to be good, you can book into a posh Shikar tent (designed and manufactured by the Maharaja of Jodhpur, no less) – huge beds, lots of space, great comfort. Although not *en suite*, banks of loos and showers are located nearby, as well as access to massages and beauty treatments. Try www.campkerala.com – it isn't cheap but it's a million miles from anything Robert Baden-Powell had in mind. From the confines of your luxurious tent you can plot your very own *fête champêtre*, or do it the easy way and get Camp Kerala to provide all the food and their 'cocktail mixer' to come up with some suitably noxious cocktails.

Much less posh and therefore much more accessibly priced is www.tangerinefields.co.uk, which gives you a comfortable way to have fun at festivals – no need to beg, borrow or hire your own stuff and lug it all the way there. The tents are all set up, have good access to loos and showers and leave you free to have fun.

Meanwhile, a whole host of other companies have set up shop to provide jolly, highly decorative tents to enable those of us who live in what geographers lightly call 'temperate climates' to make the most of a special-occasion *fête champêtre* in the summer, no matter how wet, windy or chilly. Take White Canvas Tents (www.whitecanvastents.com) as an example. Tents made from proper rainproof canvas have interiors embellished with hand-blocked Indian prints, pretty poles and finials, and come in a range of sizes, some just big enough for a small summer lunch party, others large enough for a party for sixty or seventy people. They offer a whole range of styles for hire, from a lovely cupola to the Jaipur – the largest, which has a rather more colourful Rajasthani influence than the others and is correspondingly more expensive. Their range is also for sale, which may be worth it if you're hooked on outdoor parties and see yourself throwing several per year for many summers to come.

A Tent of Your Own

Millets have led the way in stylish tents by doing a bit of lateral thinking and getting Cath Kidston and Celia Birtwell (both of whom also came up with posh wellies) to add some designer kudos. Although their tents are not particularly luxurious, they start at a very reasonable £69.99. (Cath Kidston seems on a personal mission to pretty up the world and even offers hurricane lamps with roses painted on the glass and sweetly striped blankets.) A good sturdy plain natural cotton canvas tent can be had from www.belltent.co.uk for £275.

✳ Most counties have websites full of information for those who want to explore their hills, dales and beaches. The Suffolk coast is particularly good (see www.forestcamping.co.uk and www.gocampinguk.co.uk).

Puma have got in on the act, too. They took one look at the camping arena and thought it was more or less a style-free zone to which they could add some designery oomph. They wanted 'to bring design where it has not been before – to take it outside and into nature', or so they said, and asked uber-hip Dutch designer Marcel Wanders to come up with a range, which he brilliantly called 'I Hate Camping'. The name alone is enough to win over all those who, in their hearts, think camping is a hearty outdoorsy thing, which they secretly despise but yet accept that there are times when a tent – the right tent – might come in handy. Wanders gave it a breezy touch, with lyrical filigree black and white patterns sprinkled over canvas, towels and blow-up loungers. This, Wanders seems to be saying, has got to be fun.

✱ Puma's tent, the Villa, is evidently not one that you'd take up mountains or anywhere remote, but more of a protective covering from the sun, perfect for summer lunches in the garden or on the beach. You can buy it for £162.50 and any of the accessories in the range from www.microzine.co.uk.

For the most elaborate tents of all, turn to www.lpm bohemia.com, which has proper furnished numbers with waxed cotton canvas exteriors in all sorts of exotic forms. You could have a proper Mongolian yurt with a wooden frame and tough canvas and all their tents may be hired. Most theatrically of all, a Rajasthani tent may be specially ordered, complete with hot pink linings, coir matting and antique wooden doorframes.

✳ As well as being practical for summer parties and lunches, tents also provide extra bedrooms when the occasion demands. One summer, we rented a gorgeous house in Suffolk, and to cope with large numbers of children, we used a tent in the garden – which gave the young ones a sense of adventure as well as somewhere to rest their heads at night.

Picnic Essentials

Everybody from Marks & Spencer and John Lewis to quirky little out-of-the-way boutiques have got in on the act here, which means you're spoiled for choice. You could go all pretty-pretty with Cath Kidston. You could just be practical and get lightweight, easily portable backpacks, which seems the only option if you like hiking or walking to picnic sites. If you're travelling by car, you could go for an old-fashioned charm offensive.

Carrying the Gear

* Hampers: wicker does look the part – think of all those picnic scenes from the grand days of motoring – but be warned, wicker hampers are hell to carry. In fact, they're really only worth contemplating if you're going to picnic very near where you've parked the car. And they're expensive. A wicker hamper with kit for four people, that is napkins, ceramic plates, glasses, cutlery, salt and pepper shakers, costs £149 from John Lewis. Amberley does a range of charming retro-style hampers with a series of different interior fittings (www.retrocentre.co.uk).

* Rucksacks: for picnics that are preceded by long walks, it's a good idea to share out the load in rucksacks, and some brilliant ones that hold a lot of picnic paraphernalia are available for those who want to eat on the top of hills or in remote areas, unreached by modern transport. Marks & Spencer has a lightweight picnic rucksack for £19.50, containing plates, glasses and cutlery for four, and a bottle-opener-cum-penknife – not beautiful but oh so practical. Small children could carry one. Another place to try for inexpensive picnic backpacks is Picnic Ware (www.picnicware.co.uk).

   At the other end of the scale, Daylesford Organic (www.daylesfordorganic.com) has some nice dark-green picnic bags together with a very chic rug for £175, while a pack with pockets for two bottles, cutlery, plates and glasses as well as pouches, a cheeseboard, a corkscrew and a picnic blanket can be had from www.present-innovations.co.uk for £101.08. The advantage of this one is that it can be used as a perfectly ordinary rucksack at other times.

* Cooler box: all shapes and sizes are widely available at varying prices. Lakeland (www.lakeland.co.uk) has a small one in the Polar Gear range for just £7.82.

Picnic Ware

* John Lewis has some brilliant picnic ware. A brightly coloured tiffin box consisting of four stacked containers, in neon lime green, yellow, orange and fuchsia looks summery and is practical and easy to carry. Matching

plastic cutlery, glasses, serving spoons and mugs make up a set, and a Stanley flask in shocking pink is very jolly, too.

* Gorgeous decorative wine glasses in brightly coloured acrylic are available from Graham & Green (www.grahamandgreen.co.uk) for £6.95 a time, while for all those practical and useful (though not aesthetically beguiling) essentials – wide-mouthed food flasks (£11.73), tight-lidded plastic containers for salads and endless variations on lunch-box coolers – try Lakeland.

Rugs

When it comes to rugs, I mostly prefer classic gear. As I've mentioned, it's hard to beat Glyndebourne's own picnic rug, which is made of nice sober green check wool with a mackintosh backing (see pages 90–91). If you like rather jollier versions – if you decide, for instance, to go the John Lewis brightly coloured, cheerful route – then you might like the Pod Company's range of patterned waterproof picnic rugs (£23.50 from www.thepodcompany.co.uk), and Picnic Ware has a cheap and cheerful one for under £12. For beach picnics, Runaway Coast (www.runawaycoast.com) has a padded waterproof beach mat for £68.

❋ National Trust shops often have a very good range of picnic equipment, including some enchanting metal plates (sturdy, unbreakable) that are printed with the patterns of grand china plates. They also have backpacks, wine coolers, flasks and waterproof rugs.

KEEPING THE BUGS AT BAY

One divine website (www.roullierwhite.com) sells an eau de cologne to keep the bugs away – that is, it achieves the miracle of ensuring you don't smell of repellent to yourself and those around you while at the same time putting off the things that bite and buzz. Mrs White's Unstung Hero is £15 for 250ml (you can decant it into smaller bottles for travelling) and smells of tea and lemon. The lovely Mrs White also has a natural bug-repelling candle (£12.95) and the Batard Folding Picnic Knife with an integral corkscrew (£25), which is brilliant. To deal with the quintessential, indisputably English picnic visitor – to whit, the wasp – Daylesford Organic (www.daylesfordorganic.com) sells a splendid little ceramic wasp trap for £14.95.

Simple Picnics

Omar Khayyam would have us think that a loaf of bread, a jug of wine and 'thou' was all one needed for a sublime outdoor experience. Now this may well be true in the early heady days of a passionate romance, but as the years pass I think most of us, even while still dearly loving our 'thou', would prefer a little more in the way of sustenance and company.

Personally, I love picnics even when the weather isn't at its best. Everybody born in northern climes probably has childhood memories of blustery days on hills and beaches, when somehow nothing could dampen the pleasure of being outside and, anyway, as poets and writers have noted since history began, all food tastes better out of doors. In my South African childhood, we often used to have supper on Cape Town's Clifton beach, watching the sun go down like a great big orange behind the sea. I seem to remember that ordinary Marmite sandwiches were the norm, but in that place, at that time, those picnics seemed like bliss. I also have happy memories of outings to British beaches when our children were small, in Northumberland mostly, where my brother and his family lived for a while, and on the East Anglian coast. Instead of basking in sunshine, we often ended up huddled by dunes, sheltering from the wind, with Thermoses of hot soup, sausages, crisps, some apples and chocolate. We still had a rattling good time. In Suffolk's Aldeburgh, where for many years my father and stepmother had a small house, we would buy fish and chips from the famous corner shop, where long queues are to be found round about every meal-time, and team that up with some crisp white wine for the adults, ginger beer or lemonade for the children. With strawberries afterwards, a great time was had by all. In Spain one year, also when the children were small and we were on holiday with another family, we made a simple fire outside, and using a rack from the cooker, grilled fresh fish bathed in olive oil and herbs. It was one of the most delicious meals I ever remember.

Nowadays we have rustic picnics either in France, where our son and his wife have a house in the Cevennes, surrounded by woods and hills, or in Ireland, where our daughter and her husband have a house near Kerry. Picnics are always big features of times spent with them, and although not strictly *fête champêtre* occasions, they are times of great joy, involving lots of walking and the sort of simple food there's no need to cook and it's easy to carry, although we sometimes grill some sausages or roast a couple of chickens or some fillet of beef to take with us as we're having breakfast.

Simple picnics are brilliantly easy to organise. If possible, you can even shop at local markets on the way – divine and no work. They are all-hands-to-the-deck affairs, where everybody carries something and helps lay out the food and drink. One person cuts the bread while another sorts out the cheese and so on. You need some really good fresh bread – I love soda bread with gravadlax or smoked salmon (www.hebrideansmokehouse.com) but don't forget the lemons – a selection of cold meats (San Daniele ham, pata negra or Parma ham, salamis and perhaps some English hand-carved ham), farm-made pâtés, tomatoes, olives, cheeses and fruit (strawberries, peaches or figs with some sharp cream cheese). Other than some chocolate, one doesn't need much more.

However, I am reminded of the great cookery writer Elizabeth David's cautionary tale of a last-minute picnic, when she was staying with friends in Marseille. Their house party was meeting another group of friends and everybody was going to bring some food. It soon became clear that her house party's choices, made impulsively in the market, were rather inferior to the friends' contributions, almost entirely because they'd forgotten all the little things that make a difference – the salt, the butter, the coffee, the flat white plate. She was always very keen on flat white plates or bowls was Mrs David, because they made the shiny olives, the pink salami and sharp goats' cheese look so good. There is a lesson in there, I think.

Sand in the sandwiches, wasps in the tea,
Sun on our bathing-dresses heavy with the wet
Squelch of the bladder-wrack waiting for the
  sea,
Fleas round the tamarisk, an early cigarette.

From 'Trebetherick' by John Betjeman

Chilled Soups

For summer picnics, lighter fare than the sort I've suggested
for Easter should come into play. Scarcely anything could be
more elegant or easier than chilled soups. They stay cold
beautifully in a vaccum flask and can be made the day
before. Pea soup is brilliant and so easy. There are lots of
different methods and some people don't even cook the peas
– they merely whizz together some frozen baby peas (once
thawed), a small lettuce (washed and dried), a little spring
onion, some chicken stock and a little thin cream and they're
done. My recipe is only a tad more complicated.

Summer Pea Soup

2 shallots, finely chopped
2oz/60g butter
11oz/300g spinach
1lb 2oz/500g frozen peas
30fl oz/850ml chicken stock
salt and pepper to taste

crème fraiche
fresh mint leaves

Sweat the shallots in the melted butter. Blanch the spinach in a little boiling water for just 20 seconds (the spinach gives the soup a gloriously deep green colour). Drain, refresh and drain again. You could use frozen spinach, in which case you don't need to blanch it. Stir the frozen peas into the shallots and butter and cook for 2–3 minutes. Add the chicken stock (if I haven't made any at home I use Joubere's) and bring to the boil. If you want to use fresh peas, you will need to simmer them in the stock for about 10 minutes. Add the spinach and whizz everything together in a blender. Season with salt and pepper and leave to cool. Serve with a dollop of crème fraiche and some fresh mint leaves.

＊ A great website if you're looking for more foodie inspiration is www.the-picnic-site.com

Sandwiches

I'm not mad on sandwiches but they are certainly a convenient way of compressing nutrients into a small package for ease of carrying. If you must take sandwiches, think about some interesting fillings – rare beef finely sliced and mixed with some finely chopped spring onion, gherkin and horseradish, or mix the beef with some finely sliced roasted peppers and aubergine; sliced cold chicken mixed with finely sliced roasted peppers: soft goats' cheese and sliced dried figs; salami or ham on a lettuce leaf with some sliced artichoke hearts and black olives; goats' cheese on a base of puréed peas and broad beans.

Pan bagnat is traditionally made with a French baguette but you could use ciabatta or soda bread instead. Cut the bread into pieces roughly 15cm/6in long. Split each piece in half and spread with olive oil and crushed garlic. Layer the bottom half with strips of grilled red pepper, onion rings, sliced sweet tomato and sliced marinated artichoke hearts (you can buy them from good delicatessens or bottled). If you like them, add a few anchovy fillets. Otherwise, add some torn basil leaves, and season with salt and pepper to taste. Lay the top half on the filling and wrap the sandwich tightly in foil to keep it together. One or two of these makes a good robust lunch.

The contemplation of so idyllic, so simple a delight holds a particular poignancy; yet of one thing you can be sure; whether or no the picnic is a true pleasure, the habit of it is so firmly engraved in human character that it will survive countless calamities and holocausts.

Osbert Sitwell in *Picnics and Pavilions* – written in 1944

WHAT TO DO IF IT RAINS

Firstly, that's why we've talked about marquees and tents. Secondly, always take umbrellas (a wonderful John Leech cartoon in *Punch* shows the rain sheeting down on a clutch of upturned umbrellas, and the caption reads, 'It would have been so provoking to have brought our umbrellas and then to have had a fine day'). Thirdly, always take extra layers of clothing, and if it looks really squally, take cagoules or some kind of mac. Fourthly, pack a wonderful book — or several books — and read aloud. Learn some poems. Fifthly, play guessing games. Sixthly, remind yourself of those countries (Botswana, for instance, and Somalia) where they don't have enough of the stuff. Think of its life-giving properties and rejoice.

A Grand Picnic

The grandest picnics, the nearest to the idealised *fêtes champêtres*, that we do are when we go to places such as Glyndebourne, Garsington or Grange Park Opera. But all over the country there are other grand houses staging music, and there are race days at Ascot and Epsom Downs, sports days, regattas, music festivals, open-air concerts, cricket matches. For quintessentially English summer opera outings, I like to up the ante and try to make it very glamorous. Yes, I fret. Yes, it's quite a lot of hassle, but no I wouldn't have it any other way.

I take a linen cloth of some kind, usually an antique French red and white one, big linen napkins (find lovely old monogrammed ones at the cloth shop, www.theclothshop.net) and proper china, cutlery and glass (which I wrap in cloths to protect them on the journey), and some tea lights so we can have candlelight in the gloaming. We have a cooler to keep the drinks cold and carry the rest in a couple of huge soft baskets (proper hampers look wonderful but are awkward to carry). We have a little folding table and some chairs (John Lewis sells some that fold into bags at £25 for the chair, £45 for the table, although you can get cheaper ones at Robert Dyas) but I think sitting on a rug is just as nice (see pages 90–91).

We usually try to arrive early, somewhere between 4.30 and 5.30, so there's time for some nibbles and a drink before the opera begins. Cheese straws, spiced nuts, some olives and a chunk of fresh parmigiano, crudités with hummus and smoked aubergine purée are all good. Also think of little strips of Parma ham or a thin carpaccio of beef wrapped round half a fig or some asparagus. Champagne is the drink of choice (the Glyndebourne shop, incidentally, sells a terrific champagne stopper for £7) since most people love it and those who don't can go straight into the wine – though not too much because everybody's driving home.

The main meal is taken during the interval, and in such a quintessentially English setting, with those lawns, herbaceous borders and great views, nothing too exotic seems right. I like the food to be not too elaborate but on the luxurious side – smoked salmon or gravadlax (for a change you could try it potted), Morecambe Bay potted shrimps (from James Baxter & Son), smoked trout or Arbroath smokies pâté on toast (make it by whizzing smoked trout or smokies with some cream cheese, seasoning and a couple of spring onions in a blender) or an ice-cold pea or watercress soup (transported in a Thermos flask to keep it cold). Gulls' eggs, asparagus or smoked eel are other English summery starters (best smoked eel I know comes from www.brownandforrest.com). Then we may have really tender cold beef, still pink, served with a creamy horseradish sauce, new potatoes and a salad of mixed baby broad beans, peas, mange-tout and some feta cheese, or with a mixture of roasted peppers and aubergines. Sometimes I do little racks of lamb, cooked so that they're crusty on the outside and pink on the inside (twenty minutes is all it takes). If I'm feeling energetic and not in quite such quintessentially English mode, I marinate thin strips of chicken in a mixture of yoghurt, lemon juice and spices (coriander, cumin, turmeric, ginger, salt and pepper) and then grill them and serve them cold. For the potatoes, I like Jersey Royals or Pink Fir Apples, dressed either with a classic vinaigrette (do it while the potatoes are still hot) with lots of herbs, or else with a little sour cream and some chives or spring onions.

For a different salad, try mixing green beans with a little onion, a few baby halved tomatoes and some vinaigrette. Other variations to try include shrimps cooked in sesame oil and then mixed with cold, lightly cooked sugar-snap peas (they should still have some crunch); crab and avocado mixed with a little (very little) mayonnaise and scooped into tiny white china pots; flageolet beans and ham mixed together with some sliced avocado and dressed with a lemon vinaigrette; and, if you want to be really grand, a lobster salad with an aioli to which you've added some chives. Marks & Spencer often sell dressed lobster in the summer, as well as ready-prepared mayonnaise that you can turn into an aioli by simply mixing in some puréed garlic and, if you like, a little chilli paste.

After that, we usually have fresh berries (mostly strawberries) with some crème fraiche or little French cream cheeses, or tartlets from a patisserie. If you're really pushed for time, both Marks & Spencer and Waitrose often have small individual summer puddings, which make a heavenly end to a meal, particularly if you add some sugar and thick cream. We also take along a great big slab of some splendid English cheese and some oatcakes or flat Italian olive bread and a few dark bitter chocolates.

For glamorous/luxurious ingredients (caviar, acorn-fed Iberian hams, shellfish) check www.efoodies.co.uk.

Special Occasion Picnic

Plenty of other summer events are worth celebrating. I remember making great big vats of coronation chicken (if nicely and carefully done, this makes great summer food) for our daughter's twenty-first birthday, held in May on the lawns of Clare College, Cambridge, which has some of the most beautiful gardens I know. I think I followed that with mounds and mounds of berries served with either coeur à la crème or fromage à la crème, which I make in white ceramic heart-shaped moulds with holes in them – Divertimenti (www.divertimenti.co.uk) sells them.

Coeur à la Crème

You'll need either one big or several smaller heart-shaped moulds, plus some fine muslin for lining them.

2 egg whites
5fl oz/150ml double cream
8oz/225g cottage cheese

½oz/15g caster sugar, vanilla flavoured
thick cream, for serving
bowl of caster sugar, for serving

Whip up the egg whites until stiff. Put the double cream in a blender and whizz until in mounds but not dry. Add the cottage cheese and blend again. Then fold in the vanilla-flavoured caster sugar (I always keep some caster sugar in a jar with a vanilla stick to give it flavour) and beaten egg whites. Line the heart-shaped mould(s) with fine muslin and pour in the mixture. Put the mould(s) on a plate (because the excess fluid will leak out) and transfer to the fridge. Turn out just before serving and pour on some thick cream. Serve with a separate bowl of caster sugar.

You could substitute some French cream cheese (Chambourcy for instance) for the cottage cheese, and sometimes I do half yoghurt and half cottage cheese. What is key is to serve the coeur à la crème absolutely plain – with no decoration whatsoever. Any berries or compotes should be served separately. This pudding is delicious with a glass of soft fruity wine – a Vouvray, for instance.

To decorate the table, crystallised rose petals look divine, sprinkled around the meringues, say, or displayed in bowls. They are not difficult to make, but you have to plan ahead because they take two or three days to dry. After that they will keep if stored in an airtight tin. When roses are in season, gather the petals, wash them carefully and pat dry very gently. Beat an egg white with a pinch of salt and then beat in one teaspoon of water until the mixture is foamy. (If you have collected lots of rose petals, you may need to double up this mixture.) Dip each petal very gently into the egg white mixture, or use a pastry brush to brush it on. Don't coat the petals too heavily. Shake caster sugar evenly on to both sides of the petals and then store them on greaseproof paper and leave to dry.

Luncheon at Home

For a large outdoors picnic-cum-summer luncheon party that involves no travelling on the part of the food, nothing could be nicer to start with than some dishes that used to be served in the seventies and eighties and are now coming back into favour, having acquired an aura of retro chic – jambon persille (jellied ham with parsley) and summer mousses made of cucumber, smoked haddock, eggs or chicken. They're elegant, light and a good balance for a variety of different salads.

The grand set-piece could be a vast aioli – a whole cod or haddock, baked, surrounded by steamed baby vegetables, such as carrots, green beans, artichokes and new potatoes, plus some halved eggs and a golden garlicky mayonnaise made with some wonderfully scented Provençal olive oil. Alternatively, a vitello tonnato, usually the centrepiece of Milanese tables for an Assumption Day dinner (15 August), another summer speciality is a whole rolled loin or topside of veal, thinly sliced when cold and the pieces layered with tunnyfish mayonnaise (see www.deliaonline.com for a detailed recipe).

On these occasions, I've sometimes done a very good lamb dish. Roast the meat slowly and, when it's cooked as you like it, shred it into shards. Make a sauce from a mixture of cream, yoghurt and sour cream, tasting it as you go. Add the lamb shards, masses of mint jelly, lots of fresh mint, some lemon juice, salt and pepper and serve on a bed of nutty wild rice.

As well as these main dishes, great platters of fresh prawns, charcuterie, salads, cheeses and lovely breads go down a treat.

I think piles of meringues look wonderful, and children love them. They can be crushed and scattered over berries with some cream. Another dramatic-looking pudding is whipped cream (make it lighter by adding some low-fat yoghurt and, if you like a slightly tart flavour, some sour cream) with trails of crushed mixed berries streaked through it. Bruise the berries very lightly in a tiny amount of water and sugar first to release the juices. Serve it in a huge glass dish. Chocolate tortes and cheesecakes look terrific on cake-stands as do a pile of profiteroles (they're dead easy to do – good standard cookery books have recipes for them), and brownies and flapjacks always go down well, especially with children.

Jelly and Ice Cream

I have a very soft spot for old-fashioned jellies, delicious ones made with elderflower syrup, water and gelatine poured over soft berries and allowed to set in the fridge. (One packet of Davis gelatine is enough for 1 pint/600ml of liquid.) Marks & Spencer has started selling jellies made from fresh orange juice – an idea easily copied at home and deliciously light and refreshing. Pomegranate jelly (Waitrose sells pomegranate juice) is even more exotic.

It's quite fun, if you're having a big all-generation celebration, to hire an ice-cream van for the day (www.macks-ices.co.uk) or, if you can keep them suitably cold until needed, order some of Minghella's famous ice creams or sorbets (www.minghella.co.uk). Owned by the family of the late film director Anthony Minghella, the company produces some fabulous varieties, and uses no artificial flavours, or cheap sweeteners, such as corn syrup. Unrefined brown sugar is used instead, and quantities are kept as low as possible. So how about gin and pink grapefruit sorbet? Or mint choc chip ice cream? Or absinthe sorbet? Or lemon meringue? Or one from the special low-fat, low-GI range (called La Dolce Vita)? Retailers are listed on the Minghella website.

An Elegant Picnic Tea

Picnic teas are, obviously, less burdensome than lunch or dinner from the point of view of the food. For a traditionally elegant tea, sandwiches matter because you simply can't have a picnic tea without them. Make finger sandwiches of cucumber or smoked salmon or egg and cress. Scones, good-quality jam and clotted cream are also essential, as are a Victoria sponge and some fruit cake. Cupcakes are a modern fad that I fail to 'get', but since others like them it seems churlish not to offer them, and the great thing about them is that you don't have to go far to find them. Alternatively, turn them into fun by enlisting the children's help to bake some.

As for the tea, all the camping shops have small portable burners that you could easily carry in a car and use to boil water in an old-fashioned kettle. So there's no excuse not to have a pot of your favourite tea, even if you are picnicking away from home.

❋❋❋❋❋❋❋❋❋❋❋❋❋❋❋❋❋❋❋❋❋❋❋

NO TIME?

You can pick up perfectly presentable food from the better supermarkets. Marks & Spencer's small quiches are delicious, hams (Waitrose will carve it in front of you off the bone), ready-made salads (choose carefully – some have too much gloop), tomatoes on the vine, good bread and a wide variety of cheeses are good and need little doing to them. Many of the puddings are terrific. Carluccio's will provide ready-made picnics while at the posher end of the spectrum it's hard to better those from Daylesford Organic (www.daylesfordorganic.com).

❋❋❋❋❋❋❋❋❋❋❋❋❋❋❋❋❋❋❋❋❋❋❋

The Barbie

There's a school of thought that says barbecuing is a dastardly un-English invention. Here, for instance, is somebody called Peter Rhodes writing on www.expressandstar.com '. . . barbecues are so dashed foreign and frightfully vulgar. A barbie goes with Hawaiian shorts, baseball caps and all that silly Australian nursery talk about eskies, rellies and tinnies (insulated boxes, relatives and tinned beer). The picnic is essentially English. It goes with floral frocks and big hats, with blazers, white flannels and cravats.' He might have added, 'AND NO COOKING'.

The fact of the matter is that barbecuing has rather taken hold in this country, and although most barbecues are too big and heavy to transport to far-flung picnic sites, the nation's backyards and gardens are awash with the smell of charcoal come the first hint of summer sunshine. Now, according to one Charles Ramseyer, who is a barbecue expert (www.bbq.co.uk), the key thing to note when buying a barbecue is the difference between charcoal and gas. I get the sense that he prefers charcoal ones, particularly for large numbers of people. They take some thirty to forty minutes to get going but, in compensation, retain the authentic flavour of the food. Gas ones fire up as soon as you turn them on. If you're a mad keen barbecue fan, Charles Ramseyer recommends getting one of each!

Barbecues certainly make it easy to cook a fillet of beef or a butterflied leg of lamb (see page 96) – a heavenly dish that should be cooked fast on a seriously hot grill. Certainly, there's not a lot nicer than a home-made hamburger, made from good organic beef, cooked in the open air.

In South Africa, we used to have what we called a 'braai' – an outdoor fire with a makeshift grill – and the simplest barbecue I know is still a bucket with a grill over the top, sold by John Lewis for £15. The Aussies, of course, are the barbie specialists, so it's perhaps no wonder that the Australian Weber barbecues seem to be all the rage at the moment (www.weberbbq.co.uk). There's a nice, light, portable gadget called the Weber Smokey Joe Silver on which you could cook such things as hamburgers, sausages, sweetcorn and chicken legs. As well as various cook books, Weber also produce DVDs demonstrating how to use the barbecue. Their accessories are of good quality and useful, including a basket for grilling vegetables. Weber barbecues can be ordered online, and are also available from Heal's and John Lewis.

Alternatively, there's a small tabletop barbecue grill called the Eva Solo on which you could cook prawns, sausages or marinated chicken (£211 from www.ictc.co.uk).

If you want a big summer celebration and don't have the equipment (not to mention the know-how or the energy), a company called Blistering Barbecues (www.blistering.co.uk) will come and do the lot for you. You can have it as simple or elaborate as you like. They'll do everything from tents to flowers and lighting, and they have ice-cream vans and hot-dog stands as well as the barbecued food; or you can just get them to do the food. They'll do whole spit-roasts or any combination of outdoor cooked food you fancy.

For a really special occasion, a string band playing would be lovely, or a singing act halfway through – maybe one of the guests would be willing to oblige. Although a live band would be fantastic, setting up a music system is probably more realistic – but not too loud if neighbours are likely to be disturbed.

What to Drink

Light summer wines – a Sancerre or Vouvray from France, or crisper white ones from New Zealand or South Africa – are good, and summer is a great time for pink champagne. If your *fête champêtre* is to be extra special, you might consider Laurent-Perrier's splendid Cuvée Rosé Brut. Otherwise, never forget Pimms – the quintessentially summer drink.

For a barbecue, beer or lager is often called for, and there has been something of a resurgence in the popularity of cider in recent times. Julian Temperley has some finely made ciders (www.ciderbrandy.co.uk) and, in particular, his cider brandy has been declared a good rival to Spanish calvados. The Meriadoc Trading Company (www.meriadoc.net) imports delicious cider from Brittany, particularly 'Au Breton Gourmand'. You can find it at Tom's Deli (www.tomsdelilondon.co.uk), Luscious Organic (www.lusciousorganic.co.uk) and Fine Ciders (www.fine ciders.com) for less than £3 a bottle.

Otherwise, I make an ardent plea for lots of splendidly refreshing non-alcoholic alternatives. I love wine and wouldn't want to do without it, but plenty of other liquid is needed just to quench the thirst and for that, it's hard to beat fresh lemonade. It's a good idea to provide water, apple and orange juice as well, especially if children are going to be present.

How to make Pimm's

Traditionally, Pimm's is served in wide-brimmed glasses.

Pimm's No. 1
lemonade
ice
fresh mint leaves
lemons, sliced

cucumber, sliced
ginger beer or ginger ale
strawberries, to garnish

Fill a large jug with ice and pour in the Pimm's and lemonade. Add the ginger beer and stir. (One part Pimm's to three parts lemonade/ginger beer.) Then add the fresh mint leaves, lemon and cucumber slices. Pour into individual glasses as required, adding half a strawberry to garnish.

Home-made Lemonade

From spring onwards, this lemonade was permanently on offer in my parents-in-laws' house, and nothing was nicer than finding a great welcoming jug sitting on the sideboard after a long walk over the Berkshire downs. These quantities make about 1.75 litres/3 pints.

6 organic lemons, unwaxed
5oz/150g sugar
2½ pints/1.5 litres water, boiling

Wash the lemons well, squeeze out the juice and peel the outer zest, taking care to avoid the pith. Put zest and juice in a bowl with the sugar, pour on the boiling water, stir and leave overnight. Check for sweetness, adding more sugar if necessary. You can drink it either on its own or dilute it with water.

MORE NON-ALCOHOLIC DRINKS

Quantities of the ingredients should be adjusted to suit the preferences of your guests, and your own taste:

* Mix freshly squeezed lime juice with ginger beer, add ice, some wedges of fresh lime and fresh mint leaves.
* Mix freshly squeezed lime juice with sparkling lemonade, add ice, some wedges of fresh lime, some angostura bitters and fresh mint leaves.
* Make ice cubes out of cranberry juice – they look divinely pretty. Add them to a variety of drinks, such as lemonade, grapefruit juice and pomegranate juice.
* Frozen raspberries make a lovely drink when whizzed in the blender with another fruit juice (orange, pomegranate, cranberry or plain lemonade) and some ice cubes.
* Peel and deseed a honeydew melon, peel and chop a whole cucumber and squeeze the juice out of some limes. Whizz these ingredients together with a jug of ice cubes, and serve with fresh mint leaves.
* Watermelon – to my mind, the most boring of fruits – makes the basis for a very refreshing drink. Whizz one (peeled and deseeded) in a blender with some freshly squeezed lime juice and grapefruit juice (pink makes it look nice).
* The classic cocktail Sea Breeze contains vodka, but on a very hot day it's just as nice if you make it without. Whizz together three parts cranberry juice to one part grapefruit juice and just add ice and fresh mint leaves.
* A Shirley Temple was devised for, yes, child star Shirley Temple by a bartender in Beverly Hills, California. The original recipe calls for two parts ginger ale to one part orange juice plus between a teaspoon and a tablespoon of grenadine syrup, and it's usually topped with a cherry. These days, the orange juice is often omitted and a twist of lemon peel added together with a thin slice of orange and two ice cubes.

Games

In Victorian times, a *fête champêtre* picnic always involved games and for several very good reasons – they're fun, they burn off energy and they're often memorable. It's not a lot of trouble to take some kind of bat and ball for a game of rounders or cricket, or a football for a kickabout. Badminton racquets and the lightweight shuttlecock are also easy to carry, and a set of boules, comprising eight chrome steel balls, isn't too difficult to bring along. Croquet needs a rather splendid lawn, but if you're holding a *fête champêtre* in your garden, it's worth investing in at least a mini set.

The traditional outdoor games of hide and seek, treasure hunts and grandmother's footsteps can be played by all ages. Heal's (www.heals.co.uk) sells a lightweight colourful hopscotch template-cum-rug for just £15 – good outdoor fun for the kids.

Otherwise, an intricate-sounding Swedish game called Kubb (www.kubbin.com) involves a small set of differently shaped wooden pieces and an elaborate set of instructions – could be something new to add to the mix of games. Also online, a splendid website – grandparents.about.com – has lots of ideas for making picnics more fun. There are more ideas for games to be found on www.thegardengame.co.uk.

If you think it would be fun to have a treasure hunt, you can organise it yourself (and rope in the family), or www.treasure-hunt-people.co.uk are the experts and will give you a top-notch, professionally organised one.

Mrs Beeton's Words of Warning

'Watch carefully not to provide too much of one thing and too little of another; avoid serving plenty of salad and no dressing; two or three legs of lamb and no mint sauce; an abundance of wine and no corkscrew; and such like little mistakes. Given a happy party of young people, bent on enjoyment, these are trifles light as air, which serve rather to increase the fun than diminish it. But, on the other hand, the party may not all be young and merry; it may be very distasteful to some to have to suffer these inconveniences.'

✳ Don't forget the corkscrew.

The Birthday Party

S ome people give birthday parties every year. These annual 'dos' aren't usually big, and tend to evolve into a standard formula that is much looked forward to by friends, becoming a sort of marker as the years go by. Two women friends of mine have taken to inviting small groups of their closest female friends to lunch – often, happily, in very nice restaurants, but it doesn't need to be. It would be just as jolly at home, although obviously more work for them. I presume they celebrate differently with husbands, lovers and children come the evenings.

Others, if their birthdays are at the right time of year, always mark the occasion with a summer lunch 'do', whilst yet others have small dinners with their closest friends. We have one friend who has a house in southwest France and since his birthday is in August, it has become the hot high summer invitation in their part of the world. His wife lays out long tables under the beams of an outside area, overlooking wild fields and woods. The tables look enchanting covered with Provençal cloths and jars full of flowers from the fields. She does simple starters, such as melon with parma ham, and cooks moussaka or shepherd's pie, her husband's favourites. An array of cheeses follows, and puddings from the patisserie, but what really makes an invitation so sought after is the mix of fellow guests – ranging from the local Duc (one of seven families who have been in the area forever and whom it is essential to invite) to old friends from home, new friends in the area and, of course, a couple of essential rakish British parvenus.

There's no formula. Birthday parties are all about suiting them to the person, the place, the weather, the local culture. Jeffrey Archer, in his heyday before he was packed off to sew mailbags, was famous for his annual shepherd's pie and Krug parties – he did it every year and guests would have felt cheated if he'd done something different. It was THE invitation of the season, although I suspect people didn't go for the food half so much as because everybody, but everybody, would be there.

However, proper parties are not for showing off. When I look back at the parties I've enjoyed the most, many of them have had very simple ingredients. The most important, of course, is the people, and if you're anything like most of us, they'll be a mixed bunch – some left over from school or university, some successful, some not, some funny, some charming, some clever, some married to people who are boring or difficult. They are one's friends and that seems important to me. Proper parties are for fun. Not for showing off. They're for friends and family and to introduce people who you hope will like or even love each other. We always hope that sometimes our friends will make new discoveries and fresh avenues will be opened up for them because of the people they meet. Parties celebrate years of friendship and being together, but they do take a bit of work.

MISSING THE POINT

For a successful party, grandeur is a totally optional extra and not by any means the core of the matter. Among the saddest parties ever I always think are Jay Gatsby's, where he seems like an outsider at his own events – he lays on all this splendour but where are his real friends? Every weekend he labours to please a whole lot of people he scarcely knows. You are likely to see groups of friends having more fun down at the pub every day of the week.

'Every Friday five crates of oranges and lemons arrived from a fruiter in New York. Every Monday these same oranges and lemons left his back door in a pyramid of pulpless halves. By seven o'clock the orchestra has arrived. No thin five piece affair, but a whole pit full of oboes and trombones and saxophones and violas and . . .'

The Great Gatsby by F. Scott Fitzgerald

The sort of parties that seem to me pointless are the ones that journalists all too frequently find themselves at, which is where a whole lot of so-called celebs mill around in vulgar frocks and one is supposed to be grateful for simply being in their presence, which isn't to say that some of these semi-work parties aren't sometimes done with great panache and expertise. If hosts take trouble over who sits next to whom, introductions are made and the food and wine are beautifully chosen, they can be very enjoyable. I've had some wonderful experiences at work-related parties. It's just that the best ones, the most memorable ones, are ultimately about personal connections, not merely experiencing an overpowering assault on the senses.

Sitting Down

'm a bit obsessed with seating plans. I think they matter. For a dinner party, I don't think husbands should be put next to wives, best friends next to each other, boyfriends next to girlfriends. We can – and do – talk to each other at home thank you very much. Putting people together who will have some common ground, who will amuse or charm one another, is part of the point of the party.

So, too, is introducing people to each other. Leaving one's friends to mill around (and I've been to plenty of those in my time), particularly those who come alone, isn't what a good host should do. To encourage conversation and connection, I think that having little areas where people can properly sit down makes a lot of difference. It can be done by grouping tables and chairs or hiring huge cushions and putting them in corners. Standing around for hours, particularly now that some of us (ahem) are getting a little older, isn't fun.

٭ Extras like magicians are fun – they go round the tables, giving everybody a chance to see them in action. If you're having your party in a hall you could hire a tribute band (The Rolling Stones, The Beatles, whatever takes your fancy). Blood Red Sky are a U2 tribute band (www.bloodredsky.co.uk).

If you're young and energetic it's quite fun to organise an adventure race of some kind. Guests arrive and are given clues which they have to follow and until they've done one task they don't know what the next one will be. Things like counting how many lamp posts in the road, bringing back five different flowers, you get the idea. The first one to complete wins. It all ends up with some delicious food and drink.

What to Eat?

Well that depends on the party. Cocktail parties (does anybody give them any more – except after weddings?) need good canapés or titbits (call them what you will) to balance out all the booze. They're the hardest thing to provide because they're so fiddly. Some cheese straws and nuts really aren't enough. Posh caterers do brilliant things – fish and chips in miniature newspaper wraps, tiny baked potatoes stuffed with sour cream and caviar, deep-fried prawns with a hint of Asian spice, sushi, morsels of chicken satay, fusion bits and bobs. These are almost impossible to do yourself because of the quantities required – trays need to keep coming at a steady rate – so it's worth knowing that Waitrose and Marks & Spencer both have catering services, and you can order anything from canapés to wedding and birthday cakes. For canapés, for instance, Waitrose offers little mini vegetarian wraps, tiny roulades, smoked salmon blinis, what it calls bread canapés (a selection of foods on rounds of malted bread), cheese straws, bruschetta and much more. I once used this service and found it highly efficient, although gastronomically, it has to be admitted, not cordon blue, but it was a whole lot better than being stressed and not being able to ask friends back to the house. It was also amazingly good value.

I often think that simplicity can be very elegant. I remember a friend's party, given at home in winter time – huge bowls of an amazing fish soup, with accompanying rouille and croutons, lovely bread and cheese and big bowls of shiny apples. Some other friends recently had a party with long trestle tables in an inexpensive marquee in their garden. The food consisted of two huge spit-roasts overseen by their children, one of lamb and one of a sucking pig, accompanied by lots of salads, baked potatoes and couscous (it was Moroccan themed). Puddings were bowls of berries and an array of amazing cakes. Entertainment was provided by a quartet of barbershop singers (www.singbarbershop.com), who were enchanting. Later, there was music and dancing. It was, all in all, a winner.

Some of the best parties are when everybody brings a dish – it's fun, relatively trouble-free, and no one person has to bear all the cost. Theme it from a food point of view so that the dishes work together. For example, for an Italian party, some could do the anti-pasti, some the pastas, some the main courses, some could bring cheeses and others fruit or tiramisu. Other styles that come to mind are middle Eastern (lots of meze), Greek (stuffed vine leaves, lamb, Greek salad), Mexican, Scandinavian and English (so back in vogue just now).

THEMED PARTIES

There's no doubt that themes do encourage people to let their hair down more, and to be more colourful in what they wear. I find generalised fancy dress rather daunting but if there is a theme, it's easier to come up with something jolly. The scope is endless – Arabian Nights, Heaven and Hell, Roaring Twenties, James Bond, Bollywood, Rock 'n' Roll – all offering the opportunity to have a great deal of fun. Think of the variety of great music. Austerity themes can be based on war-time, the jazz age or prohibition (the party venue being the speakeasy, of course). If you've exhausted your supply of themes, have a look at www.amazingpartythemes.com for a vast list of ideas. It also offers the props to bring the theme alive for those who aren't good at improvising, as well as all manner of party essentials.

Some of my young friends who party at the drop of the chapeau seem to have a lot of fun with the simplest of dishes. They don't fuss. They just do great big vats of spaghetti Bolognese, huge lasagnes or masses of bangers and mash – beware of cheap bangers, though, filled with unmentionable parts and too much fat (see box for where to get decent sausages). Now that you can get fantastic patisserie from good delicatessens, puddings are dead easy. My favourite is the pistachio cake from Ottolenghi's (www.ottolenghi.co.uk) – I suggest putting it on a cake-stand to make it look pretty and, once tasted, you're a fan forever. A huge platter of brownies usually goes down well, and my standby is always big bowls of fruit of the season.

What to Drink?

Mojitos, Cosmopolitans and Sea Breezes seem to be all the rage, but I think they're tricky to manage unless you decide to stick to one and so use just a few ingredients. Vodka-based cocktails seem to give less of a hangover, or you could pour a good slug of iced vodka over more crushed ice

GREAT SAUSAGES

If you have a good local butcher, he may well make terrific sausages. Otherwise, always check the meat and fat content on the packet – obviously the more meat and the lower the fat the better. The great charm of sausages is that they are dead easy to cook. Just bung them in an oven.

1. The Essex Pig Company's Cambridge sausage is made from 93 per cent meat and is flavoured with nutmeg and ginger. They sell other varieties, too. (www.essexpigcompany.com)

2. Dorset-based Denay Farms has a 100 per cent meat sausage made from pork and dry cured bacon. It's quite German in style – which is perhaps why I like it – and it isn't fatty at all. (www.denhay.co.uk)

3. Richard Woodall's Waberthwaite Cumberland sausage, made from an old family recipe, is 95 per cent meat. (www.richardwoodall.co.uk)

4. Duchy Originals has an old-fashioned pork sausage with herbs – 85 per cent pork with no flavour enhancers or GM ingredients. Find them in Waitrose.

5. Waitrose sell their own organic pork chipolatas, which children love but are often hard to track down. (www.waitrose.com)

6. I. Camisa & Son, an Italian deli in London's Soho, sells its own small spicy sausages, which are something different – it's the fennel that does it. (www.camisa.co.uk)

7. At the Ginger Pig, they make sausages from named breeds –
Gloucester Old Spot, Berkshire and Tamworth pigs – which they
raise organically themselves. The Toulouse sausage is perfect for
cassoulets. (www.thegingerpig.co.uk)

8. Porkinson's sausages, so-called because they were developed by
the late photographer, Norman Parkinson. The Porkinson sausage
came out top in a Heston Blumenthal taste-test. Find them at
Waitrose, Morrisons, Asda and Ocado. (www.porkinson.co.uk)

9. You don't have to have British bangers – I love German and
Polish sausages. Here are some sources:
   * *The German Deli* (www.germandeli.co.uk) *has a big selection,
   including smoked and dried, as well as salamis.*
   * *Kurz & Lang* (www.kurzandlang.com) *sells home-made
   German sausages, such as bratwurst.*
   * *Topolski* (www.topolski.co.uk) *sells authentic Polish sausages,
   which make a fantastic addition to a beef casserole, turning it
   into something more like a goulash.*

TO GO WITH SAUSAGES

If you're up for it, make a salsa to go with the bangers, or
roast baby tomatoes very slowly on the vine, and serve with
either baked potatoes or, better still, lots of fabulous mashed
potato – the secret is to put the mash through a potato ricer.
For a change, mash the potatoes with olive oil – I love the
olivey flavour better than butter and milk. A mustardy or
horseradish mash are other options.

and lots of pink pomegranate seeds – looks fabulous, tastes good and is particularly refreshing in the summer. (Visit www.in-the-spirit.co.uk/cocktails for loads of cocktail recipes, and see pages 29–32.)

Even if I'm not offering cocktails, I like to have gin, vodka and a single malt or fine blended whisky available, as well as some chilled white and a decent red wine. Bottles and cans of lager should be well chilled – offer them in some sort of large tub or container filled with ice (from www.elegantice.co.uk) and make sure supplies are constantly replenished. If it's summer, you could have big jugs of Pimm's; if it's winter, mulled wine.

✳ If the party is going on all night, you'll need to lay on plenty of non-alcoholic drinks (see pages 273 and 274) as well as masses of water.

Champagne and Champagne Cocktails

Good-quality champagne makes everyone feel special (see page 412), but Prosecco and some sparkling white wines are excellent, and cheaper. Caterers say that you'll need something like three-quarters of a bottle per person. Buck's Fizz is popular – the orange juice must be really fresh, and remember to add it just before serving. Don't keep ready prepared jugs of Buck's Fizz standing around. Likewise, Bellinis (champagne with peach juice) and Kir Royale (champagne with a little cassis) shouldn't be prepared in advance.

Smooth Mixers

If you're going to offer variety, you really need somebody to run the bar. Friends are often willing to help, taking it in turns, but if the party is to be rather more formal, professional help may be the answer.

* For professional bartenders, try www.shaker-events.co.uk.

* AquaDiablo take their portable modular bar (you order the number of modules you need, depending upon the size of the party) all over the country. They charge £250 per module (+ delivery), £40 an hour for skilled bartenders and £30 per hour for cocktail bartenders (minimum of four hours) and the cocktails (for complicated licensing reasons) are charged at cost.

* www.partyparties.co.uk will also set up a bar.

Where to Hold the Party?

If your house isn't big enough for a real knees-up to celebrate in style, think in terms of hiring another space. Finding the right one takes time, and prices vary hugely. Undoubtedly, some venues are more magical than others (I can think of castles and some of the wonderful old halls in various cities, not to mention National Trust properties throughout the country) but these do tend to cost more. Church and community halls, or rooms above pubs, are probably the cheapest, and they can be decorated and jollied up quite easily. If you have children, rope them in to help. Banners, ribbons, balloons and streamers all help to create atmosphere. Check the lighting arrangements – a bright light the whole time is to be avoided if possible and a dimmer switch is a must. You probably won't be allowed to have candles but some splendidly gaudy candelabras may be a possibility (£12 each at Argos). Other props can be hired from www.thepartyhire company.co.uk, www.londonlaunch.com or www.partypop.com.

✳ Always remember that party magic doesn't just last for one night – it lingers on in memories. Tina Brown, for instance, got the late Robert Isabell, one of New York's smartest florists and party organisers, to do her launch for *Talk* magazine. He created magic, she wrote on her web-site, on Ellis Island, where there was no electricity, so it was a candle- and lantern-lit night-time picnic. Each guest was given a different-coloured tablecloth to spread out on the grass and a small picnic box loaded with delicious pâtés and delicacies and small bottles of wines. Nobody who was there ever forgot it.

Getting Help

If you can afford to hand everything over to a caterer or party planner, good for you. Mostly, they do it brilliantly (oh, the grandeur and drama of some of the schemes) but the cost will amaze you. There are subtle ways of economising. Instead of canapés and a three-course menu, you could choose canapés with the drinks and a two-course menu – in other words the canapés become the first course. Instead of fancy ingredients, go for locally sourced, seasonal ingredients.

However, a more realistic idea is to hire what you have to and do as much as you can yourself, or with the help of friends. For example, if you have the space, hire a marquee or gazebo (see page 243) and the tables and chairs, and rope in friends and family to do, say, the flowers and the puddings.

ESSENTIAL FLOWERS

I'm always banging on about Nine Elms market in London (www.newcoventgardenmarket.com) simply because it is so wonderful, but there are markets all over the country where flowers can be bought less expensively than in posh florist's shops. Seasonal flowers in simple jars are always a good idea, but it's also fun to make your arrangements as dramatic as possible by putting tall stems and branches in oversized containers. Another thing I find myself repeating is how wonderful fruit and vegetables are as decoration – bowls of apples in winter, aubergines, cabbages, artichokes, lemons, all are beautiful.

A Picnic Party

A young friend of mine recently organised a summer picnic for her birthday. She sent an email of the famous Lee Miller photograph of Man Ray and friends on a picnic and invited people to meet her between 2 and 5 p.m. under the beech tree in Hyde Park below the stone hut down from the Serpentine

Gallery. Everybody was asked to bring their favourite picnic food or drink and a wow time was had by all. If it had rained, they could have cowered under the bridge, but she had umbrellas and a waterproof-backed rug in case. The food contributions consisted of quiches from Marks & Spencer (the nicest ones were still warm from the ovens), loads of sausages, strawberries, chocolates, scones and crisps, and my young friend greeted them all with a socking great Martini. Lovely! (See pages 237–276 for more picnic ideas.)

THE CHARITY PARTY

I read about a wife who wanted to give her husband a terrific 'do' for his fortieth but was strapped for cash so she organised a party in aid of one of their favourite charities. All the guests were asked to make a donation to the charity instead of bringing a present and the entertainers agreed to give their services free. The wife merely provided the food, drink and decorations. What a result.

A Surprise Party

The very notion fills me with terror (unless you're very high maintenance, most of us need a bit of notice if we're going to look our best), but there's no doubt some surprise parties have been spectacularly successful. You can always, of course, say there's going to be a small celebration so that the day is booked, the hair is done, the dress is chosen and only at the last minute is the full scale of the production revealed. Some people like the idea of a 'this is your life' party, where anybody who has ever meant anything in the life of the birthday boy or girl is rounded up (so organisation needs to start a long way in advance) and pictures from the past are deployed around the room. Getting Personal can create a book to celebrate the event (www.gettingpersonal.co.uk).

Children's Parties

These days, the competitiveness of children's parties has got completely out of hand, what with the need for entertainment, goody bags and unimaginable treats. The stress, worry and expense have taken over from the pleasure. I read recently that, before the recession set in, many a middle-class parent was somehow bullied into spending ridiculous sums on their offspring's birthday 'dos'. Party planners would urge them on with chances for child guests to record their own pop song, or they'd have 'tank' parties where children could drive military tanks. Seats in directors' boxes at top football matches, or extravagantly themed parties with karaoke, personal trainers to organise the games and heaven knows what were all the rage.

In America, a campaign group called Birthdays Without Pressure (www.birthdayswithoutpressure.org) has been formed. On their website you'll find some mind-boggling stories. Saddest of all was the eleven-year-old's party for which none of the invited guests turned up, and there are astonishing examples not just of how spoiled some children are but what sort of parents they have. One mother, it seems, stipulated on the invitation that all presents for her child had to cost $35 or more – the year before some presents had cost as little as $10 and this hadn't covered her outlay! Now I don't think we've reached that stage here in the UK, but in some circles children's expectations are abominably high and their attitudes far too world-weary.

Anyway, enough. Children's parties do need planning and thought but unless you're a hard-pressed cardiothoracic surgeon, a cabinet minister, an over-worked lawyer or one of the new hedge-fund managers left, you don't have to have professional party planners, nor do you have to have oceans of dosh. In my day, in long ago South Africa, we did do themes – I remember my mother hand-sewing a fairy dress for me and being thrilled to bits – but the main fun was the food (jellies, ice creams, meringues, Marie biscuits decorated with hundreds and thousands, chocolate cake, milkshakes) and the games. We tore around, climbing trees, riding bikes, playing hopscotch, pass the parcel, grandmother's footsteps, hide and seek and having treasure hunts. My mother was effectively on her own and very hard up, but she got it together on a shoestring. Of course, times were different then, but the principle is much the same.

✳ In Gloucestershire, a mother and daughter have got together to help with children's parties – Pretoria Woods makes divine cakes (ring her on 07971352571) whilst her daughter Elise Healey runs a company called Funky Monkey (07977925346) and she'll organise themed parties (she did a Tin-Tin one for a young grandson of mine recently), treasure hunts and generally come up with enterprising ideas.

Themes

A theme gives shape to the party and allows you to have some fun. For girls, there are ballerina parties, fairy parties and butterfly parties. For boys, there are pirates and soldiers, Harry Potter and spies.

✳ Websites to visit for themed children's party ideas are www.birthdaypartyideas.com, www.amazingmoms.com and www.thepodcompany.co.uk (which also has lots of nice little presents, plus balloons, invitations and gift tags.)

Everything from the invitations and fancy dress to the games and food can reflect the theme. Invitations are relatively easy – football-shaped for football parties, pink and glittery for fairy parties and so on. Children often love to help making them.

As for the costume, some parents are creative enough, and good enough at sewing, for this not to be a problem. If you're any good at improvising, give it a go. Otherwise, plenty of shops sell costumes these days, and kids generally love dressing up, so they'll probably want to wear them all the time. Online sources include www.sillyjokes.co.uk (masses of choice at under £10, including pirates, fairies, medieval lords and ladies, kings and queens), www.joke.co.uk and www.wonderlandparty.co.uk. eBay is also worth a try.

One young mother I know who chose butterflies as a theme asked the children to come in costume (not too stressful for the parents, since a pair of wings were enough). She made butterfly-shaped biscuits, decorated with hundreds and thousands, coloured icing and chocolate splinters. All the big supermarkets, such as Tesco and Sainsbury's, sell the wherewithal and she had a lot of fun doing the cooking with her daughter before the event. One of the games was a butterfly-themed true or false quiz, and she put little books on butterflies in the goody bags. She involved her daughter in the planning, asking her to think about how to give her guests a good time, and whom they might like to sit with or play with. Her daughter made the place names, and had to greet each guest and be on the door to say goodbye.

For small children, you could organise a picnic on a theme – *Wind in the Willows* or *The Teddy Bears Picnic*. Small hampers are available, specially geared for children. I recently saw one sporting images from Beatrix Potter (www.beatrixpotteremporium.com).

✳ Party games and quizzes can be devised at home – plenty of books are available to help, or check www.kids-party.com for lots of ideas. In my experience, children love the old-fashioned games – pass the parcel, hide and seek, what's the time Mr Wolf? Football (if it's not raining) and treasure hunts, either indoors or out, are also popular.

Entertainers

If you're having large numbers of children (sometimes you just have to have the whole class), hiring an entertainer may be worthwhile. Word of mouth is usually the best source, although be aware that some with bizarrely high reputations turn out to be duds. I have to say that one of the best children's parties my son arranged was when one of his friends came round dressed as Long John Silver (it was a pirate party) and enthralled my grandson and his friends with tales of the skull and crossbones. If you don't have a handy story-telling friend, then someone to help organise the children into teams and run a series of games – jumping, running, tag, ball games – would be great. Otherwise, you could have somebody in just to do, say, face-painting or some magic tricks.

MAGGIE AND ROSE

Rose Astor has set up a private members club, Maggie and Rose (www.maggieandrose.co.uk), for families, and will organise the whole thing from start to finish, but it's not cheap with prices starting at about £300. Members don't have to buy the whole package, though, and could opt for one or two things only – just the face-painter, for instance. Some of her ideas are brilliant. She will organise animal parties, where children can hold an owl, count how many legs a centipede has or stroke a chinchilla. She offers a cheflets cooking school, where the children make their own pizzas, cinema viewings, musical sing-songs, a magic party and a disco. There's even a 'create your own masterpiece' party – choose from Dotty Damien, Dinky Degas, Very Very Van Gogh and Monster Mania Friedman.

Days Out

A trip to a bowling alley is not difficult to arrange, or for the more adventurous and energetic you could book a dry ski slope, organise trampolining or doughnutting (children sit in rubber rings and race each other down a slope), or climbing sessions on a climbing wall at a local sports centre. If they're interested in birds or animals, visiting a bird sanctuary and an experience with a professional falconer would be terrific.

For boys who want some real derring-do, www.laser-mission.co.uk and www.skirmish.co.uk organise days to be spent in the woods in make-believe combat – defending the Alamo, for one. There are other days called Ambush and Bridge Siege. Girls tend to prefer craft sessions – plate painting, baking cakes or pizza, learning how to press flowers. You could also think about packing the party food in lunch-boxes and taking them off on a picnic.

GOODY BAGS

These, it seems, have got out of hand. Many parents say their children come home with too much junk. Everybody seems agreed that it is much better to find one small but really nice present – a puzzle, a book, some seeds to grow cress or flowers. Playdoh, a little gardening set, a flower press are other options. Add a piece of the birthday cake or a cupcake – as a party activity, you could get each child to ice their own cupcake. Hawkin's Bazaar (www.hawkin.com) is a good source of interesting puzzles and games.

Kids' Party Gear

You could use pretty plastic picnic ware, such as the
Graham & Green (www.grahamandgreen.co.uk) acrylic
range (see page 254) – plates cost about £8 each, tumblers
£4.95. They come in gorgeous colours, shouldn't break and
can be brought out for picnics, parties and any other
suitable occasions. Argos, Marks & Spencer and John
Lewis all have excellent acrylic glasses and plates, or you
could just buy the paper varieties (saves the washing-up
but is a bit wasteful).

Butterflies & Dragons (www.butterfliesanddragons.co.uk)
has a printed catalogue as well as an online shop that sells
some cute children's party gear as well as little presents.
There is, for instance, a wooden picnic set, shaped like a
basket, which has enough kit for two children (£34.99). They
also have a kit for making cards based on horsey themes, and
trinket boxes shaped like cupcakes, which would make a
sweet goody bag present (£4.99 each).

Famille Summerbelle (www.famillesummerbelle.com) is
a good source of decorative bits and bobs to jolly up the
house – among other things it sells brightly coloured paper
banners, each one just over 8ft/2.5 metres long, for £20
for a sheet. For other party ideas and supplies, go to
www.partybox.co.uk.

Food

For children's parties, the food doesn't have to be elaborate.
When I was a child, certain treats were off the menu in day-

to-day life and so when it came to party time, they were
extra special. My own birthday treat – although not on the
same day as the party, was a double ice-cream sundae at the
local ice-cream house. Of course, they were usually sugar-
laden but, once a year, does it matter?

I think traditional children's party food is best – ice cream
(Hill Station, Ben & Jerry's, Green & Black's), jellies,
sausages, hamburgers, hot dogs, crisps and sandwiches filled
with egg and cress, peanut butter or Marmite. Nigella
Lawson has a brilliant tip for combining Marmite and
softened butter so that it becomes a single spread that cuts
down time and effort. It's fun to relate the sandwiches to the
theme, if you can. For instance, for a teddy bears party, have
classical bear favourites, such as honey, banana and
marmalade. Popcorn and cheese straws, as well as dips, such
as hummus and taramasalata, with fresh carrot and celery
sticks also go down well.

For jellies, either make them from commercial jelly
packets, or use fresh orange, apple or cranberry juice or
elderflower cordial, which is heaven, with gelatine – 1oz/25g
of gelatine to 1 pint/600ml of liquid. You could set fruits in
the jelly, according to the season. As a child I used to love
a jelly my mother made with chopped-up, cooked and
puréed prunes, but prunes seem to have become rather
unpopular these days. Serve with cream or ice cream.
Lakeland (www.lakeland.co.uk) sells mini shaped moulds
for making individual jellies or cakes. A tray of ice cream
cones always goes down a treat.

Birthday Cake

This is a must. You don't have to make them in elaborate shapes – just bake or buy a Victoria sponge (see page 318) and decorate it according to the theme, icing it if necessary. If you want to make it look like a fort, a ship, an aeroplane or whatever, Lakeland has moulds to help you. You can put knights on top, for instance, or ice it in pink and add fairies.

＊ For birthday cake suggestions, visit www.marthastewart.com and www.familyfun.go.com. Jane Asher (www.jane-asher.co.uk) has lots of recipes and ideas – it's easy to copy her teddy-bear cake icing, her heart shapes and her parcels.

Marks & Spencer and Waitrose, as well as many local bakers, offer to make birthday cakes to order in a lot of standard shapes – trains, buses, boats and so on – and you can order a ready-made cake from many patisseries.

When I was child in South Africa, we children used often to make a chocolate cake that needed no cooking and was delicious. We melted some chocolate – cooking chocolate, or a bar of dark or milk chocolate – in a bowl placed over some simmering hot water. Then we'd smash Marie biscuits with a rolling pin – digestives would do – mix the chocolate and the smashed biscuits together with some raisins or nuts, press the mixture into a cake tin, lightly greased, and put it into the fridge to chill. We loved it.

✳ At TK Maxx you can buy a machine that dispenses jelly beans (£14.99), and huge jars of old-fashioned sweets, such as mint humbugs and vanilla creams, for very small sums. Marks & Spencer has also started selling old-fashioned sweets.

Ice-cream Birthday Cake

Choose a filling that doesn't freeze rock hard, such as a mousse or soufflé, and tidy up the assembled cake when it is fairly frozen. In fact, I never ice the cake, and just shake icing sugar over the top and tie a bow around it.

This serves about 20 children, depending on how greedy they are!

For the cake:
4 eggs
4oz/100g caster sugar
3oz/75g plain flour
1 teaspoon baking powder
Pinch of salt

For the filling:
1¾ pints/1 litre iced raspberry soufflé (see page 305)

To make the sponge layers, beat the eggs until they are very pale and thick. Still beating, gradually add the sugar and continue beating until the whisk leaves a trail. Sift together the flour, baking powder and salt and fold them quickly and lightly into the egg mixture. Pour the mixture into a loose-bottomed 10in/25cm square cake tin, lined with non-stick baking parchment. Bake the cake in a preheated moderately hot oven (400°F/200°C/gas mark 6) for about 15 minutes, or until it is lightly browned on top.

Remove the cake from the oven and cool for a minute or two before turning out on to a wire rack. Peel off the paper and leave the cake to cool. When it is quite cold, split it carefully into two layers, using a serrated-edged knife.

To assemble the cake, place the base sponge layer on a square cake base or plate and spread it evenly with the softened raspberry soufflé mixture. Top with the second sponge layer, cover and freeze until firm. When the cake is firm, neaten the sides with a long straight knife dipped in water.

Soften the cake in the fridge for about an hour before serving.

Iced Rasperry Soufflé

12oz/350g raspberries (fresh or frozen)
6oz/175g granulated sugar
2 egg whites
2oz/50g icing sugar
½ pint/300ml double whipping cream
2 tablespoons iced water

Purée the raspberries through a fine sieve, or process quickly in a blender and strain. Add the granulated sugar and refrigerate the purée for about 2 hours. Whisk the egg whites until foamy, add the icing sugar and continue beating until the meringue holds stiff peaks. Whip the cream with the iced water until it forms soft peaks. Combine the chilled raspberry purée, meringue and whipped cream and beat them lightly together. Freeze in one large dish, or in individual ramekins or glasses, without further beating.

✳ Have a drink and some sandwiches ready to offer the long-suffering parents doing the delivering and collecting, not to mention those helping, who could probably do with something cold and alcoholic – champagne is nice, as well as tea, coffee and soft drinks for the drivers.

Flapjacks

3oz/75g butter
3oz/75g brown sugar
1tbsp golden syrup
6oz/175g porridge oats

Put the butter, sugar and golden syrup into a saucepan and stir until the butter and sugar have melted. Add the porridge oats and stir until well mixed. Press into a well-greased tin, put in a moderate oven (350°F/180°C/gas mark 4) and bake for 25 minutes until golden brown. Cut into slices while still warm.

✳ Finally, don't forget that thank-you letters should always be written – the child who gives the party has to write and thank for the presents and the guests have to thank for the party. Start them young.

The Funeral
or Memorial Service

Show me the manner in which a nation or a community cares for its dead and I will measure with mathematical exactness the tender sympathies of its people, their respect for the law of the land and their loyalty to high ideals. Gladstone

Funerals and memorial services are really for the living, for those left behind, designed to help them come to terms with the loss of somebody they cared about. So although it may seem odd to include these occasions in a book called *Celebrate*, I think it entirely apt. Every life, even a short one, is a blessing and there is good reason to mark the passing of each one, whether family, close friend or acquaintance, with a form of thanks – and therefore celebration – for the contribution he or she made to our lives and the lives of others.

Ever since time began people have felt the need to mark death with some meaningful ritual. My father, who was in a Japanese prisoner-of-war camp in the Far East during the Second World War, always said that when they weren't able to have proper burial rites after the death of a comrade, it left the camp feeling even more mournful and depressed than ever. Something in the human psyche knows that death is the last great rite of passage and that it deserves due ceremony and a proper framework if the spirits of those remaining are to be healed.

Most societies have established rituals for burials, whether based on religious conviction or not, and the bereaved maybe find some comfort in carrying on these traditions. The British way of death is usually an understated, modest affair. The typical American burial, so brilliantly skewered by Jessica Mitford in *The American Way of Death* is, happily, not how things are done in our blessed isles. Here we have not succumbed to the commercial pressures that seem to have invaded vast swathes of suburban America, where even the language has become deformed with dreadful euphemisms, such as 'post-death care services' and 'slumber parlours' and 'Memorial Gardens of Eternal Peace', and where the whole ghastly notion of 'gracious living' has been, as Mitford put it, 'transformed as in a nightmare into the trappings of Gracious Dying'. I daresay the British funeral trade is not without some deficiencies of its own but it is still marvellously old-fashioned – just as the British public likes it. In most surveys on the matter of funerals it emerges that almost everybody wants a simple, dignified plain service – and they certainly do not want their family locked into debt over it.

Grand state funerals are another matter – nobody who saw it will ever forget the marvellous solemnity that surrounded the funeral of Winston Churchill nor the weeping and wailing that attended that of the Princess of Wales. East End funerals used to resemble something out of the movies with horse-drawn hearses, flowers and all the mourners wearing elaborate dress, often with top hats. Irish funerals are traditionally very raucous affairs with the singing of songs, lots of talking, crying and drinking. Usually, though, the Brits do things in a more restrained way. Open caskets, for one thing, are not the British way. As Jessica Mitford put it, American funeral directors often say 'England is about fifty years behind us,' which the American funeral directors clearly think is a bad thing but those of us who live in England's green and pleasant land think is something for which daily thanks are due.

Practical Considerations

LOCATION: it seems to me the proper place for the funerals of Anglicans and Catholics is in a church and not in the chapel of a crematorium. A simple service of committal can be conducted there afterwards, if the deceased is to be cremated rather than buried. Country funerals in village churches are often extraordinarily moving because the person who has died has usually been known to most of the local population for many years. The simplicity is the point and the coffin is usually carried by relatives and friends while others line the way to the church door.

ON THE COFFIN: I like the habit of putting something meaningful on top of the coffin – a favourite hat, pipe or some other emblem of the person who has died. In the case of the broadcaster, wit and raconteur Ned Sherrin, it was his famous Gladstone bag. The point is that a funeral must somehow have a real connection with the person. It marks the end of a life and every life is very particular. The ceremony should manage to allow scope for the expression of pain and sorrow while acknowledging that communal grief offers comfort and a sense of hope.

✳ Respect is essential. I remember that when we passed through the city of Oxford with my brother's hearse about twenty-five years ago, old men stopped and doffed their hats until it had gone by.

HOW MANY PEOPLE: how big or small the funeral is to be depends on many things. If there is to be a memorial service, for instance, the funeral is often small. Funeral notices may say 'family only', which makes it immediately clear that it is to be a private affair, but sometimes I have been unsure whether to attend or not – would it be intruding too much on private grief? Is one a close enough friend? If all who feel they want to attend are welcome to do so, I think it is helpful to let it be known.

WHEN: on the question of timing, Ned Sherrin in *Final Curtains*, a compilation of his brilliant reviews of 'Top-drawer Memorial Services', states a clear preference for what he calls 'the good old noon-and-on-to-lunch-and-reminiscence' over the newly fashionable time of three o'clock. Although he is referring to memorial services, I guess he'd have taken the same view of funerals. I don't think it matters much. Often it depends upon how far people have to come, and on the arrangements for taking the coffin from the church to the burial ground or crematorium.

THE SERVICE: this is what matters most and the best services reflect something of the life that has been lived. Hymns and readings should be chosen with that in mind. It's good, I think, to have some members of the family or friends give readings. These can be anything so long as they're relevant – a passage from a book or a poem, for instance. If appropriate, the wider family can be involved in discussions about the form the funeral should take and what hymns and readings to include – this prevents hurt feelings and gives a wider trawl for imaginative suggestions.

If you haven't had to choose music, readings and hymns before, the person who is going to conduct the service can be very helpful, and your local library or bookshop can turn up splendid anthologies on the subject. A little fun can be alowed – if it seems appropriate. I well remember going to the funeral of a distinctly non-religious very bibulous but much-loved journalist, and his widow had asked for 'The Night They Invented Champagne' to be played. It was absolutely perfect.

The night they invented champagne
It's plain as it can be
They thought of you and me
The night they invented champagne
They absolutely knew
that all we'd want to do
Is fly to the sky on champagne
And shout to everyone in sight
That since the world began
no woman or a man
has ever been as happy as we are tonight!
Lyrics by Alan Jay Lerner

SOURCES OF ADVICE

The Consumers' Association (or Which?) has a booklet called *What To Do When Someone Dies*, which is eminently useful on an entirely practical level. Most people choose a funeral director with premises nearby, and whichever one you select, you can be sure you will be treated sympathetically. As professionals, funeral directors know the ropes. Just be as clear as you can about what you want before going to see them, and don't allow yourself to be sold any memorial caskets or elaborate coffins if you don't want them. Here are some websites that give independent advice on how to manage a funeral:

* www.consumerdirect.gov.uk
* www.oft.gov.uk (the Office of Fair Trading)
* www.naturaldeath.org.uk gives advice for those who don't want a religious service, or who want an environmentally friendly funeral.

The grave's a fine and private place but none, I think, do there embrace. Andrew Marvell

What to Wear

In earlier times, complex sumptuary rules dictated the form that widows' weeds should take, and the appropriate dress for mourning. In rural areas of Mexico, Portugal, Spain, Italy and Greece many widows still wear black for the rest of their lives. These days, in modern urban societies there are few rules. Black, of course, can look awfully elegant. Think of Jackie Kennedy, so palely, poignantly beautiful. Amid all the brouhaha surrounding the Michael Jackson obsequies, his sisters Janet Jackson with her loosely belted black dress, pearls and chic beret, and La Toya with her sharply waisted suit and dramatic black hat, stood out in the sea of vulgarity. For those close to the person who died, black somehow feels the proper colour to wear, and for the rest of the mourners sombre clothing seems to match the mood of the moment, but these days there are few constraints. Hats, too, are optional but can be very fetching.

FUNEREAL WHITE

In medieval Europe, white was the colour of royal mourning and the Spanish-born Queen Fabiola of Belgium wore white at the funeral of King Baudoin. When Queen Elizabeth, the late Queen Mother, had to make a state visit to France while still in mourning for the death of her mother, Norman Hartnell made her a fantastic white wardrobe, which created something of a sensation. The black-and-white costumes that Cecil Beaton designed for the Royal Ascot scene in 'My Fair Lady' were inspired by the 'Black Ascot' of 1910, when the court was in mourning for the death of Edward VII.

Flowers

F uneral flowers, today almost *de rigueur*, did not make an appearance until the middle of the nineteenth century in America or England and then only in the teeth of great opposition from the clergy. I think the simplest flowers are the best. Those picked from your own garden have more meaning than any stiff and formal arrangement from a posh florist. For my brother's funeral we all made our own posies and they seemed utterly appropriate for his service in the wonderful but simple little church of Binsey. One of the most poignant sights at Princess Diana's funeral was the utterly simple yet beautiful posy of white flowers from her sons, addressed simply to 'Mummy'. Flowers contorted into teddy-bears, cushions, top hats and all the other weird creations some florists dream up seem to me just plain vulgar.

These days many people ask for family flowers only, regarding a sea of flowers that have to be left behind in the church or at the crematorium as rather wasteful. The idea of asking for contributions to a named charity instead makes utter sense to me. One has only to remember the floral deluge that followed Princess Diana's death to see why it makes sense, and it's interesting to note that the Kennedy family specifically asked for no flowers at the funeral of JFK.

When it comes to what flowers to choose, white is the conventional colour of mourning – lilies, roses and any other white flowers always look ineffably poignant and elegant – but really it's a matter of personal choice. Beside his

Gladstone bag, Ned Sherrin's coffin carried 55lb/25 kilos of John Carter's rich-red flowers. Many people like to mix some red in with the white. The top florists understand instinctively what is appropriate – John Carter, Rob van Helden, Robbie Honey, McQueen's would all give you something wonderful but won't be cheap.

Afterwards

That wonderful South Africa/Canadian writer Margaret Visser points out in her scholarly trawl through the historical traditions of eating, *The Rituals of Dinner*, that 'Full dress celebrations of coming together, of marking transitions and recollections, almost always require food, with all the ritual politeness implied in dining . . . We eat whenever life becomes dramatic: at weddings, birthdays, funerals, at parting and at welcoming home, or at any moment which a group decides is worthy of remark. Festivals and feasts are solemn or holy days; they are so regularly celebrated by people meeting for meals that "having a feast" has actually come to mean "eating a lot".'

Traditions clearly vary all around the world. I well remember the passage in Frank McCourt's *Angela's Ashes* where the author's small brother dies and his father promises 'coal for the fire. Rashers. Eggs and a tea for a celebration of Oliver's life' but instead took his week's dole money to the pub.

No matter the time of day, what most people want after a funeral is a cup of tea or a stiff drink. Inviting those who have come to share in the service back to the house is the nicest and most conventional thing to do, but not necessarily the most practical. A hall, hotel or pub somewhere nearby and convenient is the next best thing. Whether it's lunchtime or teatime, there's no need to do it grandly – some light buffet food, such as hot sausages, canapés and sandwiches, is quite enough. If you think people might like something a little more substantial, you could buy some little quiches from our old friends Marks & Spencer or Waitrose, but it really isn't necessary. Nobody's in the mood for a chic affair. If it's teatime, scones, shortbread and a Victoria sponge would probably go down well.

To drink, wine, whisky and gin and maybe some beer, are all that's required, as well as tea and coffee. There's something wonderfully reassuring about tea. I like ordinary builder's tea, but others have more delicate palates, so get in a selection. An amazing variety is available from Postcard Teas (www.postcardteas.com, see page 145, will send you on an exploratory journey of discovery. If you're in London it's worth going to the shop at 9 Dering Street, where there are tastings and tea-related events) while Pukka Teas (www.pukkaherbs.com) do the best ginger teabags I know as well as many other herb-based teas.

Victoria Sponge

What could be more comforting? You can make the cake more easily with margarine but why? Butter is so much nicer.

6oz/175g butter
6oz/175g caster sugar
3 eggs, beaten

6oz/175g self-raising flour
vanilla essence, few drops
4 tbsp raspberry jam
1 pint/600ml double cream, whipped
icing sugar to dust

Lightly grease and line two 20cm/8in cake tins. Cream the butter and sugar together until the mixture is light and fluffy. Add the beaten eggs a little at a time. When the eggs have been thoroughly mixed in, gradually sift the flour into the mixture, and add the vanilla essence. Turn into the two cake tins and bake at 325°F/170°C/gas mark 3 for 35–40 minutes, until lightly browned on top. Turn out on to a wire rack and leave to cool. Then spread one cake with raspberry jam and whipped cream, place the other cake on top and dust with icing sugar.

Alternatively, you could bake the cake in just one tin and leave it plain or ice it just on top.

Scones

These quantities make about 12 scones.

8oz/225g self-raising flour
1½oz/42g butter
1½oz/42g caster sugar
pinch of salt
5fl oz/150ml milk

Cream the butter and flour together. Stir in the sugar and salt, and add the milk little by little, mixing as you go. Knead the mixture to a soft dough (with clean hands). If it is too dry and crumbly, add a little more milk. I just arrange the dough in rough shapes on a greased baking tray and bake at 220°C/425°F/gas mark 7 for 12–15 minutes. If you prefer a smoother look, you can roll the mixture out with a rolling-pin and then use a pastry cutter to cut neat shapes. Whichever way you do it, they taste just as good. Serve with jam and cream (Marks & Spencer often sell proper Cornish clotted cream, which is gorgeous).

Shortbread

6oz/175g butter
3oz/75g caster sugar
6oz/175g plain flour
3oz/75g fine semolina

Cream the butter and sugar together. Sift in the flour and semolina and work into a soft dough with a wooden spoon. Roll out the mixture, folding it over several times until you get a neat even shape. Press the mixture into a lightly greased oblong tin and prick it all over with a fork. Bake for 1–1¼ hours at 300°F/150°C/gas mark 2. When it's cooked, turn out on to a wire rack and leave to cool. Then cut it into oblong shapes.

✳ Letters are the most comforting solace imaginable to the bereaved. Never fail to write to friends and family if someone you know and care about has died. Try to say something pertinent and loving about the person who has died to show that you valued and cared for them. Anybody who has ever lost anybody dear to them will tell you how much the letters helped.

Memorial Services

Once upon a time, memorial services were reserved for people of great public distinction. Now they are much more fashionable, as the Duchess of Devonshire notes ruefully in one of the chapters in *Home to Roost*. She herself has been unlucky, she says, never having 'been to a memorial service that has reminded me of the deceased'. She is not alone, as Ned Sherrin's splendid book tells us that Robert Morley, John Gielgud and Alec Guinness didn't want one either. The Duchess, needless to say, wants to be seen off merely with a funeral and Archbishop Cranmer's magnificent language from the 1662 Prayer Book ringing round the pews: 'For we brought nothing into this world, and it is certain we can carry nothing out,' followed by, 'man that is born of a woman hath but a short time to live, and is full of misery. He cometh, and is cut down, like a flower; he fleeth as it were a shadow, and never continueth in one stay.'

'Isn't that enough?' she asks, plangently. For some it may be. Let us respect their wishes. But I have to say I love a good memorial service, and I've been to some splendid ones. People came from all over the world to my father's memorial service, and wonderfully evoked the person he was, giving a real flavour of his life. Contributions were made by Mangosuthu Gatsha Buthulezi, a prince of the Zulu nation, and my father's great friend the South African conservationist Dr Ian Player. Baroness Thatcher read the first lesson (John 14 verses 1–6), my niece, Rebecca van der Post, and Thomas Ades (now a world renowned composer) played a part of Messiaen's wonderful 'Quatuor pour la fin du temps', composed while he was a prisoner in Stalag 8A, and the choir sang a wonderful Zulu folk tune. I think he'd have been hugely pleased.

The Eulogy

At the heart of every good memorial service is the eulogy. Somebody must speak captivatingly about the person who is the reason for the gathering, encapsulating his or her personality for all present. The key is to persuade the right person to do it, for as Andrew Motion put it in a booklet commissioned by a funeral company, 'Within the ceremony, the eulogy has pride of place. It is the moment at which the deceased is brought close, and also the time when he or she steps away. It is at once a greeting and a letting go . . . it must be specific, particular, even intimate – and thereby seal the sense of occasion. This is the secret of the eulogy's power: it might move us to tears, but it will start to heal us, too.' This is true whether the eulogy is delivered at the funeral or at the memorial service.

Angela Huth's book *Well-Remembered Friends* gives some wonderful examples of the art of the eulogy. If you're charged with this awesome task, you could do no better than to start by reading it. She has gathered together some scintillating examples of the art, mostly given by very accomplished people in memory of other very accomplished people, but they're a terrific read. She makes the point that 'while foibles can be alluded to in the name of honesty, difficulty lies in listing the character's many virtues without making him or her sound too saintly'.

There should be jokes. Life is full of jokes, and besides, sometimes it is only in the telling of the jokes that the real person comes alive. It's important to remember that memorials are celebrations of life, and although friends and family are still grieving, it is time to dwell on what was good and fine and joyful, rather than the sadness of the leaving.

Thanksgiving
& Guy Fawkes

The summer's over, the gorgeous gold and russet leaves of autumn have fallen and it's time for walking through the woods, collecting chestnuts, curling up with a good book in front of the fire, or watching the entire series of *The Wire*. It's also time to plan cosy suppers. Between the end of summer and the run-up to Christmas, cheering up the shorter days and longer nights, are three splendid opportunities to have some celebratory fun with family and friends – Halloween, Thanksgiving and Guy Fawkes night. They all come remarkably close together, and you don't have to celebrate them all, but since each of them has a distinct personality and historical narrative behind it, it could be a good way of adding some fun and enchantment to what are often dank, dark days.

Halloween (Allhallows Eve)

These days, 31 October, Halloween, is mostly treated as a chance for the kids to dress up in scary costumes, carve out some pumpkin lanterns and go trick or treating. However, its origins lie deep in history, rooted in a blending of ancient Celtic myths, Roman festivals and Christian beliefs. The Celts always celebrated their New Year on 1 November with a festival known as Samhain, marking the end of summer and the beginning of the dark, cold winter – a time they associated with human death. They believed that the boundary between the worlds of the living and the dead dissolved on the night before the New Year, and so people would feel especially close to deceased relatives and friends, and be wary of strangers in case they were from the other world. It became the custom to set places at the dinner table for friendly spirits, and to offer hospitality to strangers, to leave treats on doorsteps and along the side of the road and to light candles. Placating the gods and evil spirits was an important theme. Great bonfires were lit, animals were slaughtered, and people usually wore costumes and masks.

When the Romans came to Britain, some of their festivals became intertwined with Celtic traditions, including Samhain – Pomona, for instance, honouring the Roman goddess of fruit and trees. Then came Christianity, and Pope Boniface IV, in the seventh century, decided that saints and martyrs would be honoured on 1 November, All Saints' Day, also known as Allhallows, and Allhallows Eve eventually evolved into Halloween.

Many of these ancient superstitions live on today. Halloween has its roots in fear of the dark and an acknowledgement of death's mystery. Ghosts, fearsome and malevolent, may wander abroad, and black cats should be avoided for they could be witches in disguise.

OLD SUPERSTITIONS

* In 18th-century Ireland, a matchmaking cook might bury a ring in her mashed potatoes on Halloween night, hoping to bring true love to the diner who found it.
* In Scotland, fortune-tellers recommended that an eligible young

woman name a hazelnut for each of her suitors, and then toss the nuts into the fire. The nut that burned to ashes rather than popping or exploding represented the girl's future husband.

* Another tale had it that if a young woman ate a sugary concoction made from walnuts, hazelnuts and nutmeg before bed on Halloween night, she would dream about the man she would marry.

* Any young woman peeling the skin from an apple in one long strip and tossing it over her shoulder would discover her future husband's initial by the shape in which it fell on the ground.

* Young women also tried to learn about their futures by peering at egg yolks floating in a bowl of water, and by standing in front of mirrors in darkened rooms, holding candles and looking over their shoulders to detect their husbands' faces.

COSTUMES

As well as, witches, ghosts, devils and goblins, popular characters include the grim reaper, demons, pumpkin-men, vampires, werewolves, zombies, mummies, skeletons, black cats, spiders, owls and vultures. If you aren't up for improvising, complete costumes can be bought online from:

www.escapade.co.uk
www.halloweencostumesonline.com
www.abfab.co.uk
www.fancydress.com/costumes
www.allfancydress.com

If Halloween is something your family decides is worth homing in
on, it could be worth buying costumes, because you can tuck
them into the dressing-up box and bring them out year after year.

Dressing Up

First and foremost at Halloween, children love dressing up in
weird and scary costumes. None of the costumes need be
grand, nor should you worry about fit. Black cloaks, witch's
hats and devil's horns can be conjured up at home. Old black
dresses or jackets can be doctored and layered with black
sweaters, skirts or trousers. Anything goes so long as the
whole outline is black.

WITCHES' HATS can be made by rolling a large semicircle of
flexible black card to form a point and then gluing it down
the side. To make a brim, stand the rolled semicircle on
another piece of black card, draw a circle around it and then
draw another at whatever width you want the brim to be,
and cut out the middle piece. Glue the brim to the rim of
the hat. Make it even scarier by gluing lengths of grey or
weirdly coloured wool inside it to hang down in gruesome
fashion. Embellish it further by sticking on glitter in the
shapes of stars and moons, or ghostly shapes cut out in
silvery paper.

A CAPE can be improvised very cheaply (fine tailoring is not
the name of the game) by simply buying some cheap black
fabric, cutting it into a half circle and sewing ribbon on

either end of the top so you can tie it around the child's shoulders.

GHOSTS are easy, too. Find an old sheet and cut out holes for head and arms.

MASKS for witches, Draculas, devils and ghosts all add to the macabre atmosphere, and can be bought cheaply online – very scary ones come from www.merlinsltd.com and from www.halloween-masks.com (as well as latex gloves with hideously long nails). Paint them to make them scarier – they look particularly grim if painted bright white with brilliant red lips.

Pumpkin Lanterns

One of the Halloween essentials is a pumpkin lantern, a notion derived from Ireland where a strange light flickering over peat bogs was called 'Jack'o'lantern'. Today the name is applied to a carved pumpkin. Be careful to choose one with a bottom that is flat enough for it stand without toppling over. The usual procedure is to cut off the top and scoop out the flesh with a spoon. Then carve a monstrous face on to the outside surface – it makes it easier if you draw the face on first as a guide to where to cut. All this needs a very sharp knife, so don't let the children do it, certainly not unsupervised. Place candles or nightlights inside the hollowed-out pumpkin to illuminate the carved face, and then replace the top. Don't do it too far in advance or the pumpkin will become either too dry or too soft.

Halloween Traditions

TRICK OR TREATING dates back to an early All Souls' Day tradition. All Souls' Day follows All Saints' Day and is a Catholic day of remembrance for friends and relatives. At one time, the poor would beg for food and the better-off would give them pastries called 'soul cakes' in return for their promise to pray for the family's dead relatives. Later children began to knock on doors in their neighbourhood and it became the custom to give them ale, food and money. The 'trick' comes from the notion that if the neighbour is too mean to offer something, harm may come to them. These days, a few sweets or chocolates are enough to carry on the tradition.

APPLE BOBBING is great fun, even if those participating are likely to get a trifle damp. Apples are floated in a tub or a large bowl of water and the idea is for each 'bobber' to remove one with his or her teeth. To make it more interesting, all those having a try have their hands tied behing their backs. If that's still too easy, you could blindfold them as well.

TREACLE SCONES is often the cause of great hilarity at a children's Halloween party – possibly because it's messy. Hang up treacle-coated scones (see page 319 for a scone recipe) on a string – use a big needle to thread the string through the scones. Each person must try to eat a scone while it is still attached to the string, without using their hands.

KILL THE WITCH, another party game, could just as easily be called 'Stick a Wart to the Witch'. Draw and colour a witch on a large piece of paper and hang it on the wall. Cut out small circles from black card and put double-sided sticky tape on the back to make the witch's warts. Then, individually, blindfold the players, spin them around three times, guide them to the picture and ask each one to stick the warts on the witch. The player who sticks the wart closest to the nose wins.

A Halloween Party

Firstly, the invitations – these could be shaped like a witch on a broomstick or a black cat, and don't forget to ask guests to come in costume.

To add atmosphere to the party room, you could do worse than take advice from Martha Stewart (www.martha stewart.com/halloween). If you have enough time on your hands, you could make her wonderfully effective cheesecloth ghosts – strips of cheesecloth are dipped in thick starch and then draped over a long tube structure that has wire coming out of the top so they dry in a shape that resembles floaty ghostly forms. Dot these around the room, dim the lights and the atmosphere created will be suitably mysterious. Use black cloths on tables and pumpkin lanterns (see page 331 – but be careful to place them where they will be safe from excited children). Stick strips of torn black dustbin bags on the lintel of the door so they hang down in a witch's curtain, and scatter instant cobwebs, plastic spiders, creepy-crawlies, bats and luminous skeletons around the room. These are easily available from joke and party shops.

You'll want to play lots of games – www.party games.co.uk/halloween has masses of them, all suitably grisly although most promise 'no murder'. They also have a 'Horror Sounds' CD for £9.99.

If you're looking for a one-stop source, you will find almost everything you need at www.halloween.co.uk – from spooky stories to tell and horror movies to watch to suggestions for suitably ghastly food to serve.

John Lewis has embraced Halloween as a festival and offers a host of scary props.

Food

This is not a time for gastronomic expertise. Most children like sausages and baked beans, or soup. Spare ribs cooked in a nice sticky sauce usually go down well, too.

Otherwise, the thing to do is to make all those weirdly wonderful dishes that no sane person would eat at any other time, such as cookies that look like fingers and toes – use a pastry or a shortbread mixture and put nail-shaped cherries on the end for painted nails or almonds for plain ones. You can buy moulds for making jellies that look like eye-balls and brains and skulls – colour the jellies in suitably disgusting colours (cream or grey). Make meringues in the shape of bones or skulls, and if you feel celebrations won't be complete without a haunted castle cake, allow me to direct you once more to Martha Stewart's website (www.martha stewart.com/halloween). Look up 'recipes' and you will find incredibly detailed instructions on how to make one, with lots of admiring comments from her fans who have tried. It sounds unbelievably time-consuming and finickety but, my goodness, it looks the part. Lakeland also has a mould for a castle, ideal to turn into Dracula's wicked castle. Alternatively, improvise your own – do a layered cake of two differently sized round sponges. Cover in chocolate icing and decorate with bats, cobwebs (using trails of white icing), cats, ghosts and the rest. All this looks even more horrible served on black or deep amethyst tableware, if you have it.

TOFFEE APPLES

Toffee apples are a traditional Halloween treat since the day falls soon after the annual apple harvest. Roll whole apples, each one speared with a lollipop stick, in a sticky sugar syrup – a simple mixture of 9oz/250g of brown sugar to half a cup of water, cooked on a low heat until the sugar is dissolved and the mixture has a toffee-like consistency. Then put them on a rack to dry.

PARTIES FOR GROWN-UPS

The Last Tuesday Society (www.thelasttuesdaysociety.org) runs literary salons, events and balls to celebrate all sorts of occasions from St Valentine's Day (see page 50) to, yes, Halloween. It's the perfect occasion to indulge in a little Halloween fantasy because each year the ball has a theme – one year it was the Dance Macabre – so you need to make an effort with your costume. As well as music, dancing and atmosphere, the evening often features story-telling, readings, and all sorts of fun and games.

Thanksgiving

No self-respecting American would miss Thanksgiving for a million bucks. People trek hundreds of miles across continents to be together for this most American of holidays, which is always celebrated on the fourth Thursday in November. Historically, it was established to give thanks for the safe passages and crossings of the original pioneering families. President Washington's 1789 Proclamation perhaps gives the noblest reasons for the need for gratitude – they include 'for the civil and religious liberty', for 'useful knowledge' and for God's 'kind care' and 'His Providence'. Although the holiday has become more of an occasion for a blow-out feast than a celebration of being American and of all the freedoms and liberties that encompasses, underpinning it are echoes of the deeply held religious conviction that God was on the pioneers' side in helping them to arrive safely in their new land.

These days, more and more people in the UK are beginning to feel left out if they don't mark Thanksgiving in some way, and it has become established as a regular date among many groups of friends and families, especially those with American connections.

American Traditions

From many people's point of view, the great merit of American Thanksgiving is that it has almost no commercial dimension – you don't have to buy presents and you don't have to spend hours prettifying the house and worrying about myriad details that send many of us into a borderline nervous breakdown come Christmas. This doesn't mean the food and the table are treated casually. Thanksgiving essentially revolves around one great big feast, and many people clonk out afterwards on the sofa, watching football games or DVDs. The dinner is usually regarded as an occasion to dress up a bit, but black tie would be considered pretentious. After all, the pioneering families were renowned for the hardships they suffered and their consequent addiction to thrift – a moral perhaps for our times. In most families, the dinner begins with the saying of grace, led either by the host or hostess. Sometimes, each guest contributes a few words of blessing or thanks.

WEIRD THANKSGIVING FACTS

* The National Turkey Federation (of America) estimates that Thanksgiving day accounts for one-fifth of the annual total of turkeys consumed – which in 2007 amounted to some 46 million being eaten in a single day.
* According to the *Guinness Book of World Records*, the largest pumpkin pie ever baked weighed 2,020lb/916kg and measured just over 12ft/3.5m long. It was baked on 8 October 2005 by the New Bremen Giant Pumpkin Growers in Ohio, and included 900lb/408kg of pumpkin, 62 gallons/234.5 litres of evaporated milk, 155 dozen eggs, 300lb/136kg of sugar, 3½lb/1.5kg of salt, 7lb/3kg of cinnamon, 2lb/1kg of pumpkin spice and 250lb/113.5kg of crust.

The Meal

In effect, the Thanksgiving meal is very similar to our Christmas one, with an American twist. The essentials are a roast turkey (the Americans call it 'baked'), stuffing, gravy, cranberries in some shape or form (sauce or relish), sweet potatoes and sweetcorn, and afterwards some form of pie (instead of Christmas pudding). The most usual pie is pumpkin but in some households at least four different pies – pumpkin, pecan, apple and some form of berry – are served (which, to me, seems like hard slog).

As a child, I hated sweet potatoes, probably because in South Africa they would be served in lumpy puddles with precious little flavouring. Now, I have discovered some wonderful ways of cooking them, including Hugh Fearnley-Whittingstall's sweet potato gratin.

Hugh Fearnley-Whittingstall's Sweet Potato Gratin

1lb 2oz/1kg sweet potatoes, peeled and sliced thinly – about the thickness of a 10p piece is ideal
2 tbsp olive oil
3 garlic cloves, finely chopped
½–1 red chilli (depending on variety and heat strength), chopped finely (or 1 tsp dried chilli flakes – not powder)
8fl oz/250ml single cream
salt and black pepper

1. In a large mixing bowl toss the sweet potato slices with the oil and all the other ingredients until the slices are well coated and the garlic and chilli well distributed.

2. Transfer to a lightly oiled gratin dish, spreading out the slices with your fingertips. You do not have to layer the gratin piece by piece, but try to ensure that the slices are mostly lying flat.

3. Pour over any cream remaining in the bowl and trickle the remaining oil over the gratin.

4. Bake in a preheated, fairly hot oven (350°F/180°C/gas mark 5) for 40–50 minutes until the sweet potato is completely tender and the top is browned and crispy.

5. For extra crispness, you can finish under the grill for 1–2 minutes.

British Thanksgiving

For Brits wanting to celebrate in the UK there are two options – either to do it the traditional American way as far as possible, or to make it a distinctive gastronomic experience. Echoing the simple tastes and hardy way of life of the early pioneers, you could have pretty gingham or patchwork quilt cloths, attach little paper American flags to the napkins, or make them into a table decoration, have little stems of wheat and a huge bowl of polished apples on the table. In establishing your own British tradition, you could copy some of the American elements – pumpkin soup is divine and you could end with apple or pecan pie – but have pheasant or guinea fowl as the centrepiece of your meal.

Americans take trouble over their vegetables, which is perhaps something we could emulate. They roast parsnips and carrots in honey, serve green beans enlivened with tarragon and toasted almonds, and do all manner of different things with squash. They also go in for a deal of variety on the stuffing front – Martha Stewart in her book on entertaining (published by Ebury Press in 1994) has a heavenly recipe for a stuffing made from orzo and porcini.

Pumpkin Fritters

Since pumpkin is an indispensable part of the Thanksgiving ritual, let me give you my favourite pumpkin recipe. In South Africa, we used to be given pumpkin fritters for pudding during the pumpkin season. They are absolutely delicious and very easy to make. The key is to make sure the pumpkin is as dry as you can get it.

1 sweet pumpkin, cut into chunks
self-raising flour (2 cups per cup of pumpkin mash)
eggs, beaten (1 per cup of pumpkin mash)
salt
milk
oil for frying
brown sugar – use according to taste
cinnamon – use according to taste
lemon juice

Cook the sweet pumpkin chunks in a saucepan with as little water as possible. Drain when soft, squeezing out the water if necessary, and mash. For every cup of pumpkin mash add two cups of self-raising flour, one beaten egg and a pinch of salt. Mix well. If too thick, add a little milk. Drop spoonfuls of the batter into an oiled frying pan or on to an oiled griddle and cook as for pancakes or flapjacks. Dip in a mixture of brown sugar and cinnamon and add a squeeze of lemon juice. Serve them straightaway.

Guy Fawkes Night

Guy Fawkes was one of the conspirators who tried to blow up the Houses of Parliament (according to some cynics 'the only honest man ever to have entered the house'). The plot was discovered on the night between 4 and 5 November and the seat of government was saved, but very often the reasons for Guy Fawkes's discontent are forgotten. He was a devout Catholic who, like many Catholics, felt ill-treated by the Protestant king, James I. The conspirators thought that if they could blow up the Houses of Parliament and with it the King and much of the aristocracy, there could be a new beginning and Catholicism could be restored. Fawkes was caught guarding 36 barrels of gunpowder and later hung for his pains.

The tradition of 'bonfire night' began that very year. Londoners knew little more than that their king had been saved, and lit bonfires to celebrate. As years progressed, however, the ritual became more elaborate. People began burning effigies on the bonfires, and fireworks were added to the celebrations.

Now, the gunpowder plot has become a great reason to give a party, and if we forget its gruesome origins, it's one of the nicest of celebrations. Bonfire-night parties are usually all-age events, with everybody from the youngest children to grannies being included in the invitations. Often communities that scarcely speak to each other all year get together to make a huge bonfire and contribute to the cost of rockets, Roman candles and the rest. Public displays of pyrotechnics are common, and in town and country, the air reverberates to the sound of fireworks as they explode in dazzling arrays of sparkling colour.

Throwing Your Own Bonfire-night Party

The essentials are fireworks, a bonfire and a guy. If you don't have the space to hold a party of your own there are lots of public displays to go to. If, however, you have a large enough garden with a safe area in it, or access to a field or other open space, start collecting wood and paper for the fire, and old menswear for the guy. Better still, consider having a joint fireworks party with neighbours. Fireworks are extraordinarily expensive, and you get what you pay for, so it makes sense to get together with other people to share the cost. Afterwards, you can disperse to your various houses to warm up with food and drink.

Making a Guy

A large part of the fun is making the guy, especially if children are helping. There are lots of ways to make a guy but the simplest is to get hold of the oldest menswear you can find – a shirt, sweater or jacket, trousers, hat, shoes, socks, gloves. Tie the ends of the shirt, sweater and/or jacket and trousers so that you can stuff them with newspaper.

Attach the top to the bottom by sewing them together using strong thread and big coarse stitches. Otherwise, tie them together, or tuck the top into the bottom, if it will stay. Stuff socks and gloves to make hands and feet and sew them on. To make the head, stuff an old pillowcase and make it into a round shape, sewing on buttons for eyes and nose and a strip of red fabric for a mouth, or you could draw them on with coloured pens.

ORIGINAL FIREWORKS

The first fireworks were allegedly made in China nearly two thousand years ago by stuffing an early form of gunpowder (made with charcoal, sulphur and saltpetre) into bamboo sticks. Marco Polo is thought to have brought fireworks to Europe and the first recorded display in England is said to have been at the wedding of Henry VII in 1486.

Double, double toil and trouble; Fire burn and cauldron bubble.
The three witches in *Macbeth* by William Shakespeare

Where to Buy Fireworks

* Dragon Fireworks (www.fireworksforsale.eu) offer a mixed box of some 31 different fireworks for £98.99. For a big

party (or if you're organising one for a club or a small school) you could get their big display pack, which has large rockets, roman candles, mines and fountains, and provides up to 30 minutes' entertainment for £189. If you spend over £300, delivery is free.

* Fantastic Fireworks (www.fantasticfireworks.co.uk) come well recommended.

* Since I find fireworks extraordinarily noisy, I'm grateful to Spectacular Fireworks (www.spectacular fireworks.co.uk), because they group fireworks in packs according to the noise level. They also group them according to colour.

* At www.ghenghisfireworks.co.uk you can buy rockets and all sorts of candles, and also specific packs, such as for weddings.

* For rather more elaborate fireworks than some of the other sites, try www.fireworkfactory.com – among the more traditional offerings, they also have mammoth golden sparklers, starry starry night, psychedelic bouquet and magic carpet barrage. The powder keg mine pack is, it seems, one of their most sought-after bestsellers.

* For all manner of glow products, visit www.fireworksarcade.co.uk. Children love to wander through the gloaming with wands or bracelets that glow in the dark, plus lots of little sparklers.

'ELF 'N SAFETY

Fireworks are potentially dangerous and many a child (and adult come to that) has suffered bad burns.

* Keep fireworks under lock and key until the party, preferably in a tin with a lid.

* During the party, keep children well back, and follow all the guidelines and instructions very carefully.

* Never put fireworks in your pocket or light them with a long taper, and never go near them once lit, even if they seem to have gone out, because they could explode in your face.

* All fireworks should indicate the minimum safety distance from which they can be viewed. They usually come in two categories – to be viewed from 5½ yards/5 metres or 27 yards/25 metres.

* Only buy fireworks that conform to the British standard BS 7114.

* One person should be in charge, and should make sure to have a torch, a bucket or two of water, eye protection and gloves. A bucket of soft earth will be needed, in which to stand fireworks, plus suitable supports and launchers for catherine wheels and rockets.

* Remember to take care of pets, who can be seriously scared by fireworks.

TRADITIONAL SONG

Remember, remember the fifth of November,
Gunpowder, treason and plot,
I know of no reason
Why gunpowder treason
Should ever be forgot

Wrapping Up

Make sure everybody really is dressed warmly – I have searing memories of endless fireworks events to which kind friends used to invite us and our children. We froze. The cold seemed to seep up through our boots, so forgive me if I harp on the point – you can never have too many gloves, hats, warm socks and rugs.

It's hospitable to invite people to the house first, where you could offer some mulled wine, hot tea and coffee or hot chocolate. You could also make a hot drink of a combination of cranberry, apple and lemon juice, sweetened with some sugar and spiced up with a little cinnamon, nutmeg, cloves and allspice. Heat but do not boil.

A few hot snacks while standing around in the cold are comforting – spicy hot sausages somehow hit the spot (see pages 288–289). Wrap them in foil and hand out round the bonfire. Hot dogs – crisp buns filled with frankfurters and some mustard or horseradish – are also good. You could also hand round mugs of mulled wine and the hot fruit drink to keep everybody nicely warmed up.

Welcome to the Warmth

A few simple preparations can make the house look wonderfully warm and welcoming for when everybody troops back after the last rocket has shot skywards – a fire in the grate if possible, fresh flowers and big bowls of shiny apples and nuts. If you're having a stand-up help-yourself kind of affair, put colourful cloths on the tables as well as lots of candles. It's a nice touch to have little pots of indoor fireworks (fireworks companies label them carefully) and sparklers to carry on the fun, but supervise the children.

CHESTNUTS

Roasting chestnuts is a time-honoured autumnal and winter ritual. Sweet chestnuts are by far the nicest but not so easy to come by. Roast them in their shells in the embers of a fire – outdoors if you prefer, or if you have an open fire, roast them indoors. Make a small cut in the shell to stop them exploding, put them in the ash or on glowing coals, and you'll know they're done when the shell looks slightly blackened. Children often want to help roast chestnuts – don't let them do it unsupervised.

Bonfire-night Food

The main point of the food is that it should be warming and substantial. This is not the time for dainty morsels. Baked potatoes are good, either served simply with lashings of melted butter or topped with sour cream, grated cheddar or crispy bacon. Thick winter vegetable soups are just wonderful, or a carefully made French onion soup (the keys here are to make sure you caramelise the onions to give it that gorgeous deep flavour, and to use proper beef stock), or goulash soup (see page 94). With them, you don't need to serve much more than delicious bread, a selection of cheeses, a green salad and some fruit.

A richly aromatic boeuf en daube is perfect bonfire-night food. In an ideal world, this takes three days to make – you marinate on the first day, cook on the second, and then skim off the fat and reheat on the third. Many people, including me, don't have time for all that, but it tastes wonderful even without the elaborate marinade. The key is to add a big chunk of smoked bacon or a pig's trotter, a bottle of decent red wine and plenty of garlic and herbs to the usual onion and meat combination. Flemish stews (with ale and dumplings) also go down a treat, and other warming, comforting dishes include cottage pie, chilli con carne and an old South African favourite of mine – bobotie.

My favourite cottage pie recipe comes from Tom Parker Bowles. He adds chillis, which make all the difference, warming it up no end. Chilli con carne itself is a wonderfully good-tempered dish – once cooked, it can just be left in a low oven until everybody is back from the fireworks. But if you're tired of always doing the same thing, try bobotie. This way of cooking mince will make any homesick South African go misty-eyed at the very thought of it. Bobotie is to South Africa what cottage pie is to the Brits, lasagne to the Italians and moussaka to the Greeks. Aside from that, it is great comfort food, which is what bonfire night requires.

After all this hearty fare, I don't think most people could face a heavy pudding. A fresh pear with a small piece of Taleggio, or a crisp apple with a piece of sharp Cheddar, would be perfect. For the children, you could consider toffee apples, or give them marshmallows on long forks to toast in the fire.

Tom Parker Bowles' Cottage Pie

Serves 4

1lb/450g organic beef mince
2 medium red onions, coarsely chopped
3 Thai chillis, finely chopped (de-seed and de-vein for less heat)
3 tbsp of olive oil
1 can of Sainsbury's beef and sherry consommé
a few shakes of Tabasco
1 tsp of tomato purée
3 tbsp of Worcestershire sauce
freshly ground pepper and salt
4 medium-sized Maris Piper potatoes
generous lump of unsalted butter
splash of milk

Heat the olive oil and sweat the chillies to infuse in the oil for a couple of minutes. Add the onions and cook over a low heat until soft and brown (about 5 minutes). Turn up the heat a little and add the mince in handfuls, stirring into the onion. When all the onion and beef is mixed together and browned, add the tomato purée and mix again. After a minute, pour in the consommé. Add the Worcester sauce and Tabasco and stir. Turn the heat down, simmer and reduce for about 30 minutes. Keep tasting to make sure it is OK.

As this is reducing, peel the potatoes and throw into a large pan of cold, salted water. Bring to the boil and simmer until soft. Drain, put back in the pan and over the heat (to dry off any excess water). Add the butter, a splash of milk and mash.

Put the mince into a shallow baking dish and cover with the potato. Dot the potato with chunks of butter, season with salt and pepper and put into the oven (at 375°F/190°C/gas mark 5) for 25 minutes. Serve with peas or small broad beans, drenched in butter.

Philippa Davenport's Chilli Con Carne

The recipe comes from my old friend and colleague Philippa Davenport whose book Davenport's Dishes (published by Jill Norman) is filled with lots of splendidly comforting food for the winter months as well as old-fashioned staples that we're all beginning to turn to more and more. This recipe is for four to six people but obviously you can just double or triple it up. You need to make it the night before.

1½lb/680g steak – chuck, rump or skirt
2 large onions

6–8oz/175–225g red kidney beans
a little olive oil
1 tsp plain flour
14oz/400g tinned tomatoes
1 large green pepper
salt and pepper

For the spiced paste:
1 red pepper
1½ tsp chilli powder
2 fat garlic cloves
1 tsp each cumin and coriander seeds
2 tbsp olive oil

Warm the cumin and coriander seeds over a low heat until they smell aromatic, then pound with a mortar and pestle. Put into the blender with the chopped and deseeded red pepper, chopped garlic, chilli powder and oil. Reduce to a paste. When it is quite smooth put it into a shallow dish. Add the meat, cut into largish cubes, turn to coat evenly and leave covered in a cool place overnight.

Whiz the tomatoes and their juices in a blender until a smooth purée. Turn into a bowl and reserve. Soak the kidney beans overnight.

Next day, scrape the paste off the meat and add it to the tomato mixture. Heat a little oil in a flame-proof casserole and brown the beef in batches (if you put it all in at once it lowers the temperature and the beef stews instead of browning) and remove from the pan. Then brown the roughly chopped onions. Stir in a teaspoon of flour to soak up the remaining oil and then return the meat. Add the tomato mixture and lemon juice and bring to the boil. Cover tightly and simmer either on the top or in the oven (300°F/150°C/gas mark 2) for an hour.

Add in the drained and rinsed kidney beans (fast boiled in a separate pan for 10 minutes) and cook for another hour. Add the chopped green pepper and cook for another hour. Check whether you need to add any water if the casserole seems too dry. Check for seasoning, adding salt, pepper and chilli powder according to taste.

My Bobotie

1 thick slice white bread, broken into small bits
1 cup milk
2 tbsp butter
2lb/900g lean lamb mince
1½ cups finely chopped onions
2 tbsp madras curry powder
1 tbsp light brown sugar
¼ cup strained fresh lemon juice
3 eggs
1 medium-sized cooking apple, peeled, cored and finely grated
½ cup seedless raisins
¼ cup blanched almonds, coarsely chopped
4 small fresh lemon or orange leaves – if you can't get hold of
*   them, use 4 small bay leaves*

Preheat the oven to 325°F/160°C/gas mark 3. Combine the bread and milk in a small bowl, and leave the bread to soak for at least 10 minutes. Meanwhile, in a heavy 10 inch/25cm sauté pan, melt the butter over moderate heat. When the foam begins to subside, add the lamb and cook it, stirring constantly. Break up any lumps until the meat separates into granules and no traces of pink remain. Transfer the lamb to a deep bowl.

Pour off and discard all but two tablespoons of fat from the pan and drop in the onions, stirring frequently until they are soft and translucent but not brown. Add the curry powder, sugar, salt and pepper, and stir for one or two minutes. Add the lemon juice and bring to a boil over high heat. Pour the entire mixture into the bowl of lamb.

Drain the bread in a sieve set over a bowl, and squeeze the bread completely dry. Reserve the drained milk. Add the bread, one of the eggs, the apples, raisins and almonds to the lamb. Knead vigorously with both hands or beat with a wooden spoon until the ingredients are well combined. Taste for seasoning and add more salt if desired. Pack the lamb mixture loosely into a 5 pint/3 litre soufflé dish. Tuck in the lemon, orange or bay leaves.

Beat the remaining two eggs with the reserved milk for about one minute or until they are well combined and begin to froth. Slowly pour the mixture evenly over the meat and bake in the middle of the oven for 30 minutes or until the surface becomes brown and firm to the touch.

Public Displays

Sometimes, it's easier and more convenient to go a public display rather than becoming involved in a private celebration. Parks, commons and squares all over the land serve as venues, and public displays are usually advertised locally. Take yourselves off with plenty of rugs, Thermoses filled with hot soup, goulash or hot sausages, and a hip flask for a nip or two if it gets really cold. Wrap up warm, make sure above all that your feet are warm, and if it looks as if it's going to be bitterly cold, you could pack hot-water bottles. Here are just a few of the best-known party givers.

* Lewes in East Sussex famously has some of the best bonfire nights (www.lewesbonfirecouncil.org.uk). The whole town participates and the event is so crowded that people from outside the area are urged not to go. A huge guy – often as big as a house and made in the image of an unpopular figure of the day – is driven through the streets on the back of a truck. Processions of people in fancy dress, often carrying flaming torches, march through the town to the site of extraordinarily lavish bonfire and firework shows.

* Battersea Park is the scene of a big Bonfire Night celebration (www.wandsworth.gov.uk/Home/Leisureand Tourism/Events/fireworks).

* Leeds Castle in Kent puts on a spectacular fireworks display (www.leeds-castle.com).

Christmas

There are lots of wonderful things about Christmas but not least is the fact that it is so utterly reliable. It never goes AWOL and is never late – always turns up bang on time, year after year. Just imagine December without it – gloomy, Gothic. As far as I'm concerned, it is a marvellous focal point for the celebration of one of the world's loveliest stories in the middle of the dark days of December. You don't have to be religious to appreciate its mythical dimension or to join in celebrating all those deep midwinter pleasures – the frost, the ice, the berries, the carols, the fireside, the gatherings of friends and families. No swanky villa in the Maldives or barbie on an Australian beach could beat a truly British Christmas.

However, there's no denying that, for a single, solitary day, it looms awfully large in the psychological landscapes of our lives. Memories of Christmases past linger on in our minds and most of us can recall even the most distant ones in technicolour detail. For children, happy memories can sustain them all through their adult years, and inspire them to pass on those experiences to children of their own – all of which is why making it special matters.

Some people will tell you that they find the whole Christmas scenario a bore. Oh, the stress, the pressure, the time it takes, not to mention the cost. Now, I'm not saying I don't fret about it, too – I'm not immune from the stresses of modern-day living – but every time I start to fret I remind myself how lucky, truly lucky, I am to have so many people in my life to love, buy presents for, to cook for, to care for.

Think for a moment how desolate it would be to have nobody you minded about at Christmas time. A friend lamented that it wasn't until her husband died that she realised how much she needed to do things for other people. Having nobody to create a bit of magic for would save time and stress, but oh, the sadness.

So I think we should resist the temptation to think too much about the stress and try to think more about the joy. It's fun, after all, to dream up ways of making it the once-a-year treat it always used to be, of making the cooking, the decorating, the present-giving a joy instead of a chore. If that sounds like nothing so much as hard work, the good news is that as more and more enterprising new businesses, both big and small, offer an ever-increasing range of services, it gets easier and easier. Here, I hope to inspire, amuse and help you bring the dream to life.

Dressing the House

It isn't just people who seem to need a bit of cheering up around now – houses could do with a bit of it, too. When it comes to glamming up the house for Christmas these are not, methinks, times for minimalism. There's too much of it about. I think we should go contracyclical and indulge in a bit of over-the-top baroque, some utter fabulousness. For if there's one thing that should be prevalent at Christmas, surely it has to be generosity, particularly of the spirit but also of the decorative variety. Concentrate on scattering a sense of warmth, welcome and largesse with great decorative flourishes.

Big, I mean seriously big, bowls of just one thing – polished apples, aubergines, oranges, lemons, kumquats, lychees, walnuts, artichokes and even beautiful purply cabbages look wonderfully decorative. Pine cones, too, look and smell gorgeous. What Christmas requires is profusion.

If you're in need of decorative inspiration, I always think a good place to start is by visiting some of the chic metropolitan emporia around about Christmas time for a bit of window shopping. They all pay highly talented designers vast amounts of money to dream up splendid schemes, and I've gleaned no end of tips by wandering through the Christmassy aisles and gazing at the displays in Liberty, Harvey Nichols, Selfridges, Harrods and their ilk. Many a small boutique owner also has a witty way with decorations, so keep your eyes peeled for clever ideas. In recent years, most stores have had a rather crystally/frosty/white sort of moment – all very tasteful. Habitat stores often look magical at Christmas, and chic at the same time. The simple tactic of sticking to nothing but white with lots of brilliant, radiant lights does the trick.

✳ If you've gone in for a mainly white decorative scheme, you could add some drama in the shape of an over-the-top ruby red candelabra from Argos.

I once saw great swathes of twigs and branches at the Conran Shop, which had been painted white and intertwined with a collection of candelabra. Some florists and decorating shops sell ready-painted branches, but most people are handy enough with a brush to do it themselves.

✱ White is a favourite of the florist, John Carter. He arranges pussy willow, white roses, crystal drops and blue pine alongside nuts and gilded fruit, often binding fragrant cinnamon sticks, dried orange slices, fir cones and cloves into his decorations to make sure the house smells Christmassy.

Joanna Wood, the interior designer (www.joanna wood.co.uk), often thinks 'forest' at Christmas – 'lots of logs and pine cones, twigs and leaves. If you go to Wimbledon Common, near to the Windmill, for a fee of £10 you can fill your car boot with as much of the surplus left-over from tree cutting as you can find.'

Country town fairs and street markets often sell holly, mistletoe and other greenery for very little. A friend of mine gathers together huge branches she finds in the garden. Then she simply cuts them to length and displays them in three giant glass cylinders from Habitat, which stand on the hall table looking satisfyingly theatrical. The scale creates the drama. Put tiny stems in dinky little vases and they look puny and apologetic.

If you don't have access to woods or commons, or a garden of your own to plunder, get yourself off to a flower market. Londoners who haven't made it to New Covent Garden at Nine Elms in Battersea don't know what they're missing. For instance, you could buy white roses cheaply enough to be able to decorate your tree with nothing else – put each one into a little transparent flower holder, pin the holders to the tree, and the roses will last all through Christmas. Magic. There's a £3 entrance fee charge and it's best to arrive by 7 a.m. although I never manage it much before 8 a.m. An hour there and you can pick up masses. (www.newcoventgardenmarket.com)

It's not just for the flowers that Nine Elms is worth a visit but for all the paraphernalia – skeleton wreaths, baskets of pine cones, inexpensive containers of every size, shape and material, as well as baubles, bows, 'pearls', bobbles and all the rest. Some things you have to buy in bulk – for instance, a packet of dried limes is £35, one of dried orange slices £25 and cinnamon sticks are £25, so you would do well to rope in some friends to make it economical – but nobody could fail to be inspired by a visit.

In the Beginning

If you've just moved into your first home, doing Christmas can seem rather daunting. Paging through a glossy magazine doesn't do much for one's morale. Standards seem alarmingly high and then there's so much to do – trees to decorate, stair-rails to be adorned, windows to be swathed in lights, tables to be made visually sumptuous, living-rooms to be given the magic touch. The thing to remember is that there is nothing wrong with starting small. First time round, buy a few things that you really like. Each year add more baubles and lights, ribbons and furbelows, and in no time at all you'll have a whole collection of the decorative paraphernalia that can conjure up magic at Christmas. Children will love dipping into it to help decorate the house, and every glass bauble, fairy or reindeer will become a familiar part of the Christmas ritual.

Take us, we're grandparents now to five small boys. Many moons ago, when we had our first Christmas at home, our daughter was some nine months old, but it didn't matter that she was too young to notice – we threw ourselves into it for the fun of it, for friends and relations. We started, if I remember rightly, with a small tree, a collection of beautiful silvery baubles (which in those days, I can tell you, took some hunting down) and lots of holly and tinsel. Every year since then, we've added to the collection. Most years we've gone the rather predictable 'good taste' route – gold or silver or white. Occasionally, we've branched out into brilliant colours and experimented with a slightly more 'kitsch' aesthetic until now we have so many bits and pieces that we could orchestrate almost any theme we fancy.

There was the tartan year, which was the year I bought several metres of John Lewis's best tartan fabric and made the tablecloth that now comes out every Christmas. You could do the same with any fabric or colour scheme of your choice. Our children only have to see the cloth and it takes them back to the first year it appeared, and also to the year we rented a shooting lodge in the Highlands, filled it with friends and family and had one of the best Christmases of our lives. I bought tartan ribbons and enchanting bows from VV Rouleaux (www.vvrouleaux.com – a brilliant source for the decoratively inclined) and pinned the bows all around the tablecloth (most particularly at the corners), and tied tartan ribbons on to every candlestick in sight, and more ribbon round the napkins.

Other items in our collection include shiny, plastic droplets to be tied to candlesticks to give them a reflective glow (find them at Argos, among other places) and angels and dolls, some made by the children when they were small.

They come out year after year and top the tree or adorn the mantelpiece according to mood and moment.

UNUSUAL DECORATIONS

* Temptation Alley in London's Portobello Road (www.temptationalley.com) is a little-known Aladdin's cave filled with many wondrous props for Christmas, anything from glitter and feathers to buttons and bows.
* If you want to wave some eastern promise over the celebrations, Chandni Chowk (www.chandnichowk.co.uk) is a wonderful place to find brilliantly coloured papier-mâché elephants, horses and other animals, which make great, if non-traditional, tree ornaments. Better still, make it to the real Chandri Chowk in Delhi if you ever go – amazing for glitter and baubles.

Lights

The easiest, quickest and least expensive way to lend some enchantment is with lots of fairy lights, and not just on the Christmas tree – drape them round fireplaces, up staircases, over tables, round mirrors. Strings, garlands and amazingly imaginative and inexpensive lights of every description are available almost everywhere.

* Habitat's Cherry Blossom comes in units that cost about £48 each. Fixed to a wall, preferably white, they build into

a complete cherry blossom tree, some 8 x 3ft/2.5 x 1 metre. The whole tree needs seven units, but five also look great. Habitat also has fat ropes of lights, which burn for some 20,000 hours, for £35.

* Brooke Lichfield, when designing a press display for Daylesford, coiled simple strings of silver and white fairy lights inside a transparent Muji desk organiser, which cost about £9 – very effective.

* Lakeland (www.lakeland.co.uk – a cult company if ever there was one) has strings of 'pearl' lights for £24.99, which look terrific coiled up inside jugs or glasses. They also have red gem-cut blossom stems (£13.99 for six wired stems), which look great in vases, positioned near the lights, so they sparkle.

Candles

One lone candle in a tin lid looks forlorn and rather daft – display them in twenties, thirties and even hundreds, if you dare, and they begin to emit an air of magic. At Muji you can get a pack of 36 tea lights for £4.50 (www.muji.eu). In shops all over the country (least expensively at Lakeland and Homebase, more expensively at emporia such as the Conran Shop and Graham & Green) you can find coloured glass holders, and ceramic bowls with see-through eyelets into which you can put small candles.

CANDLES AND FLOWERS

If you run out of time, energy or money, remember that there are two simple ways of making any house look fantastic at any time – candles and flowers. John Pawson, the architect, reminds us that you can do a lot very simply: 'I love tradition and ritual – a great big bowl of polished apples looks wonderful. My father used to buy a big box of Coxes and it was my job to polish them. I always have a tree and I just put masses of tiny candles on it. I put Christmas cards out very simply on horizontal surfaces because they're lovely to look at, and get as much holly and mistletoe as I can.'

Wreaths

They add to an air of festivity and most doors on our London street adopt a wreath of one sort or another. They range from rather straggly to fat and posh. The variety is part of the fun. When, at a Spirit of Christmas exhibition, a collection of designers were asked to re-think the wreath, Clare Brew came up with a simple ring of lighted neon. Ann Shore, the co-founder of the cool shop Story (home.btconnect.com/story/), came up with a wreath made of shells, rice-paper roses and old chandelier droplets. Ercole Moroni, the hip florist at McQueens (www.mcqueens.co.uk/about/ercole.php), wrapped a disc with leaves and made a central disc of nothing but tightly packed white rosebuds.

Readymade wreaths are to be found everywhere – in shops, boutiques and online – but it's much more fun to make your own. Robbie Honey (www.robbiehoney.com), a floral magician, runs a Christmas flower school to show you how. Otherwise, buy a pre-made wreath frame (£8.50 at Nine Elms) and pad it out (they can look a bit mean) with foliage from the garden or with a pack of spruce (also £8.50 from Nine Elms). Then choose your theme. You could go for traditional baubles and bows in reds and aubergines as a change from silver; or whole dried limes, larch cones, bundles of cinnamon sticks and lavender, clusters of pink peppercorns and dried orange slices.

If you prefer the non-traditional route and like the notion of painted branches in your wreath, you can find them in myriad colours in street markets, or gather and paint them yourself. Weave them round a wire wreath frame to make a nest to which you can attach decorations of your choice. Black twigs with pearls, white branches with silver sequins, and bronze branches with bronze faux leather leaves all look spectacular.

The Tree

The ritual of choosing the tree – most particularly if you have young children – is all part of the fun. Debates about the size, arrangement of the branches and all the other important things can be marvellously involving, and since trees seem to be offered for sale in every imaginable outlet for at least a month before the day, finding one to suit is not usually a problem. Nordmann pine is the one to go for since it doesn't drop its needles everywhere.

* THE CHRISTMAS FOREST (www.christmasforest.co.uk) sells some six different varieties of trees at road junctions across London, and in addition promises to plant a tree in Burkina Faso for every one sold here.

* TREES DIRECT (www.treesdirect.co.uk) will deliver trees all over the country, and for an extra charge will provide simple decorations in the shape of little bows and ornaments.

* REAL TREES DIRECT (www.realtreesdirect.co.uk) will deliver, install and then collect the tree once the festivities are over. They'll also decorate it – and the entire house, if you wish.

* JO BOGGON (www.joboggon.co.uk) will deliver a tree, ready decorated, in central London for £50 a foot. It'll have white lights, icicles, glass and frosted balls and lots of ribbons.

* SELFRIDGES (www.selfridges.com) has what is called a ready designed tree – it will be delivered with all the non-breakable baubles and decorations, which you will then need to attach yourself. These trees range in price from £150 to £500.

* DELEGATE LIFE (www.delegatelife.com) will deliver the tree, decorate it and collect it again afterwards. They offer a Christmas package for £495 and will do almost anything from wrapping twenty presents and organising the cards to collecting drycleaning and cleaning the oven.

* WWW.CHRISTMASTREELAND.CO.UK is devoted almost entirely to things Christmassy, including wreaths, stockings

and stocking fillers, but is centred around the tree. All tree growers are becoming ever more environmentally aware and Christmas Tree Land has a whole section devoted to the ecology of the matter.

* JOANNA WOOD (www.joannawood.co.uk) is just one of a number of decorators and florists who will do the whole decorative number for you. She'll buy and dress the tree (choose traditional or modern), and she'll add lights and presents. She'll dress the house, too – everything from fireplaces to swags. Prices start at £300.

Artificial Trees

Anyone who can't face the mess that usually comes with nature, or whose sensitivities are offended by the ho-hum jolliness of Santa, reindeers, holly, mistletoe and all the rest, may find that an artificial tree is the answer. They're not just cleaner and more practical, but can be used to make a strong style statement. You could, for instance, have an all-black tree – yes, really. They were all the rage just a few years ago when John Lewis, not a store usually associated with the avant-garde, was selling them at some two and a half times the rate of the more predictable green variety.

You can see the appeal. An artificial black tree fits very well with the high gloss of metropolitan surroundings. The colour scheme can be kept monochromatic – crystal and frosted glass balls (from Paperchase) and glittery lights provide magic without muddying the aesthetic waters.

Of course, there are all sorts of other options – green (for those who want the natural look without the aggravation), blue, red, silver, gold and white – each offering up decorative possibilities of their own.

Decorating the Tree

For most of us, the tree is the focal point of Christmas, where the presents are stowed and around which we gather, so it's not surprising that we want to decorate it as prettily or gorgeously as we know how.

STYLISH LOOK: every year the Victoria & Albert Museum asks a fashionable designer to contribute to the style debate with a decorative tree of his or her own choosing. One year they turned to Kaffe Fassett, who festooned a natural tree with hand-made silk fans in rich reds, oranges, magentas and burgundies. Before that Matthew Williamson covered a tree in pale pink chiffon and velvet flowers along with golden dragonflies and butterflies. Even earlier, when it was the turn of Alexander McQueen and Tord Boontje, they chose a steel tree, which they covered in thousands upon thousands of Swarovski crystals.

Now most of this can't be replicated at home (a steel tree – how would you do it?) but you can pinch some of the ideas. Once you've hit on your theme – butterflies, silver globes or whatever you decide – head to any one of the less fancy stores, such as Argos, Habitat or House of Fraser, and buy as many armfuls of your chosen decorations as the purse will stand. Too few and it looks mean. If you find it's all looking a bit sparse, buy metres of silver ribbon and tie masses of silver bows to the branches – silver, glitter and lots of lights always produce a magical effect.

BAUBLES: the chief thing I have to say about baubles is this – have lots of them. Every year there is some new take on them, but the whole point is that families collect them over the years. Just recently, the Conran Shop had some lovely crystal, clear baubles with a little hole in the middle into which a tea light could be inserted and then lit – very pretty indeed, though you'd need to keep a watchful eye out for the flames. John Lewis often has some battery-operated tea lights, called Lifelogic, which have something of the same effect.

Some of the small niche mail-order companies sell slightly unusual baubles. Plümo (www.plumo.com), for instance, has some deliciously glittery sequin balls in all colours (six for £29). Joanna Wood (see above) has masses of frosty icicles, raindrops and teardrops to hang on the tree.

* If you're having an outdoor tree, the really modish, funky pot to put it in is the oversized Bloom pot, which is lit from inside. These come in white, pink, blue and orange and cost £175 from Aram (www.aramdesigns.co.uk) if you want to splash out.

The Stocking

'The Perfect Stocking'
A large-size golf stocking
A tangerine (wrapped in gold paper) in the toe and a tinsel ball in the heel to preserve shape

A packet of alphabet biscuits that spell 'A Happy
   Christmas'
Chocolate letters that spell the owner's name
A purse with a new sixpence in it
A box of dominoes
Happy families [card game]
A walnut with either a thimble or a toy soldier
   inside
Chocolates covered in gold and silver that look like
   money
A magnet
Some wire puzzles
A pencil sharpener like a globe of the world
A box of chalks
A little box of 'transfers'
Gay crackers sticking out of the top

Rose Heniker Heaton, from *The Perfect Christmas* (1932)

Where would Christmas be without Christmas stockings?
It's unthinkable. Planning treats for the stockings, and
the frenzied filling of them on Christmas Eve, is a major part of
the ritual. For parents, it's a rite of passage – like sewing on
name-tapes, doing the school-run and freezing on the side-lines
on sports day. When our children were small, the stockings and
the decorations were the only preparations that my husband and
I actually did together (otherwise we divided up the tasks – I
looked after food, he did the drink, that sort of thing). Late on

Christmas Eve, we took one stocking apiece (we had two children – with larger families, you probably have to start earlier). Stocking presents don't have to be beautifully wrapped – they're torn open by the children in a frenzy in the dim early light of Christmas morning. All that matters is that everything is hidden and secret. I used to use all the left-over wrapping paper and sticky tape.

Perhaps one or two presents might get some more elaborate treatment with a bow or a flower. Of course, there has to be a tangerine and some chocolate. Other traditional essentials are a small soft toy and something to read. We also used to track down little packs of cards, dice and other games, cute-shaped rubbers, coloured pencils with their names on them and other small bits and pieces. Gimmicky toys are available from www.firebox.com and www.myredpacket.com, which has such tasteless fancies as the wind-up racing grannies (they're pushing zimmer frames) and the fighting granddads (they use walking sticks).

As for the stocking itself, in the olden days – you know, those years before we all got so spoiled – children used to put out one of their own woollen socks or, if one was a bit of a chancer, a pillow-case. These days, a whole host of ready-made stockings are available to buy, from tasteful to neutral and from truly vulgar to utterly charming. Take your pick. They're in every department store and many online shops have particularly gorgeous selections – try www.thewhiteco.com.

I really think you shouldn't delegate filling the stockings but if, say, you've got octuplets, or you're a cardio-thoracic surgeon on constant standby, or simply a frenzied multitasker, then it's better surely to get somebody else to do it than witness the disappointment on all the little faces come Christmas morning. You can order stockings online, empty or filled, at varying prices via www.handpickedcollection.com, www.notonthehighstreet.com and www.santaselves.com, all of which either bring together a host of unlikely small, often craft-based, companies that don't have a website of their own, or provide links to companies that can help. If that's what it takes to keep you cool, calm and collected (or, more realistically, less frazzled), then go for it.

Crackers

Rather than buying them, why not make your own? They're dead easy, although you'll have to buy in the snaps. Take an empty loo roll, put your present, joke and the snap inside it. Lay the loo roll on the paper of your choice – tissue paper, crêpe paper, patterned paper – and cut a piece that will fold round it and extend beyond each end, making sure the snap is reachable. Glue the paper in place and tie a ribbon round it at each end of the loo roll. If you've used plain paper, you can add glitter, stars and stickers to pretty it up.

* Biome Lifestyle (www.biomelifestyle.com) has crackers that include an eco-tip instead of a joke, and the little pressies are things like wildflower seeds, which have a certain charm.

THINKING OF OTHERS

* Kids Company (www.kidsco.org.uk) works with London's vulnerable and disadvantaged children. Donate new clothing, toiletries, gift vouchers, toys that are *de trop* but do it in time for Christmas.
* Crisis (www.crisis.org.uk) needs entertainers (singers, songwriters, magicians, musicians, cabaret artists, comedians, circus artists, bands, choirs, bingo callers, DJs, karaoke hosts) to volunteer at their themed Christmas evenings at centres for the homeless across London. Apply online.
* Give new or gently used goods (food, cinema vouchers, toiletries, towels, linen, clothing, shoots) to make Christmas special at this 48-room hostel for the homeless. The Passage (www.passage.org.uk).

Cards

There are only two routes to go, aren't there? Either make your own or buy them from a charity. The old swanky way of using immensely grand family portraits seems very old millennium. Making your own is especially good if you have children as it not only encourages them to be creative and gives them something other than their Gameboys to concentrate on in the dark winter evenings, but it gets them into the whole spirit of the season. Crafts shops sell most of what you need – card paper, stars, stickers and glitter. You can easily get your child's drawing reproduced and printed (www.truprint.co.uk). Schools very often help children with this. One of our grandsons entered a competition for a Christmas Card design with Gloucestershire Wild Life and won it (well, somebody has to, so it's always worth a go) and was given a hundred free cards based on his design as a prize.

If there's no drawing talent in your house, cut motifs from books, magazines and old Christmas cards and use them to make new cards. Here is a good moment to say don't throw away last year's cards – keep them and cut out the cute bits to use again.

If rather jokey cards (not always in the best of taste) are your cup of grog, have a look at www.someecards.com – you copy its slogans free of charge.

Charity cards are widely available, but if you don't have a specific cause in mind or can't get to an outlet, visit www.cardsforcharity.co.uk where you'll find a comprehensive list.

✳ I don't think email cards cut it – unless they're lovely newsy ones from far-flung friends, which I adore. Speaking personally, my inbox was overcrowded last year with joyless e-cards, what on earth is one supposed to do with them?

DISPLAYING CHRISTMAS CARDS

If you have wide mantelpieces and acres of shelves or empty surfaces, you haven't a problem. Otherwise, the best idea I've come across is to take a long length of ribbon – tartan looks great but choose anything that pleases you – make a great big bow at the top and pin it to the top of a picture rail. Attach the cards to the ribbon with paper clips. Make as many strips as you need, pinning them to arches and architraves as well as picture rails, anywhere the cards will look nice. On bookshelves, simply slip the back of each card between the books and so make a collage with the cards covering the books.

Presents

The giving and receiving of presents isn't, as some puritans try to persuade us, yet another example of profligate consumerism that contaminates the whole notion of Christmas – it is a biological imperative. Learned studies, most particularly by Marcel Mauss (*The Gift*), have shown us that this need to exchange was deeply entrenched in all so-called primitive societies. People could only give what they had made or found. This created an indissoluble link between the person and the gift, which was what made it precious. Mauss described it as being akin to 'giving a part of oneself'. There's a lesson there. Now, I'm not suggesting that we should all go away and sit up half the night knitting or making jam but I do think it's a reminder that the presents chosen with love and care are the ones we value the most. Sitting by my desk is the little piece of tapestry my daughter sewed for one of my birthdays, even though she was in the middle of hugely important exams. I also remember the Christmas my husband tracked down three huge Chinese garden pots, which he'd noticed I'd admired – there they were in the garden come Christmas day. Then there was the time my son noticed the chaos in my office and put together a package of all the small things he thought would help – the Sellotape holder, hole-puncher, stapler, files. None were expensive but all showed he'd thought about what would make a difference to my life.

Finding something somebody you care about hadn't dared consider but turns out to love is to hit the bull's-eye. Take the woman who had most things in life but always had a hankering for a drawing by a particular Welsh artist – her husband tracked one down and there it was, under the tree. Former interiors editor at *Harper's* magazine Rachel Meddowes had a surprise when a bicycle landed at her door, courtesy of her boyfriend. She'd been thinking about buying one but hadn't got around to doing anything about it. She was thrilled. Noticing that somebody who works at home spends far too much at Starbucks makes a small Nespresso machine a great present – it may be 'stuff' but it's not superfluous 'stuff'. Something like that, for the right person, shows thoughtfulness and can chirp up its new owner's daily life no end.

✳ Paul Smith was once given a little old train set by his then girlfriend, Pauline (now his wife). He loved it so much that he took it everywhere in his briefcase and even used to bring it out in stressful meetings (a bit like worry beads). One year he recreated the train set and the briefcase for his Heathrow Terminal Five shop – idiosyncratic, of course, but charming, too.

Personalised Presents

Anything personalised usually goes down well, stationery for
the new home owner who's too busy fixing the lights to find
spare cash for the letterheads, for instance. A child's drawing
– scribbles, spelling mistakes and all – can be printed on to a
pillow-case at the Monogrammed Linen shop
(www.monogrammedlinenshop.com). It's not cheap, starting
at £200, but special. They will also transfer a name, a poem,
a sweet message on to a cushion.

Anya Hindmarch (www.anyahindmarch.com) embellishes a
handbag with a photograph of the owner's children, which
makes a terrific present for the new (or even older) mother
(from £75 to £215), as do the very chic bracelets made of gold
cubes with letters spelling out the names of children or the
nearest and dearest (www.felt-london.com). She's just started
a new service making wallets, jewellery boxes, journals to
special order, embellishing them with personal messages. Not
cheap, but very special.

I remember the pleasure with which a very successful
entrepreneur showed me the special Monopoly board his
children had had made for him. Each station on the board had
a personal reference to his home, his office, his friends or his
family. They hadn't just gone into a shop and bought a standard
model – they'd put thought and effort into it. This makes a
great present. You can either order one complete from
www.firebox.com (£79.95) or go for a Make Your Ownopoly set,
which provides just the bare bones (£19.95 from www.hand
pickedcollection.com), and customise it yourself. You'll need, as
the website warns, a free afternoon and a good printer.

Firebox has plenty of smaller personalised ideas – a puzzle, for instance, based on the recipient's home area (£19.95). You provide the post-code. For £24.95 you can have the front page of any edition of *The Times* (choose a birthday or an anniversary) made into a puzzle.

Photographs and Paintings

As for our entrepreneur, he was just as thrilled by the present a great friend had made as a thank-you for a fiftieth birthday jaunt to St Petersburg – a personalised album filled with photographs, drawings, poems, sketches and anecdotes from the whole weekend. You could adapt this for Christmas for somebody you care about. Romaine Lowery of the Clutter Clinic (www.clutterclinic.co.uk) will do it for you if you can't face it yourself. She charges £60 an hour if she comes to the house or £25 an hour for the work she does at home, and she's a fountain of innovative ideas on what to do with photographs. She'll sort the albums, have photographs blown up to make works of art (photographs of their children make great presents for new parents or doting grandparents), and have them printed on to sheets or blinds. If you prefer to do it yourself, Romaine Lowery's book *The Clutter Clinic: Organize Your Home in 7 Days* has a whole section on what to do with photographs.

If you're in digital mode, visit www.shutterfly.com, which will lead you by the hand, showing you exactly how to create your own albums.

A bit of lateral thinking, not to mention planning ahead, doesn't come amiss – if not a photograph then a painting of a child, spouse, pet, or home is always special, although not cheap. You could consult the Royal Society of Portrait Painters (www.therp.co.uk) to find an artist.

Buying Time

The Practical Princess (www.practicalprincess.com) is a regular tidier-upper. For Tamara Mellon and PR supremo Tom Konig Oppenheimer, she sorts the office, the wardrobe, the drawers or anything else that needs doing. Half a day − or if you're feeling generous − a whole day (£450) of her time would be a fantastic present.

What my husband wants most of all is somebody to put his hundreds of books into some kind of order. If you know somebody like him, booking some of Romaine Lowery's time would be well received. This is just the sort of task the Clutter Clinic (www.clutterclinic.co.uk) relishes.

These days, Rachel Meddowes (www.rachelmeddowes.com) helps the disorganised, the ill, the unimaginative or the just plain busy get to grips with doing up their houses. For the right person, some of her time would not only be a lovely present but also a godsend.

✳ Having a child's or a teenager's bedroom, or a grown-up's study, decorated is the sort of present nobody ever forgets.

Tickets

Tickets to Medium Rare (www.mediumrare.tv), a raunchy cabaret show, could be fun, but choose the recipients carefully. Otherwise, tickets to a hard-to-get-into show, opera or concert are always a treat. Our daughter once gave us tickets to the Intelligence Squared debates at the Royal Geographical Society (www.intelligencesquared.com), which we loved, and a pony-mad child would love tickets to see the Lipizzaner ponies at Olympia. Vouchers (www.seetickets.com) give access to anything from a rock concert to jazz, tennis, football or a festival.

FLOWERS FOR CHRISTMAS

I've never known anyone at all not to love flowers. If you can't think of anything else, flowers make the most gorgeous present. A bunch of roses every week for a year is wildly romantic – www.realflowers.com will deliver them for about £420. The roses are from England, in season, and from Kenya the rest of the time.

On a Budget

There was a moment last Christmas when, judging by the newspaper columns filled with bright new recipes for chutney-making, it looked as if entire families were going to be exchanging jars of condiments come the big day. Now, lovely though the home-made version is (my son makes it every year and I love it), I somehow think a giant exchange of nothing but chutney across the land would somewhat dampen the proceedings in most of the houses I know. If you're going to do home-made, I think you'll have to be a bit more imaginative.

If you can't buy a professional's time, you might think about giving it instead – my daughter-in-law has promised me two hours of techy-savvy skills (I hope to get my iPod rather better filled). You could do some gardening, sew on buttons – you get the picture.

Presents don't have to be expensive. The year we rented a house in the Scottish Highlands we decided nobody was to spend more than £15 on a present. I don't remember feeling remotely deprived. We were given divine little bottles of special oils, vinegars, packets of dried truffles, secondhand books, little antique finds from tucked-away shops. It can be done. It stops anybody feeling pressured and we found that we really enjoyed the challenge.

✳ Jasper Conran, when once asked about his attitude to Christmas present giving, said, 'My whole family is horribly discriminating. They don't mind whether a present is expensive or not, but it has to be unusual, interesting, and capture their imagination, which takes a lot more thinking about.' Imagine the pressure of trying to find something to please his father, Sir Terence Conran. Think on *that* and count your blessings.

Presents that upgrade on a few of life's essentials go down well – gorgeous coffee, a good virgin olive oil from an interesting Italian estate, fine soap (Prada had a beautiful boxed set for £24 last Christmas), a classy scented candle (Rigaud, Diptyque, Cire Trudon), a pair of soft gloves, a luxurious bath oil (Ren's Moroccan Rose Otto or Jo Wood's organic oils), a rare vinegar (raspberry, a fine Balsamic), a spot-on cookery book, a fine scarf, a terrific pepper-grinder or pestle and mortar, or set of good knives. The difference between the bad and the best is often not extortionate in monetary terms but huge in terms of pleasure. Beware of the cheap versions – nasty soap, vulgar scented candles or rough gloves give no pleasure and are truly a waste of money.

✳ A secondhand book carefully chosen, makes a lovely present. My husband, for instance, tracked down three old books on the history of the region in France where our son has a farmhouse, and they gave very special pleasure. The books weren't expensive either. (www.abebooks.co.uk is a good source.)

My tactics when shopping for presents on a budget are to plan ahead so there's plenty of time, and to make shopping seem like fun instead of a stressful chore. It's when you run out of time and begin to panic that throwing money at the problem seems like the only option that it can begin to stir up feelings of resentment. So I try to do a bit of disciplined list-making (not something that comes naturally but needs must) – people to buy for, what sort of thing they might like and what shops to hit. I then clear the decks to give three Saturdays in a row to the campaign, but the key thing is that each and every shopping day is broken up by a very jolly lunch with whoever can be persuaded to join in – friends, husband, children. That may add to the cost of shopping, but I defy anybody, even Paula Radcliffe, to shop all day without a cheery hour or two spent with the feet up and a drink in hand.

Since I live in London, I allocate one day to Notting Hill

and its quirky little boutiques, another to a couple of
department stores and the final Saturday to trawling the
antique shops in Camden Passage, where I've often found
my most satisfactory presents. The strategy can be adopted
for all sorts of other cities, and those who are better
organised – and willing to forego lunch – could possibly do
it all in one day.

The most perfect presents, of course, are those that are
most appropriate to the recipient. In the end, it comes down
to putting some love, thought and imagination into the
matter, and it is easy to see that the right thing need not
cost very much money.

Specially for Men

In the case of the men in our lives whose reluctance to lust
after worldly commodities is endearing for most of the year
but inconvenient come Christmas, we just have to think
harder and deeper. I am married to the least consumer-
minded man I know, so when he actually mentions
something he'd like, I pay attention and leap to. The presents
therefore tend to be few but rather expensive – a 1930s black
lacquered desk from a Brussels antique shop (before that, he
was using a trestle table from Habitat); antique library steps
to reach the topmost bookshelves – he now has two sets in
two different places and loves them both; antique cuff-links;
a fantastic light for his desk or bedside table to help eyes
that aren't as good as they used to be. Gew-gaws, trinkets,
and all the cheaper, smaller gimmicky gadgets the mail-order
brochures purvey as suitable presents for men interest him

not a jot, and I think he's not alone. Here are some more ideas for a special present.

* A VINTAGE WATCH: if he needs a watch, keep an eye on the auction sales – the bargains to be found there are often fantastic. As a specialist source of vintage watches, it would be hard to beat Tom Bolt (www.thewatchguru.co.uk). Tom cruises all the auctions, buys the best vintage watches wherever he finds them, and if you have something specific in mind, he'll do the scouting for you.

* ARTWORK: originals are tricky – that old problem of taste raises its awkward head – but for somebody interested in modern art it is worth looking at Countereditions (www.countereditions.com), who commission work from a roll-call of young British art stars. The limited editions at London's Serpentine Gallery (www.serpentinegallery.org/shopping) are often surprisingly good value – prices start at £100.

* GADGETS AND GIZMOS: this is where precision really counts. The wrong laptop or mobile phone is not only a grievous disappointment but a waste of large sums of money. What many men would really love is a gift voucher for one of the top-end specialist stores, such as Cornflake (www.cornflake.co.uk) or Selfridges (www.selfridges.com), where the Ron Arad-designed electronics department is everything a gadget-minded man could wish for. There, experts will engage him in esoteric discussions on such matters as surround sound, VCR taping, plasma screens, home cinemas and all the newest home entertainment systems on the market.

* FOOTBALL SEASON TICKET: obtainable from the club in question, this would have to be an early present – the season starts in August.

* CLOTHES: cashmere jumpers of the highest quality and utmost simplicity are usually loved by all the men I know. If you can afford a grand label, well and good, but if not, Marks & Spencer and Uniqlo sell them gratifyingly plain, and they are terrific value for money. Pyjamas with a bit of provenance have also been, as they say, 'well received' by the men in my life – some steely grey ones from Armani in a silky cotton were a particular success. Classy but modern ties, far from being a boring cop-out, are a useful standby. Richard James (www.richardjames.co.uk) is a good source.

* KITCHENWARE: if you have a foodie to buy for, you're in luck – firstly food itself is consumable and therefore needs constant replacing (great for present-givers) and secondly it takes time to acquire the full *batterie de cuisine* the ardent foodie requires. The secret here is never to buy cheap. As one young foodie I know put it, 'I want the really good, plain classic things that are of high quality and I can't afford myself. For instance, last Christmas I was given a wonderful frying pan – it never burns, never catches, I use it all the time. It probably cost about a hundred pounds but it's a present to last a lifetime.' High-quality saucepans (Le Pentole are beautifully engineered from heavy stainless steel), strong, sharp knives (Sabatier or the Japanese Global range – from Cucina Direct, www.cucinadirect.com) or a proper Le Creuset casserole

dish are good choices. For a chap who can't get going in the morning without a strong shot of caffeine, Gaggia make some of the best coffee machines around (see the House Party chapter for more on coffee machines). You could spend anything from £200 to £700 on a fine machine. Divertimenti (www.divertimenti.co.uk) has a good selection and will dispense useful advice.

* WINE GLASSES: for the real wine buff there is only one glass to drink out of – the Riedel glass. They're absolutely plain, not the tiniest bit of decoration in sight, but what makes them special is that they are made of finest crystal, and every single glass is the result of serious study of the correlation between glass shape and the characteristics of the particular wine it is holding. Buy top of the range – the Sommelier collection – and start with the Burgundy Grand Cru or the Bordeaux Grand Cru. At £42.95 each they're not cheap but it solves present-giving for years – you can just gradually build up the collection. The Wedding Shop (www.weddingshop.com), Harrods (www.harrods.com) and really good glass shops sell them.

Specially for Women

Christmas makes me realise what a spoilt puss I am. 'What can we give you?' wail my nearest and dearest to no avail. Well, I don't need a lot, but there are things I'd love, and if I'd love them, I think that most probably so, too, would lots of other women.

* BOOKS: I love books that introduce me to ideas, or writers that I wouldn't have discovered on my own. I'm a sucker for reference books – particularly on design or art themes – and read them for pleasure. Membership (minimum £10) of the talking book club (www.travellerstales.co.uk) is a great idea. Tapes of anything from a terrific thriller to Anna Karenina can be bought or rented and played in the car or on holiday (not so heavy to carry around as the real thing).

* CDS: a version of a special concert or by a favourite composer.

* HOMEWARE: look for things that are individual and one-off and trawl the antique shops. Cushions from the Designers' Guild (www.designersguild.com) would perk up any room. Classic cable-knit throws in pure cashmere are not cheap but for those of us who live in draughty houses are an everyday luxury that really makes a difference. Although Zara Home has some lovely and cheaper alternatives (www.zara home.com). Stylish Art-Deco-ish, hand-made mirrors, bevelled and properly joined with leading, would look great in any room. Find them at local antiques markets, plus Oka often has some pretty pieces (www.okadirect.com). Every year there seems to be a gadget of the moment – one year I remember longing for a floating radio, perfect for listening in the bath. Otherwise, something as simple as candles may be the answer, although they have to be beautifully scented or plain cream.

* STATIONERY: since scribbling is my stock-in-trade, I can never have enough of those beautifully soft, moleskin-

wrapped notebooks of the sort that Ernest Hemingway and Bruce Chatwin never went anywhere without. Most stationery departments sell them at prices starting as low as £8 (www.moleskine.co.uk).

* FOOD: a hamper filled with goodies (www.esperya.com) would be pretty nice to come down to on Christmas day – can't have the cook going hungry, can we?

* CLOTHES AND ACCESSORIES: since women's wardrobes need updating it's good to look for ways of doing it that don't break the bank. Jigsaw (www.jigsaw-online.com) is perfect for cardigans that are just a little different, or for the jacket that is just the right shape and material for the season. Small boutiques, such as Musa where I once found a silk embroidered antique shawl and a brilliant crystal necklace with a beautiful old clasp, The Cross (www.thecrossshop.co.uk) and Mimi (www.mimiboutique.com) often have charming or witty little numbers that you won't find anywhere else. For fantastic antique watches on leather straps, pretty and witty accessories and jewellery, try Paul & Joe (www.paulandjoe.com). John Lewis (www.johnlewis.com) sells extremely tempting costume jewellery for about £30.

* FROM A SPECIAL SOURCE: anything from www.re-foundobjects.com would be gorgeous – there's hardly a classier bath oil than Cote Bastides Fleurs d'Oranger and their crackle-glazed bowls and pitchers look as if they've come straight from a romantic old French farmhouse. I also love individual, one-off finds from antique shops.

Some of my most successful presents have come from that source, from old lorgnettes to antique picture frames, wine glasses, jewellery, silver jugs and all the other singular and precious things that give pleasure.

Specially for Children

Parents will know what's really hot in any given year because their children will tell them, and if you are buying for other people's children, it's best to consult with the parents. If you can't think what to buy, don't forget treats – a visit to a theatre, a concert or a trip to a theme park all make great presents.

CHRISTMAS TREATS

If I could wave a magic wand, every child would get a free ticket to a pantomime each Christmas. They're the all-time Christmas treat. The bad news is you need to book early if you want a decent seat – and take it from me, where you sit matters if you don't want to miss a lot of the action. For information, visit www.pyramidpantomimes.com (touring pantomime company) and www.thisistheatre.com.

Everybody should try once in a lifetime to go to the Festival of Nine Lessons and Carols, which has been held on Christmas Eve at King's College Chapel, Cambridge since 1918. John Betjeman called the chapel 'the most beautiful building in Britain . . . a forest glade of old coloured glass and between the great windows columns of shafted stone shoot up and up to fountain out into a shower of exquisite elaborate fan vaulting. It is the swansong of Perpendicular architecture, so immense, so vast, so superbly proportioned, so mysterious, that no one can enter it without gasping.' The combination of sublime architecture, the beauty of the music (it always starts with 'Once In Royal David's City' and every year there's a newly commissioned carol) and the purity of the boys' voices makes it an unforgettable experience. It's primarily designed for the people of the city of Cambridge but members of the public can start queuing at 1.30pm on Christmas Eve for some of the remaining seats. The service starts at 3pm and finishes at 4.30pm (www.kings.cam.ac.uk).

Small but lovely children's shops are tucked away all over the country, but if you don't know of one and don't fancy the nightmare that a visit to the big emporia usually entails, all you have to do is browse through numerous great websites, sit back and get everything sent to you.

* www.hawkin.com is great for stocking fillers. It has a section called 'pocket money' where kids can go for inexpensive small presents, and there are splendidly quirky ideas, such as 'Adopt a reindeer', as well as party paraphernalia.

* www.letterbox.co.uk has a wonderful selection of toys for all ages. They're not particularly cheap but it's worth paying a bit extra to make sure they don't fall apart.

* English Heritage's online shop (www.english-heritageshop.org.uk) has a children's section. One of my grandsons is quite astonishingly interested in weaponry, so it provides a great source of presents for him.

* www.the-green-apple.co.uk has quirky ideas for presents for eco-conscious children – a rocket, doll's house and castle made from cardboard, for instance, as well as dominoes and skittles made from bamboo.

* www.carouseltoyshop.co.uk sells all those little plastic figures that children love – pirates, fairy-tale characters, scary knights – individually as well as in groups.

* www.pedlars.co.uk has some nice quirky ideas, including a remote-control plane for £19.50.

* www.notonthehighstreet.com and www.handpickedcollection.com are two beautifully put-together sites that have great taste and are adept at uncovering interesting small companies.

* Most museums have great shops. The Natural History Museum (www.nhmshop.co.uk), the Science Museum (www.sciencemuseumstore.com) and the British Museum (www.britishmuseumshoponline.org) are fantastic, full of dinosaur-related items, skeletons to put together, scientific experiments to do and wonderful books and puzzles. The actual shops are worth a visit, as well as browsing online.

PERSONAL SHOPPERS

Last Christmas, just as I was leaving Selfridges, bent at the knees having spent a whole Saturday there, I happened to glance into the personal shopping suite. There I saw a beautifully edited collection of the best the store had to offer – I could have done it all in the comfort of the suite and made the personal shopper do all the work. If you've got a long list and want special things, it's a great way to shop, but it's not really on if you're merely looking for a bargain.

❋❋❋❋❋❋❋❋❋❋❋❋❋❋❋❋❋❋❋❋❋❋❋❋❋❋❋❋

Gift Wrapping

You may be of the school of thought that thinks that wrapping up the pressies can be dealt with by using any old paper and sellotape minutes before Santa is expected down the chimney breast. Now if you've got a full house, with decorations to organise and stockings to fill, are cooking for twenty on the day and have a full-time job, then you're excused and perhaps the answer is to delegate. Some stores will do it, although not always automatically and it's usually mighty time-consuming involving long queues. More and more websites, though, are coming to the rescue.

* www.notonthehighstreet.com not only sends everything out ready-wrapped in tissue paper with a label, but also sells the wherewithal to do your own wrapping, if you prefer to do that. It could be just some plain brown paper with white ribbon (black would be just as chic) and a wooden letter – a good way of identifying who the present is for at £3.60 a time.

* If you're a slightly hopeless, out-of-touch godparent or grandparent, and aren't up to speed with children's tastes,

www.wickeduncle.com lists children by age and suggests presents for them – these are then sent ready-wrapped with a hand-written message.

* For techy, jokey, gadgety toys that boys love, www.firebox.com is the place and it will also send them ready-wrapped. Firebox offer six wrapping options and you may be surprised to learn that the third most popular of them is its Crap Wrap. Crap Wrap consists of the sort of botched old paper and sticky tape combo that looks as if it has been done in two minutes flat by somebody with zero artistic flair. 'This uniquely shoddy process,' it states clearly on the website (you only find this fabulous item once you've bought something and are checking out), 'may result in one or all of the following: product highly visible, evidence of nail scissor use, hair found on sellotape, rips and tears.' There you go.

Doing it Yourself

For those who like to make some kind of a personal effort and jazz up the wrapping – possibly to make more of the diminished present inside – here are a few ideas:

* Do as Annabel Lewis, the owner of VV Rouleaux (www.vvrouleaux.com), does. She uses petal paper, left over after they've made their paper flowers, to wrap small presents, and it comes in heavenly colours (£2.95 a sheet).

* For bows that hold their shape, always use wired ribbon, which is available in myriad colours, patterns and widths.

* Save every scrap of spare, or at least not torn, paper and ribbon each Christmas in a war-chest. In there, you're bound to find enough material to make some wild rosettes – take one small scrap, fold it ends to centre, tie another over that and another and another to build up layers until the rosette looks crazily wonderful. You could also use the odds and ends to make a great stream of rag ribbon, and add butterflies, small birds or roses (all sold by VV Rouleaux).

* For children's parcels, you could add pink mice, lollipops or candy sticks.

* If you hate the idea of waste and are thinking eco, go to www.naturalcollection.com for recycled paper and tags (six sheets of paper and six tags for £2.25).

* Choose a colour scheme (bottle green with a bottle green-based tartan ribbon is my choice). Newspaper can look quite creative tied up with black-and-white checked or striped ribbon. Colour code presents by keeping different ribbon for each person, or different tissue paper – either works a treat.

* Best idea I've come across for treating something very small but precious, such as jewellery, is to take an unwanted hardbacked book and with a sharp knife cut a hole in the middle, slip the tissue-wrapped item into it and then wrap. Brilliant.

* Theme the paper according to the present or the interests of the recipient. Wrap a foodie's present in paper with pictures of great dishes. If you're giving a travel book, wrap

it in a road map. Otherwise, use several sheets of a favourite magazine taped together.

* Empty coffee jars, cereal boxes or other containers can be conscripted for Christmas duties.

* Little imaginative touches can make a difference. For instance, you could tie a miniature whisk to a kitcheny present, or a magnifying glass to an atlas.

* Leaves, greenery, flowers, berries and pine cones all pretty up a present no end and make it look personalised.

* Pieces of fabric are a wonderful substitute for paper, and if you also use some as a tie, the wrapping can look really individual. A scarf or a belt could also be used as a tie.

* As for those elusive tags — it seems to be an immutable rule that they run out on Christmas Eve — make your own using cut-outs from old Christmas cards or pictures from magazines stuck to old labels or business cards.

✳ Counsel of perfection: do your wrapping by degrees. Deal with a few parcels at a time, as you watch *Newsnight*, or whatever else you fancy on TV.

The Table

So, the house is looking great, the turkey (free range and organic) has been ordered, the tree's in place, the Christmas cards are written and posted — now you're

SAVING THE PLANET

If you want to shop, wrap and generally celebrate Christmas without wasting resources, here are some ideas.

* Keep away from traditional wrapping paper. This is a key commandment – buy recycled wrapping paper, or, better, re-use newspapers, comics, magazines, fabric remnants or brown paper bags. All can be prettied up with leaves, pine cones, stickers and children's candy (www.use-less-stuff.com has some good ideas).

* Stockings made from Fair-trade cotton, and eco-friendly crackers, can be bought from www.biomelifestyle.com. This website is also a source of eco-friendly presents, such as recycled glass, bamboo coasters and Alpaca slippers.

* John Lewis usually has crackers that are not only made from recyclable materials but a percentage of the profit goes to Save The Children.

* For eco-friendly stocking fillers from ethical sources, visit www.adili.com, www.ecocentric.co.uk and www.traidcraftshop.co.uk.

* Green Ribbon (www.greenribbon.org.uk) sells crackers, cards and wrapping paper made from natural or recycled materials while its biodegradable ribbons are made from wood pulp and are gorgeous.

* Buy your tree from a sustainable source. Visit the British Christmas Tree Growers Association (www.bctga.co.uk) for advice.

* Buy a potted Christmas tree, if you have somewhere to keep it, so that it can be re-used every year. If you buy a cut tree, make sure it can be turned into mulch. To recycle the tree – or anything else – visit www.recyclenow.com for advice.

* Baileys (www.baileyshomeandgarden.com) sell baubles for the tree made from recycled glass. Tree decorations become part of a family tradition, reminding everybody each year of the Christmases that have gone before, so buy them to last.
* Use solar-powered or LED lights on the tree – www.nigelsecostore.com sells them.
* Buy as much of your food as possible from local sources – www.thelfd.com has a list of small, local suppliers.
* Finally, don't buy jokey tat. Just don't. It's a waste of money.

wondering how to make the day itself special. Well, since most of the day usually centres round the table, that's where most of the effort should go, and there are as many ways of making the table look terrific as there are decorative styles.

COLOUR SCHEME: start by choosing a colour scheme. Focusing on just one colour always looks good. You could go for all white with perhaps some touches of silver and myriad lights – very Scandinavian. Tie-on chair covers in the same colour fabric are an added touch, or, failing that, you could tie matching ribbons to the sides of the chairs.

Another idea is to indulge in, say, a gold table. Gold-bedecked glasses that you might not normally dream of using look very celebratory at this time of year. Christmas, in my view, isn't the time for minimalist chic – it's for exuberance, extravagance and a bit of over-the-top kitsch. Talking of extravagance, Astier de Villatte gold-plated cutlery is available from the Designers' Guild (www.designers guild.com) – £24 for a knife, £17 for a fork and £17 for a spoon, but they could be brought out come party-time year after year.

TABLECLOTH: you may have a gorgeous table that doesn't need a cloth, but otherwise it's nice to have a special one for Christmas day. Antique shops and antique fairs often have old embroidered sheets that you could use, or you could buy a length of inexpensive fabric and make your own. If you have a really large table, and dream of it covered in a vast damask cloth, start saving. The Volga Linen company (www.volgalinen.co.uk) sells them in off-white or natural with a paisley self-pattern. The largest is 98½ x 216½in/ 250 x 550cm for £295 while the linen version comes in black or natural for £340.

The interior designer's trick of using two cloths – say, a coloured heavy one (or bedspread) underneath, topped by a shorter white or cream one – looks very grand. Take a trip to Southall, or any local Indian market, if you can. There you will find saris in almost every colour, gauzy and garish, silky and beautiful, with which to clad your tables for a fraction of the price that tablecloths command.

Runners down the table add a festive air – John Lewis have some terrific voile, satin and velvet table runners (£35) in rich red and gold. SIA (www.sia-homefashion.com), a Swedish company, also sells table runners, starting at £9.95, and they have a vast range of crystal candleholders and candelabras, and collectible baubles, too. The company has just one shop (in Wimbledon) but Selfridges, Harrods and John Lewis all stock its wares, and its website is filled with inspirational ideas that you could plunder.

USING PLANTS, FRUIT AND VEGETABLES: Stephen
Woodhams, the garden designer, is a past master at conjuring
up magic round the table. For a grand dinner he used long
sprays of pussy willow interspersed with fat creamy candles and
masses of deep red roses. The red roses are the most expensive
item – it needs lots to create the magic – but buy them at a
market and they become affordable. I did the same thing at
home a few days later, and it was a doddle (as Christian Dior
used to say, 'It's the idea that costs'). Pine cones, nuts, fruit, fir
branches or anything else that takes your decorative fancy can
be used to equally good effect. Big bowls of lychees or purple
cabbages look sumptuously decadent. Robbie Honey, the florist,
runs garlands of spruce down the length of the table,
embellished with piles of satsumas, walnuts, chestnuts and tea
lights. He'll also circle huge candlesticks with dried rose heads
(buy them cheaply at Nine Elms). You can use artichokes as
candlelights – cut out the hearts, flatten the base and insert a
candle in a small glass holder – ravishing. It's got to be done
sumptuously if you're going to do it – don't stint on the fruit
and veg (you can always eat them afterwards).

Another suggestion is to fill Victorian-style terracotta pots in
different sizes (usually available from markets, gardening shops
and garden centres) with hyacinth bulbs and put a run of them
down the table for a more rustic effect. Emphasise them with a
row of night lights wrapped in bunches of galax leaves.

LIGHTING: a selection of glass candelabra and glass candlesticks
of assorted shapes and sizes (that is important, matching
doesn't work the same magic) looks wonderful lining the centre
of the table. The Conran Shop stock them, and a whole flock

of its pink pigeon candles would also look fantastic (they come in gold or silver, too, at £6.80 each). Argos has quite elaborate sparkly candelabra in jewel colours, which add some decorative panache to the table, while www.notonthehighstreet.com has them in a pretty French style.

Giant hurricane lamps are terrific imbuers of glamour. They can be found at Baileys (www.baileyshome andgarden.com) and Marks & Spencer, and more expensively at India Jane (www.indiajane.co.uk), the chain that sells a decorative, Christmassy look all year round, and Oka (www.okadirect.com). Marston & Langinger (www.marston-and-langinger.com) has gorgeous oversized hurricane lamps, lanterns and all sorts of other table magic.

EXPERT HELP

I think it's much more fun to get the family to help with all the preparations for Christmas – a joint effort with everybody piling in, searching around in the linen drawers and the boxes where the decorations are kept, makes it a sociable activity and not a chore. However, for those who, for one reason or another, want expert help, plenty of it is on offer.

* All the big florists and decorators – from Kelly Hoppen to Joanna Wood, John Carter, Robbie Honey and Rob van Helden – will decorate the entire house, from table settings to the tree, but, as you'd expect, it costs.
* Concierge services will do anything at a price:
– www.quintessentially.com (annual fee £1,000) has special

departments to take care of everything from food and flowers to finding a venue for a party. The gifts department has an array of personal shoppers who will do the shopping for you.

- Concierge London (www.conciergelondon.co.uk) will arrange most things for you – from buying and decorating the tree and sorting the presents to booking the travel and finding a cook – but the annual membership fee is high (£5,000) and you need to be proposed. Once you're a member, an hourly fee of £30 applies.

- www.cushiontheimpact.co.uk doesn't charge an annual fee at all and will track down experts to do whatever it is that's required. Want somebody to shop for presents? Fine, they'll sort it. Want to give your husband an iPod and fill it with his favourite music? No problem, they'll get somebody to load the lot. They'll organise your Christmas cards, do all that's necessary to hold a dinner party for eight to ten people, order the food, whatever you need. You buy blocks of hours and use them as you like – five hours' worth of labour costs £135, ten hours costs £250.

- Consider it Done (www.consider-it-done.co.uk) charges £295 (plus VAT) a month for eight hours' worth of services. You can buy add-on packages, blocks of time and extra hours as necessary. The 'Now and Again' package (£325 plus VAT) entitles you to eight hours of labour – they'll order the turkey, decorate the house and the tree, send off the Christmas cards and search for presents.

- Rachel Meddowes (www.rachelmeddowes.com) suggests ideas for original presents, tracks them down, buys and wraps them. She says the purpose of presents is 'making dreams come true'.

Food

M y view on food at Christmas is that it's not the time for
culinary pyrotechnics. In the midst of all the tinsel, booze
and general chaos, I don't think anybody is going to know or
care if the bread sauce, brandy butter, cranberry sauce, chestnut
and other stuffings have been lovingly made by hand or merely
lovingly bought in. Most of us crave tradition and you can
provide the annual reassurance that these age-old rituals are still
alive and well without having to slice and chop from morning
until night. Come Christmas, there are more important things to
do than get red-faced round the cooker – spending time with
friends and family whom you don't often see, for one.

I believe in ordering and organising ahead so that on the
day you need do as little as possible. There's no getting round
the fact that the best birds and hams come from small
suppliers. If you have a good local butcher or farmers' market,
well and good, otherwise visit www.thegoodwebguide.co.uk,
which lists literally masses of small suppliers with links
through to them. So choose your supplier and then order your
free-range, organic, bronze turkey (I get mine from
www.swaddles.co.uk), your beef (grass-fed from Donald
Russell, www.donaldrussell.com), your ham (I get a large
Alderton ham, deliciously moist, from the Country Victualler
at www.alderton.co.uk) and your cheeses. I like traditional
English cheeses – Cheddar, Stilton, Stinking Bishop – which I
buy from small local cheese shops. These sources are not
usually cheap, so be selective. If you're really strapped for cash,
you could follow the example of an impecunious artist I know

(who clearly has nerves of steel) and wait until Christmas Eve when your local Waitrose may well be selling turkeys at a marked-down price.

Otherwise, simple but good ingredients are what you need and these days supermarkets offer perfectly good versions of all those fiddly extras that used to get the cook so het-up – they sell bread sauce (add some cream), brandy butter (add a tad more brandy), Brussels sprouts and chestnuts ready prepared (if your local shop doesn't sell them, get the chestnuts tinned or vacuum-packed, peeled and ready to caramelise in butter before adding to the sprouts) as well as potatoes ready to roast.

When it comes to stuffing, I do make my own – bought versions are too heavy on the bread and the dried herbs – but this can be done ahead so that it isn't a headache. I stuff one end of the turkey with a Caroline Conran recipe I've had for years (simply combine stoned prunes pre-soaked in brandy, walnuts, browned pancetta or bacon bits and caramelised baby onions) and the other end with a Nigel Slater recipe.

If you're a vegetarian I'd counsel against too much reliance on nut roasts. I rather go along with Nigella Lawson, who thinks it's best to go for everything except the turkey. In other words, there's so much else, what with delicious roast potatoes, heavenly vegetables (roasted parsnips, Brussels sprouts with chestnuts and red cabbage cooked slowly in the oven with some chopped onions and apple). Top it all with bread sauce, if you like. If you're catering for vegetarians, remember to roast the vegetables in something other than animal fat, and not round the meat. Check the *Guardian* website for Allegra McEvedy's suggestions – her rather complicated-sounding Strata of Savoy dish (a combination of butternut squash, cauliflower, savoy cabbage, onions and lots else) sounds suitably celebratory and gets some rave reviews.

If you're a small family, newly married or just a couple of friends, or, as happened to us one year when both children were with what I call the outlaws (i.e. their partners' families), you might take up Nigel Slater's sensible suggestion of asking your butcher to bone a turkey leg or two, and then stuff them – cheap and delicious, and much better, in my view, than one of those pale rolled-up turkey breasts.

One year, a long time ago, when we had to give lunch to one set of parents (oh happy days, when they were all still with us) before setting off for Christmas with the others, I did a quick and easy meal of two roasted pheasants with a huge green salad and crisps, preceded by smoked salmon and followed by a light orange cold soufflé. I do remember that it was exceptionally elegant and beautifully light. If you're a small group, it's worth thinking about.

Pudding – well, it has to be the proper plum pudding, doesn't it? If you love cooking and you have a ritual of making it *en famille*, with the children doing the stirring, way back in September (to let it mature), then stick with it. Me – now the children have children of their own – I buy Marks & Spencer's most luxurious version and it's delicious. Slight variations on the theme are not difficult to find – Meg Rivers, Daylesford, Fortnum & Mason all offer them. Try one if you feel like a change. Children don't always like the traditional version, so I sometimes make another pudding – a white Christmas pudding.

White Christmas Pudding

Serves 12

2oz/50g raisins
2oz/50g sultanas
2oz/50g currants
2oz/50g dried apricots, chopped
2oz/50g prunes
juice of 2 oranges
splash of brandy, optional
zest of 1 orange
½ tsp cinnamon
½ pint/10fl oz/300ml double cream
½ pint/10fl oz/300ml whipping cream
3 egg whites, stiffly beaten

Soak the raisins, sultanas, currants, apricots and prunes in the orange juice – plus an optional splash of brandy (although not if the pudding is for children) – for at least two hours. Add the orange zest and cinnamon. Then whip together the double cream and whipping cream, and add the beaten egg whites. (A shortcut is to use the best vanilla ice cream, i.e. made with real cream and eggs, instead.) Finally, fold in the dried-fruit mixture, transfer to a Christmas pudding-shaped bowl and freeze – it makes a great treat.

Christmas Day Routine

Let me tell you how we organise the day in my family. We start
with a simple breakfast. Since everyone has very conservative
tastes in food at this time of the day, we stick with cereals,
orange juice, croissants and coffee. Anyway, going to town at
breakfast takes the edge off the appetite for the treats to come.
Then the family turns to and helps prepare the main meal – the
turkey goes in the oven, vegetables are peeled (or, if I'm doing it,
I simply decant the ready-prepared versions – time is what
matters more to me at Christmas) and a check is made that the
pudding and all the trimmings are ready to go. At about
midday, we gather round the tree for pressies and smoked
salmon (from the Earl of Granville's Hebridean Smokehouse –
www.hebrideansmokehouse.com) on rounds of brown bread. If
I'm feeling energetic, I sometimes serve gravadlax with dill and
mustard sauce on toasted bruschetta. After the present giving, we
all go out for a blow of fresh air. By 4 p.m. we're back and it's all
hands to the decks so that we have the meal sometime round
about 6 p.m. as there are always lots of small children. We like to
eat after dark – so much more magical with all the candles lit –
but not too late, leaving time for games or a great DVD
afterwards.

* Special Christmas foodie treats include chocolate truffles – Rococo is
hard to beat but there are masses of suppliers of very fine chocolate
(see pages 82–86). If I do a starter – which I don't often, because it
can be too much – I may choose a cold jellied consommé, topped
with sour cream and huge dollops of Danish egg roe. If you like
oysters, nothing could be more elegant.

Boxing Day

On Boxing day I like to keep things simple. A good soup is wonderful. Jerusalem artichoke soup looks like washing-up water but tastes divine – add lots of chopped herbs to take away that pallid look. Beetroot or leek and potato are also nice and warming. Follow that with left-overs, if there are any, teamed with baked potatoes with sour cream, and some crisp salads and cheese. The best salad I ever came across for using up cold turkey, if you don't want to play it straight, is to mix thin strips of the meat with chopped spring onions, dark wild rice (cooked of course), some skinned and chopped tomatoes and pomegranate seeds. Add some soy sauce to a vinaigrette dressing.

The ham could come into play as well, and it's nice to have a pie or terrine on hand – but it must be good. Donald Russell does a terrific pheasant terrine, and Daylesford does wonderful game pies. At this point, chutneys actually come into their own – Daylesford (again) does wonderful ones but you've probably been given something home-made.

An extremely expensive Christmas treat is pâté de foie gras en croute, which is really just a grander and more delicious version of a meat pie, except that the meat is substituted by foie gras. It's expensive at £110 but as a one-off convivial delight, perhaps it's worth it. Pass it round with some beautiful Sauternes before the meal. Each person uses a warmed spoon to scoop some out, and if you happen to have brioche on hand, that would be good. Otherwise, foie gras mi-cuit is too rich for every day but terrific once a year – you just slice it into fat pieces, fry them quickly in butter and serve on brioche (from www.gourmetfoodstore.com).

You could finish with Cantuccini biscuits (from Carluccio's everywhere) which you dip into some chilled Vin Santo, or the quickest hot pudding in the world, which is white of egg soufflé.

The Quickest Hot Pudding in the World

4 egg whites
2oz/50g sugar per egg white
6oz/175g fruit purée
scrape of butter
scattering of sugar

Whip up the egg whites into stiff peaks with the sugar and add the fruit purée (you can buy delicious prune purée, which is divine). Put into a buttered and sugared soufflé dish and cook in a hot oven (275°F/150°C/gas mark 2) for twenty minutes until risen.

What to Drink

by Chris Orr, Managing Director, Quintessentially Wine (www.quintessentiallywine.com)

Deciding which of the big birds you're going to have on the merriest day of the year, as you gather friends and family around you, is certainly one the principal challenges of the festive season. However, once you've plumped for your fowl, and drawn up an extensive menu of titbits with which to delight your fellow revellers, an even bigger challenge remains – what to drink with it.

Now, if you're up for a bit of cheating, I would happily recommend that you drink champagne from breakfast through to the final snooze in front of the annual Bond movie, keeping things simple, fizzy and fun – but not everyone likes fizz and not everyone is partial to a handful of Rennies every half-hour to keep the rampaging acid at bay.

Champagne should, of course, appear at some stage. Personally speaking, I find that some smoked salmon and a glass of something as special as you can afford (a bottle of Dom Perignon or a magnum of Krug would be sublime!) is the perfect way to spoil your guests and yourself. Once that's over and done with, though, where do you go next?

Well, assuming you've splashed out on the above, there's probably good cause to ease off the spending, and go for some more reasonable options. If you follow three simple rules, you should find the perfect wines to go with an indulgent Christmas lunch.

Rule 1: Don't opt for heavy. Stick to light to medium-bodied wines. It's a big day, almost marathon-like in terms of food and wine consumption. If you choose wines that are too heavy and too rich, some of the party are going to end up feeling very ill before the plum pudding's arrived.

Rule 2: Usually when matching food and wine, you try to pick out a few essential flavours and find a wine to match. At

Christmas time, however, goose or turkey are often racked up with Brussels sprouts, devils on horseback, chestnuts and sage stuffing. Again, go for whites and reds that have character but are more likely to cleanse and soothe your mouth after this taste assault, rather than add to the melée.

Rule 3: Choose wines that are low on alcohol. Go for whites around the 11–12% abv mark, and reds around the 12–13% mark. If you go for a big ballsy red at 15%, for example, not only will you be breaking Rule 1, but you'll be all over the place by mid-afternoon, and barely able to focus on the television.

Stick to the above rules when choosing your wines, and I'm pretty sure you'll not go too wrong. But what are the best combos for typical Christmas fare? After all, however experimental you are, a glass of port is not going to be first choice to kick off a nice light, fluffy salmon mousse, nor is a light white going to hack it with the plum pudding or the Stilton.

Ideal Matches

SMOKED SALMON, OYSTERS, CRAYFISH, LOBSTER: these are invariably the first course of any Christmas blowout, which makes it very easy to choose the wine. I'd avoid heavily oaked Chardonnays, opting instead for a crisp, clean, young Chablis, or alternatively a Sauvignon Blanc, with its salty nose and gooseberry fruit flavours, ideally suited to these fish options.

GOOSE: great big fatty birds deserve something with a little kick of acidity, so I'd opt for Riesling or a dry Gewurz if you favour whites, and Pinot Noir (preferably from the New World, as the juicier the better) from the red camp.

TURKEY: funnily enough, turkey is a little more robust than goose, so go for a lightly oaked Chardonnay, or perhaps a Viognier from the Rhone (if you fancy spending some serious money on something cold and white). Alternatively, if you're a red fan, something slightly more tannic than Pinot would be a good choice, so perhaps a luscious Grenache from Spain, a young tempranillo in the form of Rioja, or a classic Chianti from Tuscany.

PLUM PUDDING: the classic wine to drink with Christmas pudding is a Sauternes (d'Yquem if you're feeling very extravagant, but most supermarkets have lots of much lower-priced alternatives – look for Sauternes with an 's', which is from Bordeaux, rather than Sauterne, without an 's', which is a different white wine from California). However, I'd also advise trying a traditional sweet sherry. If you go for one of the top brands, such as Lustau, you'll find this much-maligned drink is like Christmas pudding in a glass – which means it's perfect for this.

CHEESE: if it's Christmas, it should be Stilton, and there's nothing that goes so well with Stilton as a bottle of decent port – unless, of course, you count a top-class Claret. I often prefer it to the port, which is lovely but a big whack of alcohol to take at this stage in the proceedings.

Acknowledgements

Nobody who is published by John Murray can fail to be aware of just how lucky they are. Quite apart from the thrill of being part of its awesome publishing history I owe them so much. So huge thanks to Eleanor Birne whose idea – yet again – it all was. But also I'm grateful to Roland Philipps for his endless encouragement, to Nikki Barrow and Shona Abhyankar for their imaginative support and to Helen Hawksfield for her patience, her helpful prodding and her hand-holding when the going got tough. As ever I can't quite think how it is I got so lucky as to earn a more than decent living doing a job that is quite so much fun. I owe all the newspapers and the many editors who've supported me through the years more than I can say.

The author and publisher would like to thank the following for permission to reproduce copyright material: Philippa Davenport for her chilli con carne recipe from *Davenport's Dishes*; extract from 'Trebetherick' by John Betjeman from *Collected Poems*, reproduced by permission of John Murray (Publishers); sweet potato gratin recipe © Hugh Fearnley-Whittingstall, reproduced by permission of Greene & Heaton; J. Sheekey Oyster Bar and Head Chef Richard Kirkwood for J. Sheekey's shellfish cocktail recipe; extract from 'The Night They Invented Champagne', composed by Frederick Lowe and Alan Jay Lerner © 1957 and 1958 by Chappell & Co., reproduced by kind permission of Warner/Chappell Music Ltd, London w8 4EP.

Index